November '16
the Best

I hope
the play

STUDENT PLAYS FOR DRAMATISTS

P.S The "underlines"
+ capitalized words
are stage directions
for the student
actors.

Student Plays

FOR DRAMATISTS

BY D.S. HUTCHEON

PORTLAND • OREGON
INKWATERPRESS.COM

*Scan this QR Code
to learn more about
this title.*

Publisher: Inkwater Press | www.inkwaterpress.com

ISBN-13 978-1-62901-278-0 | ISBN-10 1-62901-278-5

Printed in the U.S.A.

1 3 5 7 9 10 8 6 4 2

TABLE OF CONTENTS

The Third Agenda

I Am Myself Alone

STROKED

CHARACTERS

DR BILL WINTHROP Ed.D (35) .... PERSONNEL DIRECTOR

DR TOM JONATHON M.D (55) .... CHIEF OF STAFF

DR ALEX DOOLEY Ph.d (35) .... NEUROPSYCHOLOGIST

DR DON CARMICHAEL M.D (28) .... PSYCHIATRY RESIDENT

ALICE MAYFIELD (30) .... NURSE THERAPIST

DR SUSAN CRAWFORD M.D (50) .... CHIEF PSYCHIATRIST

GENERAL STANLEY MORGAN (45) . . . INPATIENT

CHRISTOPHER (45) .... INPATIENT

JIM (40) .... INPATIENT

DANIEL (28) .... INPATIENT

STEPHEN (25) .... INPATIENT

WAITER (50) .... RESTAURANT

MAITRE DE (45) .... ELEGANT RESTAURANT

TIME: Fall 1988

PLACE: The exterior of a Psychiatric Hospital in Central Kansas. The buildings are white and four storied. The facility is a sombre, squared structure with a paucity of windows.

In front is a large manicured lawn to offset the starkness of the buildings. It is early morning about 9:00 A.M. The attendants and medical personnel have been on duty since 7:00 A.M. The sound of patients' shouting is heard in the background.

Two staff psychologists are standing in front of the hospital's main entrance. They are discussing their upcoming duties for the day. Both men are in their mid thirties, well dressed and their conversational tone is serious. One man carries a clipboard and cradles it in both arms. The other man holds a ballpoint pen tightly in his right hand and compulsively presses and depresses the pen's button. His conversation is animated, often punctuating his sentences with broad gestures in the air, while waving his pen back and forth like a pointer stick.

ACT ONE SCENE ONE

BILL WINTHROP:

Alex, I'm deeply concerned about the government cutbacks that may hit the State in the new fiscal year. If it happens how can we operate effectively, we're understaffed as it is.

ALEX DOOLEY:

Winthrop we went through this three years ago and came out relatively unscathed. A few jobs were cannibalized to provide additional funds to maintain the status quo. Apart from that minor set-back, nothing major happened.

BILL WINTHROP:

Nothing major happened? Three of the staff sued the hospital for wrongful dismissal and collected a bundle. Subsequently a number of departments including the Personnel Unit were told to cut down on 'extraneous service delivery' Whatever that means? The joint went bananas for six months because of those lawsuits.

ALEX DOOLEY:

Bill, Bill . . . Bill keep your shirt on.

Your unit doesn't have an 'extraneous service delivery" because it doesn't deliver any real service . . . take a valium. Drift through this period of uncertainty one day at a time. If cutbacks happen, they happen. What can we do about it, besides everyone knows you haven't made any 'faux pas' to generate concern. You know the government . . . I think your mediocrity should pull you through.

BILL WINTHROP:

It's easy for you to talk, your operational funds have increased on a yearly basis for three years. Your research is deemed 'high profile' by the administration and most importantly your uncle <u>is a state congressman.</u>

ALEX DOOLEY:

Winthrop quite frankly my Uncle's position has no bearing on any funds my unit receives. Neuropsychology is THE new field . . . obviously the most appropriate area to provide research endowments. Stop trying to cover up your unit's raison etre <u>which is questionable</u> to put it mildly and <u>denigrating the only cogent scientific research done at Orangeville Psychiatric.</u>

BILL WINTHROP:

DOOLEY YOU'RE A POMPOUS ASS.

STAGE LIGHTS DIM – END OF SCENE ONE

ACT ONE SCENE TWO

(Bill walks away lights dim set change. Lights raise Bill is reading various reports at his desk. The office is filled with momentous from the past, numerous photographs of patients with arms around Bill. A large plant stands by the door and a plaque on the wall behind his desk reads STO PRO VERITATE. The clock on the wall shows 9:35 A.M and Bill begins to muse about his conversation with Alex Dooley. Bill looks up to see Susan Crawford staring at him from the doorway. She is a striking brunette, 5'8", slim, attractive features with a flashing smile. She is the senior psychiatrist at Orangeville Psychiatric Hospital)

BILL WINTHROP:

Hi Susan, what can I do you for?

SUSAN CRAWFORD:

Bill, what's all the gossip I'm hearing about hospital cutbacks in the new fiscal year?

BILL WINTHROP:

I know, I just had a brilliant commentary from Alex Dooley about the subject. That man has the biggest ego I've ever encountered! Apparently Neuropsychology is THE cogent area to research and receive funding these days! Alex sounded like he's cornered the market against cutbacks. I think his ability to accurately prognosticate anything is open for debate! I remember his first wife telling me how brilliant he was at income tax. Two years later the I.R.S hit him with $24,000 he owed in back taxes. So much for Alex the investment genius!

SUSAN CRAWFORD:

He can be a pain in the ass but I must admit his research on the tertiary zones of the left hemisphere in relationships which are logical or symbolic was brilliant. His argument that these relationships are quasi spatial I agree with totally. His usage of a mathematic paradigm to highlight this postulate was well thought out and in my opinion proved that patients with lesions in this region will break down well below the level they are expected to function. An amazing man <u>yet a first class jerk.</u> Too bad he couldn't be put in his place but it appears he covers his ass too well with management. I hear Tom Jonathon thinks the sun rises and shines with Dooley. Typical management myopia. A stupid self perpetuation of ego dystonic stroking between the lizards of the joint.

BILL WINTHROP:

Susan . . . your thesis about Dooley nearly put me to sleep. For God's Sake speak English in this office. Hey how are things with your boyfriend Kenneth, or is it Trevor? I can never keep track . . . your sex life is like Dooley's opinion of himself . . . <u>vigorous.</u>

SUSAN CRAWFORD:

It's Trevor and it really doesn't matter . . . lets say he meets a need and that's all I want out of the relationship. I mean he's bright articulate and bi-sexual. Show me a New Yorker who's left the State and I'll show you a man of questionable sanity. He hates the mid west . . . is not happy at his job and wants to marry me. A disturbingly acute problem don't you think?

BILL WINTHROP:

Susan get outta here I've got work do. Even though Alex 'Boy Wonder' thinks personnel is a waste of time.

(two patients walk by the open door looking at the ceiling)

I wonder if those guys think Personnel is crap? Hey . . . Hey

(shouts at patients who keep staring at the ceiling as they walk down the corridor Dr Tom Jonathon enters Bill's Office as Susan Crawford leaves).

DR TOM JONATHON:

Bill . . . have you got a moment? I want to talk to you about the horrendous rumor concerning cutbacks in the next fiscal year.

BILL WINTHROP:

Tom, just one question . . . will it happen?

DR TOM JONATHON:

God only knows I've got two phone calls into Topeka. I hope to hear one way or the other by late this afternoon. If they say 'Yes" I'm going to fight this tooth and nail. I remember 1981 and those three she-males THAT SUED. They won a $340,000 settlement! Money we could ill afford Bill.

BILL WINTHROP:

Yeh seems to me I had a recent conversation about that one. I remember the Personnel Department getting it from all sides that year! They wanted us to join the class action on the grounds that the hospital was mismanaging departmental funds and all the employees should go for the jugular. As I recall I said 'No' because I'm still here. Seriously Tom, you better find out whose spreading this gossip and nip it in the bud. Your butt could be on the firing line if things escalate.

DR TOM JONATHON:
IF I FIND THE BASTARD . . .

Oh God, I can't afford another lawsuit at this institution. What irresponsibility <u>I'm going to find the creep and do him in.</u>

BILL WINTHROP:
What happens if it's a group and getting one person doesn't resolve anything?

DR TOM JONATHON:
I'll cross that stream with hip waders Bill. Never fear . . . but I appreciate your concern.

BILL WINTHROP:
Tom, keep your eyes open, your wits about you and try to remember all the enemies you've made during the past nine years.

DR TOM JONATHON:
Yeh, you're right, it could be anyone of fifty people on staff or even ex-staff I'll wait 'till I receive information from Topeka and then firm up a plan of action. Thanks Bill I appreciate your support have a good day.

> *(Tom Jonathon leaves abruptly, Bill looks at the clock on the wall and then at his notes. Alice Mayfield walks by his office and then doubles back to his doorway. Alice is respected by her colleagues and has an Iowan accent)*

ALICE MAYFIELD:
Bill, you look hopelessly lost in your work how 'bout a coffee?

BILL WINTHROP:

Alice

(absorbed in reading looking up mildly startled)

that's the most enticing offer I've had all day, why not. But on one condition, we drink it in here. I can't stand the incessant shop talk and gossip in the staff lounge.

ALICE MAYFIELD:

You drive a hard bargain Bill but after deliberation of your suggestion I concur.

(both laugh)

BILL WINTHROP:

Not you too, I talked with Sue Crawford this morning and she went on and on about Dooley's scientific acumen. It frustrated me to no end! But more out of envy than anything else. I guess he contributes the most in this place ... no dummy.

ALICE MAYFIELD:

<u>That scumbag.</u> I wouldn't trust him with one syllable of information about work related issues. Screw his 'scientific acumen'. He has the morals of an alley cat and would 'eighty six' his grandmother to get ahead.

BILL WINTHROP:

I think he's already tried that as a tax shelter and was given a one-time exemption, I'm wondering about our coffees Alice?

ALICE MAYFIELD:

Bill I need a good listener. Don Carmichael has been sabotaging my group sessions with the guys. I'm ready to scream. . . he gives me the creeps and I think I know why he's such a jerk these days. I dated him two or three times . . . he came on too quickly the 'M.D routine' and all that crap. It makes me sick I told him to get lost and since then he's used his Connecticut charm with your pal Crawford to oversee as many of my job duties as he can.

BILL WINTHROP:

Why don't you complain to Susan. Make sure you can back up your complaints with plenty of concrete evidence.

ALICE MAYFIELD:

Bill, he's too slick, plus his interference is subtle except if you're right there observing through the one way mirror. I've noticed a marked decline in the patients' general comfort level during our 'T' groups. I'm ready to commit an axe murder against one Don Carmichael . . . psychiatric resident at Orangeville.

BILL WINTHROP:

Alice, why don't you confront both Don Carmichael and Susan Crawford about his inappropriate conduct. I know it sounds somewhat irregular but if Carmichael is the slime you say he is, any other confrontational strategy could blow up in your face — like you rejecting his appeals to satiate his libido . . . I could use some coffee.

ALICE MAYFIELD:

Let me think on it Bill I mean about Carmichael. I don't want Crawford on my case too — she can be a 'bitch on wheels' if you challenge her professionalism. I feel caught Bill . . . Carmichael is here for three more years. I hate first year residents they are such 'know it all glory seekers'. Why doesn't he leave me alone. I almost wish I could turn the clock back and say YES I'LL LET YOU SLEEP WITH ME . . . JUST DON'T BUG ME.

BILL WINTHROP:

Alice, how long have we known each other . . . three years? I know you'll find a solution to your problem. I haven't seen you make too many errors in your life thus far.

ALICE MAYFIELD:

Yes yes. . . little miss perfect practitioner the Doctor's pet I have problems too you know.

BILL WINTHROP:

Look why don't you come back later on and we can talk about this at greater length. I haven't seen you so agitated since your unit assistant was assaulted by one of your guys.

ALICE MAYFIELD:

Thanks Bill . . . how 'bout 3:00 this afternoon?

BILL WINTHROP:

Sounds good, see yah later.

> *(Alice leaves and Bill resumes his reading — the clock reads 12:25 General Stanley Morgan walks unannounced into the office. Stan, as he is called by the staff and other patients was relieved of his military command after sexually assaulting a Co-ed at a nearby college. A thirty day psychiatric assessment revealed that Stan has an antisocial personality disorder. He is currently awaiting discharge)*

BILL WINTHROP:
(senses he is being observed and looks up from his work)

Hi Stan, what's new?

GENERAL STANLEY MORGAN:
Bill, I hear the old man was in to see yah today about potential cutbacks at the 'Shrinkery' what gives?

BILL WINTHROP:
Stan, what makes you think Dr Jonathon would confide in me anyway if he did I'd have to maintain confidentiality.

GENERAL STANLEY MORGAN:
(sits down on the floor and rests his back against the wall while continuing to talk)

I also hear Don Carmichael is screwing up Alice Mayfield's 'T' group sessions. A bunch of us were thinking of sending a written complaint to the 'old man'. Why the hell does the hospital have to be a teaching center for 'baby shrinks' to practice playing God? If you want I can phone Topeka and get Carmichael's residency revoked?

BILL WINTHROP:
That's not necessary Stan. I'm sure someone will talk to him and things will be resolved.

GENERAL STANLEY MORGAN:
Bill . . . what is your opinion of the administration?

BILL WINTHROP:

Stan, I'm a staff here . . . I can't ethically comment on that question.

GENERAL STANLEY MORGAN:

In my opinion the 'old man' is a right wing politico in a left wing eco-system! His staff are antediluvian but generally competent. But most importantly his 'jag-ass' management style 'erks' the crap out of his staff. He should learn to relax. Loosen up. . . take a mistress 'get laid' do something in his life that is out of character. His staff are fearful of his command style . . . not good Billy. That breeds mistrust and contempt. I know there are times <u>when even I get insecure.</u>

BILL WINTHROP:

Stan maybe we could change the subject, how is your treatment going?

GENERAL STANLEY MORGAN:

(changes sitting posture to a prone position on the floor cradling his head with the palm of his hand)

Oh that stuff, A-OK I guess. I think I've got the baby shrink eating out of my hand . . . he uses buzz words like 'impact' resistance' and 'counter productive'. He also has interesting theories about me and my so called problem of relating, he calls our situation 'unique and intriguing'. Whatever turns you on I guess. Bill, in combat he would have been shot by his own men! You don't snow a bullshit artist, I mean I wasn't born yesterday . . . <u>come on.</u>

BILL WINTHROP:

Stan have you ever been involved in 'T groups?

GENERAL STANLEY MORGAN:

Only 'Y' groups if you know what I mean. No . . . seriously you mean Alice's 'T' groups?

BILL WINTHROP:

Any 'T' groups Stan, they can help you come to terms with some of your problems. The members of the group and its facilitator challenge your ideas and help you work through those issues you find threatening to face alone. The group as a reference point and support system is a powerful tool for precipitating change.

GENERAL STANLEY MORGAN:

(moves into a sitting position, cross legged)

Bill, enough of this crap. If you're referring to the case with the girl, she came onto to me not vice versa. I'm still appealing my committal with the army. I mean there were no witnesses and it was her word against mine. I had twenty-one years in the service, graduating third in my class from Virginia Military Academy. I was half-colonel at twenty-eight and made Brigadier General by thirty — five. Where the hell does a military tribunal court martial send me to a CIVILIAN hospital for nut cases . . . in the Sunflower State no less.

BILL WINTHROP:

Stan, there was conclusive evidence linking you to the Anderson rape it's called DNA. Besides your alibi was crap . . . your testimony had holes shot through it by the prosecuting attorney. Subsequently he requested a thirty day psychiatric evaluation which determines your mental status. Stan to reiterate . . . I think a 'T' group would be advantageous at this juncture in your life. Please reconsider what the long-term payoffs might be.

GENERAL STANLEY MORGAN:
(stands up slowly and leans on the door knob)

Bill, you sound like the prosecuting attorney at my court martial. WHERE THE HELL DO YOU GET OFF PLAYING SHRINK . . . You don't even have psychiatric training.

BILL WINTHROP:

Stan you're right. I'm sure you will come to your own conclusions about why you're here. Now if you don't mind I must request your indulgence

(motions Stan towards the door)

I've got some papers to review.

(Stan leaves the office and Bill returns to reading again).

LIGHTS DIM — END OF SCENE TWO

ACT ONE SCENE THREE

(Stage lights rise — Bill Winthrop stretches in his office chair and rubs his eyes. He turns around and looks out the window at the highway traffic in the distance. After a few seconds he re-directs his gaze to the plaque on the wall behind his desk which reads STO PRO VERITATE. Bill shakes his head and sits down again this time looking at the wall clock which reads 1:10 P.M and then at his appointment book. He looks up standing at his door is a soft bellied, dark featured man in his late twenties/early thirties gazing intently at Bill. Bill has never formally met this man)

BILL WINTHROP:

Hi I'm Bill Winthrop can I help you?

DON CARMICHAEL:

Yeh I'm Don Carmichael a first year resident in psychiatry and I hear my name's being taken in vain. You being the Director of Personnel I thought it best to make an appointment to meet with you as soon as possible.

BILL WINTHROP:

O.K Don that sounds good but lets forgo the title crap. I'm a Counseling Psychologist by training. Administrator second . . . a distant second. I took this job nine years ago after qualifying.

DON CARMICHAEL:

Hey somebody around here is human, I like that . . . no crap no veneer when can we talk.

BILL WINTHROP:

How 'bout now I'm hungry, why don't we go for a bite off-site?

DON CARMICHAEL:

Sounds good where 'bouts?

BILL WINTHROP:

'Romains' you know the place?

DON CARMICHAEL:

Yeh down the highway and then into town on seventeenth avenue for a mile or so, isn't it on the right hand side of the road with a large red sign?

BILL WINTHROP:

Yeh how much time have you got?

DON CARMICHAEL:

Well I have supervision with Susan Crawford at 4:30 and should be back by 3:30 to prepare.

BILL WINTHROP:

I have a meeting at 3:00 so we have plenty of time for an extended lunch. Your car or mine?

DON CARMICHAEL:

How 'bout yours?

BILL WINTHROP:

Sounds O.K lets go.

(Bill gets up from his desk and walks to the coat rack by the door. Bill puts on his overcoat and they leave the office shutting the door behind them)

LIGHTS DIM — END OF SCENE THREE

ACT ONE SCENE FOUR

(The lights are raised slowly, both men are seated in an ethnic restaurant. They are the only clientele. Bill is looking at the menu as Don Carmichael talks in a quiet, articulate manner, often using 'street' vernacular to highlight a point)

DON CARMICHAEL:
(sitting beside Bill looking around the room)

It is a good spot to chat a good choice Bill have you been here often?

BILL WINTHROP:

Once in awhile, why don't we 'cut to the chase' as they say . . . so I can give you as much time as you need to discuss your problem.

DON CARMICHAEL:

That's what I like . . . a man who is direct . . . to the point. No extraneous verbiage with Bill Winthrop. O.K here goes . . . I've just begun my first year in the residency as I told you and think I've really blown it by offending a psychiatric nurse who runs the 'T' groups. Her name is Alice Mayfield. Why don't I start from the beginning and state the salient points of my dilemma.

(Bill folds his hands on the table and leans forward)

About three months ago I arrived at Orangeville to begin a four year psychiatric residency. Shortly thereafter I met a nurse. . . you probably know her Alice Mayfield. She runs the in-patient 'T' groups at the hospital. I was assigned to her ward to fulfill my residency duties one of these being a participant-observer in her 'T' groups. Susan Crawford, my supervisor, told me to get my feet wet . . . this being my first year the major emphasis is on in-patient work. You know, learning the various assessment strategies and taking on individual and group cases. Anyway after approximately three weeks I asked Alice out for a drink after work. She accepted and we met at Gerry O's . . . the lounge. The date went well although uneventful she was straightforward direct . . . a solid citizen. It kind of surprised me because of the nature of her work I thought she might be a flake 'off the wall' different sort of character. Not so . . . I really enjoyed her company and wanted to continue seeing her. Anyway . . .

(interrupted by the waiter coming to take the order, both men order fettuchini and a glass of red wine)

BILL WINTHROP:

Don, what made you feel Alice wanted to begin a relationship with you?

DON CARMICHAEL:

I dunno her smile, body language alright . . . now I feel two sizes smaller.

BILL WINTHROP:

Don could you be more specific in what she discussed?

DON CARMICHAEL:

Hmm yeh I remember . . . 'Don I've grown to appreciate your insight with the patients'. She was also smiling a lot and eager to talk about herself in the context of her job. Things like 'sometimes I wish my work with the patients could be appreciated by the brass'. She also talked about 'clues for survival' at Orangeville and mentioned that Dr Crawford had washed out several residents who weren't carrying their weight. How am I doing so far Dr Bill?

BILL WINTHROP:

Good Don, I appreciate your comments. Did you make arrangements to see her again?

DON CARMICHAEL:

Yeh, we dated three or four times in the next month. Things were going smoothly she and I clicked and then it all changed. One day I came into work and she was a 'grade A' bitch. I tried to find out what was troubling her but she wouldn't have anything to do with me. Work became impossible, she was 'game playing' to beat the band . . . incredibly sarcastic. Insidious barbs about my therapy skills and inability to deal with the patients effectively. I racked my brains trying to think of a specific case that caused her change in attitude and came up with a blank.

BILL WINTHROP:

Did you mention anything that might have been taken out of context? At work or during your dates?

> (The waiter arrives with the wine, Bill sips the red wine and nods his approval. Don also takes a sip and then responds to Bill's question)

DON CARMICHAEL:

I can't recall her over reacting to anything I said. We talked about clinical themes . . . issues pertaining to the patients, other personalities at the hospital, past experiences in life. It was like one day things were great and the next I was 'persona non grata'.

> (the food arrives, both men look eager to dig in and enjoy the pasta)

BILL WINTHROP:

It sounds like one or two things may have happened (a) she got hassled by her colleagues patients etcetera for dating you, or, (b) the woman thought the relationship was becoming too involved and felt pressured in seeing you while attempting to have a collegial relationship at the same time. I dunno, how do these two hypotheses sound is there a third I've overlooked? It certainly was an abrupt change in attitude, almost as if she felt anxiety or guilt about seeing you and then felt a compulsion to punish you with insults.

(Bill stops talking to swallow his food to let his colleague speak)

DON CARMICHAEL:

Bill, I'm too close to the problem to be able to differentiate anything these days. Apart from Alice hating my guts I'm really worried about her sabotaging my residency. She is respected by her colleagues and the administration gives her free reign as a therapist.

BILL WINTHROP:

Don I'm not sure what I can do but if you want I'll keep my ears open. Why don't we set up another time to meet . . . lets say the 26th at the same time?

DON CARMICHAEL:

I didn't bring my duty book but it sounds O.K. Can I get back to you to confirm the date? Bill I appreciate your help and support.

(Don lifts a glass of wine in salute)

BILL WINTHROP:

No problem Don it's important I'm aware of interpersonal problems between staff members before things get out of control.

DON CARMICHAEL:

Thanks Dr Bill hopefully my problems with Alice will be resolved. I appreciate you listening and with a 'third ear'.

BILL WINTHROP:

Let's get outta here before I get sick.

(both men laugh stand up and leave the restaurant)

STAGE LIGHTS DIM — END OF SCENE FOUR

ACT ONE SCENE FIVE

(Stage lights are raised — Bill Winthrop is sitting at his desk reading a textbook entitled, " Treatment of Mental Disorders". He is oblivious to any other sound, he pauses and looks up at the clock on the wall, it reads 2:50 P.M. Bill glances down at his duty book on the desk and looks up, standing at his doorway is Alice Mayfield. Bill smiles and motions her to enter, she does so closing the door behind her. Alice chooses to sit in a large comfortable chair directly across from Bill, she is nervous and eager to engage in conversation)

BILL WINTHROP:

Hi Alice good timing I was just about to call you and reconfirm our meeting was still O.K.

ALICE MAYFIELD:

Bill why did you go out for lunch with Don Carmichael? Even the patients are talking about that one.

BILL WINTHROP:

Alice about an hour after talking with you Don showed up unexpectedly and we decided to go out for a luncheon meeting.

ALICE MAYFIELD:

I can imagine your conversation.

BILL WINTHROP:

Alice I can't breach confidentiality but it appears that he is concerned about his professional relationship with you. I'm eager to hear your point of view . . . if you wish to talk. I guess that's why I wanted a meeting . . . to clear the air.

ALICE MAYFIELD:

Bill I'm so angry right now I COULD SCREAM.

(Bill raises his finger to his lips and shakes his head while waving his hand back and forth)

BILL WINTHROP:

Alice why don't you go over what's troubling you with Don Carmichael . . . professionally... personally from that information I'm sure we can come up with a solution.

ALICE MAYFIELD:

It all started when we began dating. Don had just begun his residency and I was very impressed with his skills. Honest interaction with the patients. . . excellent retention good process notation. Hey I thought Orangeville is going to benefit from this guy's abilities. About three shifts later he asked me out I was impressed. A little chubby around the gut but what the hell he was a good person or so I thought. Our first few dates were great I really thought I was falling for the guy. Then one day . . . a Monday night as all the guys were watching Monday night football a strange event occurred.

I was going over the afternoon tapes to draw information for my contact notes. Somebody walked past my office door I paused and got up to see who it was you guessed it Don Carmichael. At the time I thought nothing of it. You know the hours residents keep especially first year residents. I noticed what looked like a bunch of hospital record files under his arm. Which by the way are locked up in the main filing station after each shift. Bill . . . you know that residents are only allowed to read them in the central reading room adjacent to the filing station. I remember wondering how Don Carmichael had the guts to sachez 'round with confidential documents under his arm . . . access to the files after hours are under signing privilege only. He needs a co-signing authority on duty during his first year residency. Anyway I went back to reading my notes and forgot about the incident. Two days later I saw him just for a few minutes and commented on the file thing. He said he was reading journal articles, so apparently I was mistaken. No big deal I thought a case of mistaken assumption . . . Bill not long afterwards I received a reprimand from Susan Crawford for a number of inconsistencies in my case recordings. One critique was inappropriate verbal leads during 'T' group sessions with the guys. Another was too much commentary with some of the group members. Preaching to the guys can you believe that. I was still in the dark until I figured out that these types of critique were only occurring in those groups that Don Carmichael attended. I put two and two together . . . that he's debriefing Susan Crawford in their supervision sessions and she's giving me the 'shiv'. Subsequently . . . I overheard him talking on the pay phone to someone . . . 'B.S'ing about how ambitious he was and that he had to cover all angles or get screwed in the ear. That did it . . . from that day on I was damned if I was going to be a pawn in his political game. He wants to play games, lets play games . . . only on my terms. I decided to make his life so damned miserable that he wouldn't last the year. Not on my unit anyway and not using me or my guys as peons in his little game plan. Well, that's it Bill . . . sorry for dragging on . . . what's your prognosis Doctor?

BILL WINTHROP:

Alice, have you discussed Don's behavior with anybody in the hospital?

ALICE MAYFIELD:

No . . . just you why do you ask?

BILL WINTHROP:

I'm wondering if people will misunderstand or more accurately, make false assumptions about you because of your obvious contempt towards Don? You know . . . 'Hey Carmichael dumped Alice and now she hates his guts'.

ALICE MAYFIELD:

Bill I don't give a damn what people think . . . <u>Carmichael's a 'slimeball'</u>.

BILL WINTHROP:
(stands directly over Alice)

Alice you know the politics around here and if you don't seek a resolution of sorts with this guy you could get 'whacked' to coin a phrase.

ALICE MAYFIELD:

'Whacked'?

BILL WINTHROP:

To be totally frank he's a resident who feels he has to be in control of his environment in order to survive. He'll do it at all cost . . . you could be victimized before the end of his residency. He understands Susan's power as the Resident Supervisor . . . who knows what he tells her about your competency as a therapist?

ALICE MAYFIELD:
(begins to cry)

I'm goddamned if I'll kiss his butt or hers for that matter.

BILL WINTHROP:

Forget Susan for a moment how 'bout your patients picking up on this behavior and manipulating you by disclosing their concerns to one of the management? They would love to manipulate such a scenario. You know, sit back and watch the action. Alice . . . I'm talking major power plays and potential harm being done to your career at this hospital . . . go talk to Don Carmichael and try to resolve things.

ALICE MAYFIELD:

Oh god . . . I'm going to puke if I have to go near that guy. Where's the justice in the world.

BILL WINTHROP:

There is no justice . . . a balance once in awhile . . . but no justice. Alice for God's sake get hold of yourself. Be a little more objective . . . do you know how you could be set up and by how many different people? Do you honestly think this guy would sit still for any abuse? He's no moron. Don't forget M.D means 'medical deity' in this State.

ALICE MAYFIELD:

Bill, I will think about your suggestions.

(interrupted by Bill's phone, he answers and talks in a low tone and then hangs up)

You are right about the political crap, repercussions and all that . . . oh well it keeps you young. I've got to go and you have work to do.

(Alice stands up and faces Bill)

BILL WINTHROP:

Alice . . .what are your plans later on tonight?

ALICE MAYFIELD:

(throws back her head laughs and looks at Bill directly for a second)

Sex, drugs and rock and roll . . . why? d'ya wanna join me?

BILL WINTHROP:

No thanks . . . last time I saw you in spandex pants I had to 'thought stop' lust messages all night.

ALICE MAYFIELD:

Bill you're a beautiful man thank God you're around to keep this joint from exploding. If you change your mind about tonight give me a call. Actions speak louder than thoughts Bill.

(Alice speaks seductively teasing Bill)

I would allow you lots of freedom to express yourself (cut off by Bill)

BILL WINTHROP:

Stop stop . . . alright already . . <u>get outta here.</u>

(Alice leaves Bill's office laughing quietly shutting the door behind her . . . Bill bursts out laughing)

STAGE LIGHTS DIM — END OF SCENE V

ACT TWO SCENE ONE

(Two weeks have elapsed, it is early December and the atmosphere among the hospital staff is tense . . . rumored fiscal restraints in next year's budget. Bill Winthrop has been besieged with personal requests for meetings, often with little notice. 'Back biting' is at its all time high. Dr Jonathon has called a mandatory staff meeting of all heads of departments in an effort to 'clear the the air'. The time is 9:00 A.M. Present are: Bill Winthrop, Alex Dooley, Don Carmichael, Susan Crawford, Alice Mayfield — Dr Jonathon has not yet arrived).

BILL WINTHROP:

Well, I wonder what Tom's going to say to try and put out the fire . . . these cutback rumors are ugly.

ALEX DOOLEY:

What the hell can he say Winthrop. I mean cuts are going to be made and the axe is going to fall. El finito, the axe man commeth.

BILL WINTHROP:

Alex . . . why the hell are you so goddamn flippant all the time? I've got half a mind to steal your research data one night.

(mild laughter from the group)

ALEX DOOLEY:

That's right Winthrop . . . you've got half a mind

(Bill stands up abruptly)

and I wouldn't put it past you to try something stupid.

(Bill lunges at Alex, grabs his lapels and pulls Alex upward out of his chair, they are face to face)

BILL WINTHROP:

YOU ARE SUCH AN ANUS DOOLEY. <u>Don't ever play comedian at my expense again</u> . . . just shut your goddamn mouth.

(flings Alex back down into his chair and then sits down)

SUSAN CRAWFORD:

Bill . . . Alex would you guys <u>keep your cool.</u> Bill . . . anymore physical aggression and you could be suspended without pay until further notice.

ALICE MAYFIELD:

Bill I've never seen you blow it . . . <u>calm down.</u>

DON CARMICHAEL:

Bill . . . Alex . . . as a first year resident I look to you guys for leadership around here. Especially when budget cuts are imminent.

BILL WINTHROP:

(composed, breathing is paced and he straightens his hair with his hand)

Alex . . I didn't mean to lose control . . . please accept my apology

(cut off abruptly by Alex)

ALEX DOOLEY:

THAT'S IT WINTHROP . . . I'M SUING YOU FOR ASSAULT AND I'M NOT GOING TO QUIT UNTIL YOU'RE OUT OF THIS PLACE.

BILL WINTHROP:

Alex

(cut off by Susan Crawford)

SUSAN CRAWFORD:

Alex we're all under a lot of pressure these days . . . look, Bill apologized and in my opinion was

(cut off vociferously by Alex Dooley)

ALEX DOOLEY:

<u>Susan take a valium and then challenge your</u>

(sardonic tone)

<u>irrational beliefs. The next time I talk with pea brain</u>

(Bill leaps from his chair and attempts to grab Alex who stands behind Don Carmichael)

<u>is with senior management.</u> Tom Jonathon or better still the <u>hospital board.</u>

SUSAN CRAWFORD:

Alex . . . what's wrong, you can dish it out but you can't accept the consequences . . . you can be such an <u>insidious little man.</u>

ALEX DOOLEY:

What's wrong Crawford . . . has PMS snuck up <u>and bit your psy-</u>
<u>chiatric</u> ass?

SUSAN CRAWFORD:

Alex . . . I won't give that remark the dignity of a response. Look
everyone let's wait for Tom's explanation and strategies for next
year's cut backs. He hasn't let us down before . . . at least not in the
years I've been here.

ALEX DOOLEY:

The eternal optimist . . . good ship Crawford sucks her 'lolley pop'.
God you irritate me, you're such a goody two shoes, myopic little

(cut off by Bill Dooley)

BILL WINTHROP:

<u>Shut your goddamn mouth Dooley</u>

ALEX DOOLEY:

<u>Hail the conquering lobotomy</u>

BILL WINTHROP:

(Bill begins to stand up as Alex pushes the chair back ready to run)

THAT DOES IT

*(the door opens abruptly interrupting Bill's sentence. Dr Jonathon
strides into the room and sits down at the head of the board table
everyone regains composure)*

DR TOM JONATHON:

(authoritative air)

Bill . . . were you about to say something, continue, please continue. We are all interested in your opinion.

ALEX DOOLEY:

<u>What were you going to say Winthrop?</u>

(cut off abruptly by Dr Jonathon who gives him a laser stare, Alex looks down at the table)

DR TOM JONATHON:

Shut up Dooley... Bill as you were saying?

BILL WINTHROP:

Tom, to be frank Alex and I were having an altercation about the general morale of the hospital . . . we were concerned

(cut off by Alex Dooley who jumps up from his sitting position and stands facing Bill who looks up at Alex with an air of confidence)

ALEX DOOLEY:

AN ALTERCATION . . . YOU ASSAULTED ME WINTHROP.

(Alex attempts to gain composure by deep breathing for a few seconds)

This is going to the hospital board <u>for disciplinary action Winthrop.</u>

(Alex begins his deep breathing exercises to gain control again)

In addition I'm calling the cops <u>and charging you with assault.</u>

(Alex sits down abruptly Bill looks over at Dr Jonathon who motions him to be quiet)

DR TOM JONATHON:

Bill is this accusation correct? Did you assault Alex?

BILL WINTHROP:

Tom . . . he provoked me with his sarcasm I lost control.

(Bill looks down at the table and blushes)

DR TOM JONATHON:

(Dr Jonathon losing composure begins to shout)

FOR GOD'S SAKE WINTHROP YOU'RE ONE OF THE MAINSTAYS 'ROUND HERE.

(Dr Jonathon pauses and gains composure)

I want to see you and Alex in my office immediately following this meeting. That is a directive . . . <u>do I make myself clear?</u>

(Bill nods in agreement and Alex smiles across the table at Bill)

BILL WINTHROP:

I'll be there Tom.

ALEX DOOLEY:

O.K Tom, I'll be pleased to talk about it but I'm still charging

(abruptly cut off by Dr Jonathon who glares at Alex Dooley for several seconds)

DR TOM JONATHON:

Alex . . . that is your right . . . now onto other business.

*(Dr Jonathon stands up and begins to move around the Board room
as he talks)*

Alright . . . I should start by thanking you all for attending this
meeting at such a short notice. I hope my memo didn't offend anyone? I guess it reflects my general feeling about the budget situation. O.K from the top, a couple of months ago . . . I can't remember
exactly when . . . a rumor began to circulate about budget cuts. How
it got started is beyond me . . . it just started and hasn't stopped.

*(Dr Jonathon looks at each staff member sitting around the board
table with a long penetrating stare and then begins to speak again)*

Today it stops. There will be budget cuts as of April 1st next fiscal year.

(staff groan in unison except Alex Dooley who smiles)

We faced this problem in '81 and we'll face it again next year. At this
point Topeka states all hospitals of Orangeville's size will have their
budget's trimmed in an effort to meet the federal government's fiscal restraint measures. So when more detailed information is avail-
able you'll be the first to know.

*(Dr Jonathon pauses and then looks around the board table at each
staff member)*

Until then I'll keep you posted on a regular basis via the memo route.
In the meantime I want to be the first to know if there are any prob-
lems in your respective portfolios. I also want everyone to lean on
Bill's expertise . . . he's had a lot of experience in conflict resolution.

*(staff laugh in unison which becomes a hysterical catharsis — Alex
Dooley gives Bill Winthrop an icy stare)*

O.K it's a rap . . . any questions?

ALEX DOOLEY:

Why the hell do I have to utilize Winthrop when

(cut off by Dr Jonathon)

DR TOM JONATHON:

Dooley . . . <u>don't ever play 'Prima Donna' in my meetings again.</u>

(Alex abruptly looks down at the board table)

SUSAN CRAWFORD:

Tom . . . I appreciate you telling us about the cut backs post haste . . . at least we know and can hopefully develop an action plan that

(cut off by Dr Jonathon who smiles broadly at the compliment)

DR TOM JONATHON:

Thank you Susan . . . just wait for my memo addressed to all the staff regarding the cut backs. Please keep me posted of any internal dissention. Anybody else?

(Dr Jonathon looks around the table for several seconds no one meets his gaze)

Well Dr Carmichael . . . this must be quite an experience . . . I expect a real show of strength and leadership from you. I'm aware of your appointment as the spokesman for the first year residents . . . could you please inform them as soon as possible about the cutbacks next year. Obviously it could have a direct impact on their jobs and I want them prepared. I would also request that you firm up three alternative meeting times when I could meet with them as a group.

DON CARMICHAEL:

Yes Dr Jonathon . . . its been quite a meeting.

(staff laugh except Alex who glares at Bill Winthrop and then at the board table)

I know your schedule is crammed these days . . . I'll get those times to you this afternoon.

ALICE MAYFIELD:

Dr Jonathon . . . I'm wondering what to tell the guys?

(Dr Jonathon looks puzzled)

I'm sorry sir, the psychiatric patients? My guys seem to get contaged whenever the hospital has budget gossip floating around . . . you know 'less staff more agitation'.

DR TOM JONATHON:

I appreciate the question Ms. ah

(pauses then smiles)

Mayfield . . . in situations such as this I would advise you to be as supportive as possible. I do understand the problem of manipulation and contagement. However, I anticipate my memo will clarify the situation to the line staff . . . who in turn can explain the problem to the patients. I do not want any deception or misrepresentation . . . you may request a meeting between them and I if you think it would help Ms. ah.

(Alice states her last name with a firm voice)

ALICE MAYFIELD:

Mayfield

DR TOM JONATHON:

Thank you Ms. Mayfield.

ALICE MAYFIELD:

Thank you Dr Jonathon . . . I'll wait and see how things go.

(Alice glances at Don Carmichael who returns the glance)

DR TOM JONATHON:

In respect to Ms. Mayfield's concerns and before we adjourn . . . I wish to reiterate a few points. Number one, please inform the staff about my memo . . . it should be out by the end of the day. Number two, I would like weekly Summary Reports from each of you regarding the general morale in your respective units. Please be frank and suggest any recommendations you think would be beneficial for your respective unit's ah . . well — being. Number three . . . please arrange for me to speak to your staff if you deem it necessary. I will be having an open forum at a later date . . . obviously I'm holding off as I anticipate new developments as you know cut backs are politically driven and we'll have to ah. . . Look, if there are any new developments I'll be sharing the information with you people first. If there are staff who want it from the 'horses mouth' tell them to be patient. I believe in chain of command. Number four, the last issue is probably the most important. I would appreciate your support in putting aside any pettiness . . . I do know there exists some professional differences

(staff laugh except Alex who glares at Bill Winthrop and then at the Board table)

of opinion . . . please, <u>stop the bickering.</u> I depend on you to help me raise the morale of the hospital.

(Dr Jonathon walks towards the door and stops he then turns to face the staff)

Well that's it . . . O.K Drs' Winthrop and Dooley, I want to see you both in my office immediately.

(Bill and Alex stand up in unison and leave the board room with Dr Jonathon as the lights dim to the scene)

STAGE LIGHTS DIM — END OF SCENE ONE

ACT TWO SCENE TWO

(The lights are raised, Dr Jonathon is seated behind a desk, there are medical diplomas on the wall and the furniture is very expensive. There is a large plant by the door and a coat rack, on which Dr Jonathon's 'whites' are hanging. Alex Dooley and Bill Winthrop are seated beside each other. Bill is looking around the room and Alex is 'dead pan', looking ahead expressionless)

DR TOM JONATHON:

Gentlemen I'm going to listen to both sides of the story and then make a decision which you will abide by. I will not tolerate my staff acting like 'Jack Ass's', especially in front of a first year resident. When you leave this office that point will be understood.

(both men nod in unison)

Bill . . . could you give me your version of what happened this morning.

BILL WINTHROP:
(Bill looks at Alex who is staring straight ahead)

Tom Alex and I have been getting on each other's nerves . . . today was the final straw. Alex goaded

(Alex snorts with a stifled laugh while maintaining his gaze straight ahead)

me in front of my peers. Alex do you want me to get witnesses?

(Alex continues to stare straight ahead)

Tom . . . Alex does not, nor has ever respected anyone in the soft sciences. When he sees a chance to denigrate a colleague he takes sadistic pleasure in doing so. <u>Right Alex.</u>

(Alex continues to stare straight ahead dead pan expression is maintained)

DR TOM JONATHON:
Bill could you give me some concrete examples of how Alex denigrates?

BILL WINTHROP:
(Bill shrugs before talking pausing to think of his answer)

He becomes caustic and abusive . . . anytime he's in close proximity to me. Today his insults were intolerable and I lost control . . I 'm sorry.

DR TOM JONATHON:
Anything else Bill?

BILL WINTHROP:
No not really Tom . . . but I do wish to say in Alex's defence I think he's been driving himself the past year or so and I'm wondering about the effect on his mental health.

ALEX DOOLEY:
(Alex stares abruptly at Bill and then straight ahead and responds abruptly)

Since when does a Doctorate in Education make you a shrink Winthrop?

DR TOM JONATHON:

Alex you'll get your turn and I am a board certified psychiatrist. Are Bill's accusations true?

ALEX DOOLEY:

(blasé in manner)

Tom . . . I am caustic when I'm forced to interact <u>with a fool.</u>

(cut off vociferously)

DR TOM JONATHON:

<u>Keep it civil Dooley.</u> One more smart ass remark and you'll be brought in front of the hospital review committee and I don' give a damn about your relative in high places.

ALEX DOOLEY:

(Alex relaxes in his chair and looks thoughtfully around the office before speaking)

Tom . . . why don't I provide the salient issues regarding my animosity towards Dr Winthrop . . . a title lightly coined.

(Dr Jonathon begins to talk and is interrupted by Alex Dooley's apology)

Sorry Tom. Subsequently Dr Winthrop may tear into me with gusto and disprove my hypotheses as the meanderings from a demented <u>Scientist </u>a title heavily coined.

(Alex smiles at his quip)

DR TOM JONATHON:
Alex cut the B.S and get on with it.

ALEX DOOLEY:
O.K O.K. . . from the top . . . Number one

(Dr Jonathon becomes visibly upset in his seat behind the desk)

I have worked diligently on building a research team in my Neuro-psych Unit and received very generous funding from the government and private sector . . . <u>which I wish continued.</u> More than occasionally I drag my body down the hall after a hard day's work and what do I hear emanating from Winthrop's office? Party noise vulgar language deleterious references about colleagues

(Alex looks directly at Dr Jonathon and pauses for effect and then at Bill before continuing)

<u>and it infuriates me.</u> In sum . . . my logical deduction is that Winthrop is abrogating his responsibilities and taking the hospital <u>for a gigantic </u>ride. Number two . . . I'm of the impression that Winthrop is frightened of being found out and subsequently pumps staff for information regarding the weaknesses . . . real or imagined of his colleagues. I've been aware of this for the past year or so and hence the defensiveness when I'm forced to interact with Mr . . . I mean <u>Dr Winthrop.</u> Tom . . . I find Winthrop's accusations about my low stress tolerance . . . which is a blatant lie . . . <u>highly offensive.</u> Quite the opposite is true . . . Winthrop is a dangerous man in this system Tom.

(Alex looks directly at Bill who is visibly angry and trying to control his behavior)

Number three . . .

(Alex enunciates Number three which visibly erks Dr Jonathon who glares at Alex)

My final complaint focuses on the rumoured cutbacks

(cut off by Dr Jonathon who responds)

DR TOM JONATHON:

Alex they are not rumored.

ALEX DOOLEY:

Sorry Tom but until today no one knew what was true or false . . . exaggerated or fabricated. I believe the rumor was begun by Winthrop to justify his Unit's questionable role in the hospital bureaucracy. I feel he is and has constantly proven to be an impostor playing out his fantasy as Psychiatrist on a white charger. He has used his role as 'Personnel Director' which I state sparingly to ingratiate himself with the staff and thus solidify his preposterous assumption that he is truly needed at this work site. It continually astounds me why no action has been taken to control this man's <u>megalomania.</u> <u>Alright Winthrop let's go . . . am I lying? I'm not the only one that</u> <u>feels this way.</u>

BILL WINTHROP:

(Bill is noticeably enraged but controls his voice and choice of words)

Tom . . . I've worked my butt off at Orangeville . . . over nine years and to date have never been subjected to this type of character assassination. Yes I've had staff parties both planned and impromptu but <u>after work </u>and for the right reasons . . . to release staff tension and <u>build morale.</u> Orangeville can be an incredibly brutal environment . . . at all levels of bureaucracy. As for point two on Dooley's shit list . . . my role as Personnel Director of the hospital demands that I get involved in both clinical and vocational counseling. This requires wearing several professional hats. Yes I do question staff about their relationships with their peers superiors and patients. I am privy to a lot of provocative information in the course of fulfilling my job duties. Potentially damaging material about people's job performance as perceived by others . . . as well as their personality quirks. Alex you are for instance admired by some and hated by others . . . the most controversial staff member at Orangeville.

(Alex interrupts Bill with a wave of his hand before talking)

ALEX DOOLEY:

Watch your step Winthrop you're breaching confidentiality here.

DR TOM JONATHON:

Point well taken Alex . . . but I was aware of your reputation without Bill's disclosure . . . proceed Bill.

(Dr Jonathon stares at Alex who looks down at the floor)

BILL WINTHROP:

Thanks Bill . . . Dr Dooley's work is considered valuable by most staff no doubt but his personality and outrageous contempt for those he views as inferior is his major drawback. I truly believe Alex is close to a

(Alex abruptly cuts off Bill with a sardonic response)

ALEX DOOLEY:

Break through not breakdown Winthrop and that's number two . . . Tom do I have to listen to

(Dr Jonathon sits quietly and waves off Alex and then looks at Bill)

BILL WINTHROP:

Tom . . . I believe Alex views his research as a sanctuary from the real world politics of the hospital . . . which over time has had 'a deleterious effect'. To use Alex's expression on his ability to relate to many of his colleagues he views inferior.

(Alex sits quietly but looks increasingly frightened)

Alex . . .

(Bill looks at Alex for a number of seconds before continuing)

I believe you have a need to be perceived as a great man . . . and I think a rest away from Orangeville's rigors would do you a world of good . . . a leave of absence.

(Alex abruptly cuts off Bill Winthrop and jumps up from his chair)

ALEX DOOLEY:
YOU BASTARD WINTHROP.

(Bill slowly rises from his chair trying to maintain his composure and faces Alex directly approximately one yard away)

BILL WINTHROP:

Alex . . . as for point three on your 'shit list' . . . my conduct as Personnel Director has received many accolades from the staff. Why the hell would I want to sabotage the hospital by spreading malicious rumors about impending cut backs? Your accusation is completely erroneous and based on your hatred towards me. Tom . . . if Alex takes this allegation to anyone else I will sue him for defamation of character and request . . . at the very least his dismissal from Orangeville.

DR TOM JONATHON:

Bill thank you for being frank and Alex . . . your comments were candid as usual . . . Gentlemen it is obvious that the animosity and mistrust is much deeper than I thought. But I wish to have closure on these issues . . . I've known both of you for many years and appreciate you for different reasons. However I cannot condone nor allow your conduct to continue as was demonstrated in the staff meeting today. Bill . . . I'm writing a letter of reprimand regarding your conduct in the staff meeting today which will remain on your personnel file for the duration of your employment at Orangeville. Further breech of professional conduct will result in immediate termination forthwith . . . is that perfectly clear.

(Bill begins to speak and is waved off by Dr Jonathon)

Alex . . . you can be a caustic and arrogant son of a bitch who probably deserved in spades whatever Bill dished out. If I witness or ever hear of you baiting or demeaning anyone in a public forum . . . your employment will be jeopardized . . . is that perfectly clear.

(Alex stands quietly and then nods)

Gentlemen . . . I have another appointment waiting outside. I appreciate you both and hope things get worked out. Please heed my warnings . . . I do not make idle threats nor do I 'shoot from the hip'.

(both men nod in unison and leave Dr Jonathon's office closing the door)

STAGE LIGHTS DIM — END OF SCENE TWO

ACT TWO SCENE THREE

(The lights are raised, the stage reveals a hospital meeting room with a circle of chairs. Sitting in one of the chairs is Nurse Alice Mayfield reading notes on a clipboard. The door opens suddenly behind Alice and in troops five male patients dressed in various apparel. Three patients are over forty two patients are in their twenties. General Stanley Morgan is present and dressed in loud, brightly colored clothing. Alice looks up and stares at each man as they sit down in the circle. This is the weekly group therapy session and is viewed with fear and trepidation by the patients. Alice Mayfield is a no nonsense therapist, direct and to the point)

ALICE MAYFIELD:

Hi guys I hope everybody's ready to work today . . . I know I came prepared.

GENERAL STANLEY MORGAN:

Oh God Alice how officious . . . whose gonads are being crushed today? C'mon.

CHRISTOPHER:
(tall man in his twenties very anxious)

Alice do we have to talk about ourselves today? I mean everybody knows my story . . . it's boring.

(exaggerated yawn by Christopher the group laughs)

ALICE MAYFIELD:

Christopher I thought we'd continue our discussion on issues that perturb each of you . . . sharing these feelings with the group could be very therapeutic.

GENERAL STANLEY MORGAN:

Oh for God's sake . . . I left 'Wheel of Fortune' for this crap . . . come on

(folds his arms abruptly and looks disgruntled)

Alice can't we

(interrupted by Alice)

ALICE MAYFIELD:

Stan the agenda is set . . . please bear with me for the next hour or so your comments are important.

DANIEL:

(Dan is in his forties, paranoid and extremely aggressive)

Morgan shut your mouth and let the girl alone. I like the agenda today at least we can talk about things that make us crazy.

(Daniel stares menacingly at Stan)

GENERAL STANLEY MORGAN:

O.K Dan 'Sto Pro Veritate' . . . keep cool . . . don't decompensate . . . not today anyway.

DANIEL:

How would you like a punch in the mouth?

ALICE MAYFIELD:

Dan why don't we start by discussing your ideas about people . . .
relationships and how we maintain them. What are some character-
istics you look for in someone you wish to befriend?

DANIEL:

I've been screwed in the ear so many times people have little rel-
evance in my life. I get angry when I have to talk with people . . .
I prefer being alone with my thoughts . . . my wife understood but
then she was killed by a Goddamn drunk driver.

ALICE MAYFIELD:

Does anyone wish to comment on Dan's statement?

*(no one talks each group member is busy looking at the floor, ceiling,
around the room)*

C'mon don't be shy . . . Stephen how 'bout you? What about Dan's
comments on people?

STEPHEN:

(Mid twenties, young jewish man very insecure)

Alice whenever Dan talks about people or generally anything there
is so much anger and resentment. Maybe

(cut off by Daniel)

DANIEL:

WHO THE HELL DO YOU THINK YOU ARE SIGMUND FRI-GIN' FREUD? PICK A WINDOW.

(Daniel leaps from his chair and stands over Stephen who cringes)

STEPHEN:

Dan I'm not trying to denigrate you . . . I mean I'm not trying to put you down in anyway . . It's just an honest observation . . . I don't mean to hurt your feelings.

DANIEL:

Kiss my ass milksop. What is this touchy feely B.S?

ALICE MAYFIELD:

Dan let Stephen know what you feel without threatening him. I believe he was being frank in a way that was genuine and not meant to hurt you.

GENERAL STANLEY MORGAN:

Oh for God's Sake I'm missing 'Wheel of Fortune' for this crap . . . give me a break.

(Stan looks to the ceiling and points his hands in prayer)

Hey Alice can we take a vote?

(cut off by Alice)

ALICE MAYFIELD:

Stan what are your feelings about Dan's earlier statement?

GENERAL STANLEY MORGAN:

If I say something can I leave?

ALICE MAYFIELD:

No Stan you know the rules and you voted to uphold them when we began this group in September.

GENERAL STANLEY MORGAN:

Yeah but that's before you changed the time on me . . . this is an ungodly hour of the day.

> *(Stan looks at his watch and stirs in his chair)*

ALICE MAYFIELD:

Stan . . . what is your opinion of Dan's statement?

DANIEL:

MORGAN IF YOU DON'T SAY SOMETHING YOU'RE DEAD. I'LL PUNCH THE CRAP OUT OF YAH AND

> *(pregnant pause the rest of the group is visibly intimidated and are restless in their chairs. Dan mutes his voice)*

. . . sell your body for hamburger meat. Now say something . . . you're wasting the group's time.

GENERAL STANLEY MORGAN:

O.K O.K O.K . . Dan . . . you're ideas about people are interesting . . . now . . . can I leave the group Alice?

ALICE MAYFIELD:

Stan if Daniel promises to stop threatening you will you open up? How 'bout it Daniel? I'm wondering how the other group members feel about your manner with people?

(Alice looks around the group slowly pausing when she comes to Daniel)

JIM:

(Jim is forty, with greying hair and muscular physique)

Alice I've been coming to groups like this for over ten years and have yet to see a guy disrupt things so much. Dan . . . calm down . . . everyone is trying to work through their problems. They don't need further aggravation by you threatening them.

(Jim maintains eye contact with Dan and is not intimidated — Dan is subdued)

DANIEL:

(Dan looks at Jim and then pauses before responding)

Jim my beef isn't with you . . . you haven't caused any trouble so far . . . it's the other guys that bug me . . . especially Morgan . . . he needs a good shot in the mouth . . . <u>hey why don't we talk about Stan the sex maniac?</u>

ALICE MAYFIELD:

Dan please stop it . . . we are tired of your macho approach to everyone. I know you can be civil and I would appreciate a little more co-operation from you.

DANIEL:

O.K Alice. . . how's this? Stanley you are a royal 'pain in the ass' and if you continue to provoke my anger I will lose my temper and break your nose.

(the group laughs except Stanley who looks at the floor)

ALICE MAYFIELD:

Dan . . . just keep in mind what I said and try and remember your pact as a group member. We are here to learn about what makes us hurt inside and there will be times when we challenge the negatives and reinforce the positives. Do you follow?

DANIEL:

(Dan beams with a broad toothy smile)

Yeh I'm challenging the negatives

(Dan points abruptly at Stan and then towards himself)

and reinforcing the positives . . . ME.

(group laughs except Stan who grins and looks at the floor)

STEPHEN:

(Stephen cups his hands nervously and flips his hair with an effeminate jerk of his head)

Dan I wish for once you'd stop being such a bully. You force people to be angry with you when you continually come on like a macho man.

DANIEL:

(Daniel leaps up from his chair)

SHUT UP SHIT FOR BRAINS. I WAS UP TO MY GODDAMN
NECK IN RICE PADDIES WHEN YOU WERE COMING DOWN
YOU'RE OLD LADY'S CHUTE . . .

> *(the group is intimidated and agitated in their seats Dan pauses
> before continuing)*

<u>Have you ever killed a man with your bare hands . . . eye to eye . . .
watching him die?</u> You smell him and watch his eyes roll and then
he's done. No more life . . . you play God . . . and he's done. You're
such a nimrod limp wrist

> *(Dan stands upright fists clenched looking at Stephen who shrinks
> in his chair)*

ALICE MAYFIELD:

<u>Dan please sit down.</u>

> *(Alice speaks in a soft therapeutic voice)*

Dan . . . please sit down.

DANIEL:

In a minute . . . I just wanna say something . . . I killed men . . . I
hated slants and still do. They'd sneak up and do the men in the
perimeter . . . no sound . . . nothing . . . cut their throats and watch
'em die . . . sometimes to make a point they'd emasculate 'em and
stick the organs . . . sorry Alice but it happened. Next morning
you'd come out to relieve your buddy and he's . . .

> *(Dan begins to cry)*

You end up trustin' nobody . . . especially the officer jerkoffs who
sent you out everyday. Those ass wipes like Morgan leave you out on
point waitin' for you to draw fire. They could give a damn and you're
left out alone to die. Those little slope bastards knew it too . . .

(Dan's voice trails off the group is stone silent he sits down and looks at the floor)

ALICE MAYFIELD:

Gentlemen I think Dan has shown lot of courage today.

GENERAL STANLEY MORGAN:

Alice . . . I know we must be a bunch of demanding bastards at least I am anyway. Why do hospitals like this bring out the worst in all of us? I mean life has its ups and downs but Dan's experiences

(Dan leaps from his chair strides over to stand over Stan menacingly)

DANIEL:

SHUT UP MORGAN YOU TWO FACED GUTLESS

(Alice interrupts Dan who walks over to face him)

ALICE MAYFIELD:

Dan . . . could you please sit

(cut off by Stan)

GENERAL STANLEY MORGAN:

Dan . . . I never saw action . . . Dan

(cut off by Dan)

DAN:

(spotlight — soft light on Dan — center focus as he talks to Stan)

<u>You hypocrite garbage in garbage out bastard.</u> I know why you're here . . . you raped a girl on campus. Morgan you are filth you don't

breathe the same air I do. I was a decorated goddamn grunt completing two days rear guard action . . . twenty - two confirmed kills while YOU GUTLESS JERKOFFS were wining and dining Nixon.

(much reduced voice)

Just shut your goddamn mouth around me.

GENERAL STANLEY MORGAN:

Dan

(cut off by Dan)

DANIEL:

(shouts, fists clenched)

SHUT UP YOU DON'T EXIST

Just shut your goddamn mouth around me.

ALICE MAYFIELD:

(still standing beside Dan)

Dan . . . could you return to your seat please . . . Dan . . . please return to your seat.

GENERAL STANLEY MORGAN:

(Stan seated looks at Dan)

Dan I never saw action . . .

ALICE MAYFIELD:

Dan please return to your seat.

(Dan slowly returns to his chair and sits down he gazes around the room)

GENERAL STANLEY MORGAN:

I started a rumor.

ALICE MAYFIELD:

Stan could you elaborate . . . what are you talking about?

GENERAL STANLEY MORGAN:

I started the rumor about the cutbacks.

ALICE MAYFIELD:

Stan this afternoon we had a

(cut off by Jim)

JIM:

(leans forward intensely)

<u>Morgan do you know what you've done?</u> If it's true your life is worth zero . . . <u>less than zero</u> on this ward. Whether the cutbacks are coming next fiscal year or not isn't the point . . . <u>do you know the fear and anxiety you have provoked on the ward?</u> People thinking they could be moved or worse still forgotten about . . . THANKS FOR NOTHING.

DANIEL:

THAT'S IT YOU'RE DEAD ONE WAY OR THE OTHER YOU'RE DEAD.

(leaps up and is restrained by the other group members, regains composure and sits down glaring at Stan)

ALICE MAYFIELD:

<u>Stop it Stop it</u> . . . Stan and the rest of you Dr Jonathon held a staff meeting this afternoon to inform.

(cut off by Stan)

GENERAL STANLEY MORGAN:

Alice shush . . . to reiterate I started the rumor abut the cutbacks a few months ago. It didn't take a genius to figure out what might happen. <u>Look at the fiscal restraint measures</u>

(mock exaggeration)

the past five or six years. <u>I mean it ended up true didn't it? You're going to tell us that aren't you.</u>

(Dan leaps from his chair and lunges at Stan, they fall entangled on the floor. Jim overpowers Dan and pulls him off Stan and walks him away in an arm lock, the other group members are huddled together hiding behind Alice)

ALICE MAYFIELD:

O.K guys I think we should call it a day. I want you to help me tidy up . . . could you put the chairs back the way they were before. I also want you guys to head back to your rooms . . .Group is finished.

(the patients slowly leave the room Dan turns to shake his fist at Stan, Jim motions Dan to calm down)

Jim . . . could you walk Stan to his room and spend some time with him. Thank you.

(Jim acknowledges with a nod and he and Stan leave the room, Stan is smiling and Jim is solemn)

STAGE LIGHT DIMS — END OF SCENE III

INTERMISSION

ACT THREE SCENE ONE

(The lights are raised it is one week later. The stage is brightly lit. Bill Winthrop is sitting behind his desk writing a memo. His door is open the patients are quietly walking by an occasional 'Hi Bill' is heard from the hall. Bill looks up periodically from his work to acknowledge the patients. However his serious expression reflects the task at hand — reading staff exit reports. Bill looks up from his work Don Carmichael is standing over him looking visibly upset. Bill motions him to sit down.)

BILL WINTHROP:

Don how's your day going?

DON CARMICHAEL:

Dooley is such a jerk I hate his guts . . .why the hell does he enjoy being such a cruel bastard to everyone?

BILL WINTHROP:

Why don't you start from the beginning Don?

DON CARMICHAEL:

The man needs a 'Mental Status Exam' I swear to God he's a 309.30.

BILL WINTHROP:

I beg your pardon?

DON CARMICHAEL:

A 309.30 you know . . . the DSM 111-R classification. Adjustment Disorder with Disturbance of Conduct. He's quite disturbed Bill. The residents in first year psychiatry hate his guts and are asking me to go to Dr Jonathon. They want a harassment charge laid.

BILL WINTHROP:

How has he been harassing people? I need specifics Don.

DON CARMICHAEL:

Ah . . . at this point I'm not sure I want to get into it . . . but I need to ventilate . . . can I trust what I say won't be disclosed . . . to anyone Bill? There are pressures from my student peers to take decisive action . . . be a leader . . . in short <u>nuke the bastard.</u>

BILL WINTHROP:

(Bill laughs)

Don . . . Alex tends to categorize people . . . strong or weak . . . he needs control and will seek control at all costs. There are victims out there that wished they never crossed his path. That's off the record of course.

(both men laugh)

DON CARMICHAEL:

Bill I'll lay it on the line. I think his research techniques, experimental approach and ethical standards are highly questionable.

(Bill looks startled and leans forward intensely)

I'm also aware of a phone call he made to Topeka which further confirms his lack of integrity . . . what am I saying? Who the hell am I you say? A lousy first year resident. I've got to keep my nose clean or risk

termination . . . my colleagues are expecting me to blow the whistle.
Bill . . . you're the only one I can trust . . . one positive thing in your
favor . . . Dooley hates your guts too. So I guess you ain't too bad.

(both men laugh)

BILL WINTHROP:
Could you be more specific with your allegation? I mean I can't
help you if you won't be more specific in your disclosure.

DON CARMICHAEL:
Bill cut the counseling crap . . .I'm a psychiatric resident albeit first
year . . . what are your credentials Ed.D? Please cut the crap and
let's talk man to man . . . I like you much better when you forget
to clinicize.

BILL WINTHROP:
Don I do want to get to the bottom of this

(cut off)

DON CARMICHAEL:
Bill much better. I knew you could do it.

BILL WINTHROP:
Sometimes I wonder if all residents take a test in logical positivism.

DON CARMICHAEL:
Only on Mondays and Tuesdays.

(both laugh)

Seriously you have a point . . . working with Dooley is like standing in purgatory. He's Satan and you're the poor bastard atoning for past sins. He robs you of pride, ethical principles and is so goddamn predatory you forget to duck after awhile. Bill his idea of social intercourse is a crude attempt at foreplay . . . let's face it.

BILL WINTHROP:

Don . . . could we move from the commentary and deal with the salient issue . . . what has Alex done?

DON CARMICHAEL:

You got it . . . from the hip . . . you know all those double blind experiments he did with the schizophrenics a couple of years ago? You know the hypotheses he made that were subsequently validated in his experiments? I have reason to believe he knew the results he was testing for <u>prior to the experiments being conducted.</u>

BILL WINTHROP:

WHAT?

DON CARMICHAEL:

The studies assessing the clinical effectiveness of chlorpromazine on chronic hospitalized schizophrenic patients <u>are invalid. The results are complete crap.</u>

BILL WINTHROP:

Are you sure about

(cut off)

DON CARMICHAEL:

Bill it's my contention that he was aware of how much medication was being administered in twelve studies. In a real 'double blind' neither the experimenter nor the patient are made aware of which drug . . . medicine . . . or placebo is being administered. The subsequent data was biased towards one of the medications on the patients' condition and its chronicity.

(cut off)

BILL WINTHROP:

<u>That phony pretentious</u>

(cut off)

DON CARMICHAEL:

No wait I'm not finished. I tell you Dooley is one tricky bastard. He wrote up his discussion section in such a way that camouflaged his biasing of the results. He knew they would be invalid if he didn't finesse the description of how he completed his research method.

BILL WINTHROP:

I'm not following Don.

DON CARMICHAEL:

In the thirty-eight studies utilizing the chlorpromazine medication with the schizophrenics, the percentage of patients who improved from moderately to better that average ranged from five percent to eighty-five percent . . . the median was fifty-eight percent. Twelve of the studies were 'double blind . . <u>only thirty-seven percent of the patients showed improvement. Well below the median.</u> Bill . . . Dooley's brilliant hypothesis had stated that the results from the 'double blind' utilizing this drug would be significantly lower than the overall median of improvement by the other newer drugs.

BILL WINTHROP:

So he forecasted accurately is that a crime?

DON CARMICHAEL:

Bill, Bill, he already knew the pre- determined dosages prescribed for those twelve studies. They were supposed to be randomly chosen for the 'double blind' experiments. Remember in a 'double blind' neither the researcher nor the patient are aware of the conditions with which the independent variable . . . namely the chlorpromazine interacts with the patient

(stage whisper)

IT'S A SECRET.

BILL WINTHROP:

Don please get to the point.

DON CARMICHAEL:

I have information which suggests that Dooley knew the dosages of both the placebo and the chlorpromazine prescribed in the twelve 'double blind' studies. Hence his prediction or

(mocking tone)

'hypothesis' that chlorpromazine as compared to other more recently developed anti-psychotics would have markedly inferior results is pretentious 'BS'. Alex already knew the dosage levels before the experiment was conducted which invalidated the results but allowed him to prove his hypothesis. It's called fraud Bill . . . scientific fraud and he should be hung out to dry by the authorities. I wonder how often he's played this game over the years?

BILL WINTHROP:

Where is your proof Don? Unethical research is a pretty tough accusation to banter around . . . let alone prove beyond reasonable doubt. Especially in this place during these times.

DON CARMICHAEL:

About two months ago I overheard him talking to a graduate student on the phone . . . long distance and by the sound of it University of Kansas. Alex was being grilled about the results from the double blind studies. He couldn't answer a damn thing which is highly irregular don't you think. What clued me in was his phony erudite manner whenever the questions became too detailed or they zeroed in on his uncanny ability to accurately prognosticate in so many double blind experiments over the years. Boy genius . . . right . . . like hell. I could tell by the way he was hedging his comments that he was hiding something. He was trying very hard to avoid any incriminating statements regarding the nature of the experimental procedure.

BILL WINTHROP:

Strange?

DON CARMICHAEL:

Bill you know Dooley . . . he's a Barracuda since when is he ever insecure about his lab work? Never . . . unless he was caught in a lie of such magnitude that knew his credibility and career were in jeopardy. To top it off he ended the conversation with a 'sorry I couldn't be of further help' tone that totally disturbed me. His manner was completely out of character throughout the phone call. What's the big deal you say? <u>I hate the guy how's that.</u>

(both laugh)

Look . . . everything started to come together after awhile . . . his lab assistants quitting ad nauseum . . . or being fired without prior warning. Dooley's brilliant prognostications and lab results which backed up his soothsayer reputation . . . like clock work every year <u>what total B.S.</u> It was all there under the surface . . . you just had to dig. Can you imagine his contracts with the pharmaceutical companies? Well it's time to close the loop.

BILL WINTHROP:

Don . . . Don . . . God I'm at a

(cutoff)

DON CARMICHAEL:

God had nothing to do with it. Anytime one of Dooley's assistants requested more instruction than he felt they required . . . you know . . . seeking more exact information . . . they were given the boot. No chance for investigation which could lead to dialogue . . . you know . . . to air their grievances regarding his fraudulent research practices. <u>Phony bastard.</u>

BILL WINTHROP:

Don what made you suspicious initially . . . you know inconsistencies in his research data . . . specifics that would incriminate him?

DON CARMICHAEL:

Ah the sine qua non of my argument. Easy . . . it was discovering that by coincidence the dosage level was the same . . . for twenty-eight percent of the most seriously disturbed patients. That high a percentage is an anomaly . . . it's too pat. He covered up by interspersing the regularity of each drug dosage with other dosage levels. So . . . he might have used two, three or four different drug dosages for the total number of cases. But then made sure the dosages were frequently the same for those patients who reacted negatively to the drugs' increased level of toxicity. Thus consistently proving his working hypotheses that chlorpromazine as compared with other newer drugs has markedly inferior results

(reduces volume to normal speaking voice)

and gaining a reputation of being the mid western genius of pharmacology . . . guaranteeing 'moo-cho' drug research grants from the pharmaceuticals. Smart boy . . . but how did he sleep at night?

BILL WINTHROP:

My God.

DON CARMICHAEL:

Bill take a valium . . . God had nothing to do with it.

(both men laugh)

Just to make sure that I wasn't decompensating I put the frequency patterns of the tampered dosage trials on the computer. I then matched the probability of this dosage being administered randomly with the probable effects . . . negative, positive, skewed for all types of schizophrenic patients.

BILL WINTHROP:

<u>What were the results?</u>

DON CARMICHAEL:

The probability of getting the negative results Dooley received with the chlorpromazine double blind trials <u>was 1 in 2.3 million. Statistically an impossibility.</u> In my opinion and probably the opinion of a few doctoral candidates who questioned him. Dooley cooked the experimental procedure to get the results he needed to prove his working hypothesis and maintain his reputation. This would result in more and more drug companies seeking fat research contracts with his lab to help market their pet drug. What drove him to jeopardize his career?

(pregnant pause as both state simultaneously)

309.30.

(both men begin to laugh hysterically and then gain control)

BILL WINTHROP:

Where do we go with this Don . . . you're a genius.

DON CARMICHAEL:

'Genius smenius' . . . any computer geek worth his salt could find the inconsistency. What is more interesting is calculating the probability of me overhearing his phone call making a fool of himself with a grad student innocently questioning how he is so consistently right with double blind experiments. Bill . . . <u>Alex is one dead 309.30.</u>

BILL WINTHROP:

Do you want to phone Tom Jonathon?

DON CARMICHAEL:

<u>Hell no.</u>

(both men laugh)

He thinks Dooley's another Einstein . . . no amount of information brought forward will topple Dooley.

BILL WINTHROP:

Unless he's caught beating up a patient and even then . . . stranger things have happened at Orangeville. Don . . . we can't let this information die. He must be stopped . . . I know Tom Jonathon would listen.

DON CARMICHAEL:

Bill . . . it's my word against an acknowledged expert in the field of psychopharmacology and a big revenue earner for the hospital doesn't hurt either. Quite frankly I don't want anymore headaches right now . . . hero . . . scapegoat . . . proof or no proof <u>not me.</u> I'm handing it off to you . . . which you can say you received from an 'interested third party' or some such B.S. I can discretely coach you through the technical stuff and <u>my</u> working hypothesis

(both men laugh)

of how he conned his staff during the clinical trials . . . how 'bout it?

BILL WINTHROP:

O.K . . . for now I keep quiet and respect confidentiality. But this issue must be reported . . . it's our duty to expose such unethical practice. If we don't we're no better than the Alex Dooley's of the world. I am not letting this rest Don . . . please reconsider and face this thing head on . . . I can be a valuable resource.

DON CARMICHAEL:

<u>Winthrop you naïve bastard.</u> Dooley is corrupt with connections 'up the ying yang' . . . do you think you can defeat him? There is no justice in the world . . . haven't you heard?

BILL WINTHROP:

There is no justice . . . but once in awhile we tip the scales. Let me talk to Tom Jonathon.

(pregnant pause Bill allows Don to reflect on the request)

Don . . . I won't breech confidentiality without your sanction in this matter . . . I want your support and help . . . as a colleague and friend.

DON CARMICHAEL:

O.K O.K. . . let's meet with Tom Jonathon but I know what will happen. A written deposition from me disclaiming Dooley's research as a hoax and then what . . . I guess I knew that before I came here . . . you would help me make a decision. One way or the other. God . . . <u>what a catharsis.</u>

(both men laugh and then state simultaneously)

<u>God had nothing to do with it.</u>

BILL WINTHROP:

Who knows maybe I'll do a Post Doc at Harvard next year.

(both men laugh)

DON CARMICHAEL:

Bill do you think you can précis the information I gave you? I threw a lot of technical jargon at you and was excited.

BILL WINTHROP:

Why don't we arrange a time to meet jointly with Tom Jonathon and present your case against Dooley. Let Tom call the shots after that. I've known him for many years and I think he's fair.

(phone rings interrupting Bill who bends over to pick it up)

Hello . . . Dr Winthrop can I help you? Oh hi Tom what's new? Yes as a matter of fact

(pauses while looking directly at Don Carmichael)

Hmm

(pauses then hangs up the phone)

Don . . . that was Tom Jonathon . . . apparently he's just received a written complaint from Alex Dooley about your professional conduct. He's concerned that this complaint constitutes a second action take against you in three months. He wants a meeting in thirty minutes in my office. Look . . . why don't you go back to your office and put something on paper. I'll call you when we're ready to meet.

(Don looks at Bill stands up and leaves the office, leaving the door open behind him, Bill looks at his sign on the wall behind his desk STO PRO VERITATE)

STAGE LIGHTS DIM — END OF SCENE ONE

ACT THREE SCENE TWO

(The lights are raised. Bill Winthrop is sitting in his office chair looking pensive. In five minutes both Tom Jonathon and Alex Dooley will be arriving for a meeting to discuss Don Carmichael's behavior. Bill tries some relaxation exercises flexing and relaxing his fists and forearms. Closing his eyes and breathing in a regulated manner he continues to flex and relax his fists. Two patients walking by his office stop and peer at Bill through the open door. Both patients drop down to the floor in the doorway and mimic Bill's relaxation techniques. At this time Alex Dooley and Tom Jonathon arrive stepping over the patients without missing a step or uttering a word)

DR TOM JONATHON:

Bill are you alright?

BILL WINTHROP:

Oh hi Tom . . . Alex . . . just doing my morning relaxation exercises. Sit down . . . can I get you some coffee?

(both men sit down opposite Bill)

ALEX DOOLEY:

Winthrop . . . you never fail to amaze me. What's with the two patients? Your protégés?

BILL WINTHROP:

Alex don't start up again. O.K guys

(looks at Jim and Stephen)

I've got a meeting . . . see yah later.

(Bill slowly closes the door and the two inpatients start to laugh)

JIM:

See yah Bill have a great day. I always feel great after watching you do your relaxation exercises.

(Jim digs Stephen in the ribs and the laugh increases in intensity)

STEPHEN:

Yah I really feel great

(Bill cuts him off)

BILL WINTHROP:

Jim . . . Stephen . . . I've got a meeting with these gentlemen.

(closes the door completely leaving the men alone in the hall)

DR TOM JONATHON:

Bill thanks for seeing both of us on such short notice . . . this is the crux of the matter. Alex has lodged a serious complaint against Dr Carmichael the first year psychiatric resident. I think you're familiar with

(Alex interrupts)

ALEX DOOLEY:

With due respect Tom . . . <u>Carmichael</u> is a leech of the first order. An impostor he deserves to be canned. A phrase running rampant these days. I believe you should understand this

(interrupted by Dr Jonathon)

DR TOM JONATHON:

Dooley shut your mouth and <u>don't interrupt me again.</u>

BILL WINTHROP:

Tom . . . I'm wondering whether I should phone Don . . . he's expecting to sit in on the meeting.

DR TOM JONATHON:

Not right now Bill . . . I'll talk to him later. Bill . . . Alex has laid some pretty serious allegations against our young resident. More specifically that Dr Carmichael intercepted experimental data from Alex's current research project and contacted 'Grant' agencies to discredit Alex. Apparently Alex's contacts at the University thought it prudent to let us know. Bill . . . Alex wants Carmichael's residency terminated. Does that about size it up Alex?

(Alex nods and leans forward)

BILL WINTHROP:

Tom . . . if these allegations are true then Dr Carmichael should be appropriately reprimanded. Put him on probation for the duration of his residency . . . but termination . . . it's too extreme.

ALEX DOOLEY:

May I talk Tom? Winthrop . . . for the past three months Carmichael has been seen in and around my lab an inordinate amount of times. Something in the order of six times per week. At first we thought it was a legitimate interest in our research project. We should be so lucky. A psychiatrist taking interest in psychological research . . . I thought their pocket books took precedence.

DR TOM JONATHON:

<u>Dooley . . . comedians I don't need</u> . . . get on with your story.

ALEX DOOLEY:

Sorry Tom . . . the issue became more extreme about two weeks ago when I noticed him outside my door. Apparently eaves dropping on a phone call I was making. Subsequently a day later the Librarian phoned me about a request by Dr Carmichael for several photocopies of a recent publication of mine . . . on double blind experimentation. She couldn't find the manuscript and wondered if I had a 'galley' copy? I saw no problem and gave her my copy.

DR TOM JONATHON:

Dooley for God's sake

(cut off by Alex)

ALEX DOOLEY:

(becoming more animated as his confidence rises to the occasion)

Sorry Tom . . . I'll get to the point. Coincidently the phone call Dr Carmichael overheard concerned a graduate student at Kansas . . . <u>challenging the double blind results on schizophrenics.</u> Two or three days later I met Carmichael in the cafeteria and queered his interest in double blind methodology. He balked at my question and then stated he enjoyed 'walking on the edge' or words to that effect. I found his comment inane and took no notice at the time.

(interrupted by Dr Jonathon)

DR TOM JONATHON:
Alex . . . get to the point.

ALEX DOOLEY:
I am not in the habit of receiving such liberties lightly. I want him banned from my lab and his residency terminated. He has received other complaints since his arrival Tom . . . Winthrop knows this.

BILL WINTHROP:
Alex I have talked with Don Carmichael and

(interrupted by Alex Dooley)

ALEX DOOLEY:
I knew it there is a conspiracy

(cut off by Dr Jonathon)

DR TOM JONATHON:
Shut up Dooley and let Bill finish.

BILL WINTHROP:
Tom I can't breech confidentiality . . . why don't I call Dr Carmichael in to 'clear the air'?

(looks at Dr Jonathon)

How 'bout it?

DR TOM JONATHON:

Bill I hope Carmichael is a bright young man who wants to keep his nose clean. I don't need anymore scandal at Orangeville . . . do you 'catch my drift'?

(Alex smiles while looking at the floor)

ALEX DOOLEY:

Winthrop . . . is that the best you can do? Obviously there's a cover up and you're a major player. <u>Out with it . . . come clean.</u>

BILL WINTHROP:

Alex I don't know what motivates you to antagonize so many people so often. <u>I've reached my limit with your crap</u> . . . OUT.

(Bill points to the door and stands up)

ALEX DOOLEY:

Tom now do you see

(cut off by Dr Jonathon)

DR TOM JONATHON:

<u>Alex out.</u> I want you in my office at 9:00 A.M tomorrow morning.

(Alex stands up slowly and walks to the door slamming the door behind him at the same time stepping over Jim and Stephen still completing relaxation exercises on the corridor floor outside the office)

BILL WINTHROP:

He must be eager

(cut off)

DR TOM JONATHON:

Bill . . . maybe you could level with me?

BILL WINTHROP:

Tom ethically I can't go into detail but I can say Carmichael came to my office a few days ago very upset. He felt he was in a predicament regarding a research issue. Subsequently upon disclosing his concerns I felt it should be taken up with you. It can't wait in my professional opinion . . . let me call Don.

DR TOM JONATHON:

As you wish . . . call him.

BILL WINTHROP:

(leans over the desk picks up the phone and dials)

Don . . . hi . . . it's me again . . . look I need you're O.K to divulge the matter we discussed to Tom Jonathon. Yes . . . he's sitting here. Alex . . . no he's not present . . . yes I can remember the salient points . . . yes O.K thanks.

(hangs up the phone walks over to a chair by the desk and sits down with a flop)

Tom . . . Don Carmichael came to my office with an indictment against Dooley's research methodology and ethics.

DR TOM JONATHON:
WHAT?

BILL WINTHROP:
Apparently Alex cooked the statistics to bias the results in favor of his hypotheses concerning 'double blind' studies . . . and it appears this has been going on for years. Remember all the accolades he got a couple of years ago? Don Carmichael systematically debunked Dooley's hypothesis on the basis of the results being statistically impossible without Dooley cooking the dosages and subject sample being researched. Anyway . . . Carmichael would like to talk with you about the whole matter. I guess this is common knowledge among the other residents and they want action taken Tom . . . could we arrange a time to meet with

(cut off abruptly)

DR TOM JONATHON:
Bill . . . I've always admired your principles. From the first time I interviewed you I said to myself 'this is a man I can trust'. You have been a 'tower' Bill . . . an icon of strength . . . <u>but now is not the time.</u>

BILL WINTHROP:
FOR GOD'S SAKE WHY NOT?

DR TOM JONATHON:
(a pregnant pause while Tom gathers up his thoughts)

Politically I can't afford Orangeville's reputation being dragged through the sewer. No . . .

(shakes his head while talking)

not at this time . . . what with the impending cutbacks . . . low morale and the media's scrutiny. . . another scandal is all I need. Our credibility is at stake Bill . . . I think we should wait for six months.

BILL WINTHROP:

Tom I never thought I'd hear

(cut off)

DR TOM JONATHON:

Bite the bullet . . . lay low for awhile until this tidal wave of uncertainty is . . . Bill . . . go have another talk with Don Carmichael. Tell him poor timing mitigates against such disclosure . . . anything. How 'bout 'Do you know what impact this would have on Dooley's career? He'll see the light Bill.

BILL WINTHROP:

<u>Are you demented? Do you know what you've just said?</u> You are the Chief of General Staff . . . a man I respect <u>where the hell do you get off taking such a 'chicken shit' attitude?</u>

DR TOM JONATHON:

Go ahead Bill let it out.

BILL WINTHROP:

Carmichael's young and idealistic and uncovered a lie that besmirches Orangeville <u>and you ask me to cover up.</u>

DR TOM JONATHON:

Bill I'm afraid my request is a directive. I'll accept your resignation if you can't . . . or won't carry it out. Look . . . we go back a long time . . . don't make any hasty decisions. I'm not saying 'no I won't look into the matter' <u>but now is not the time.</u> It's January and April 1st is just around the corner as in <u>new fiscal year.</u> Once I know where we stand financially I'll look into Dooley's alleged misdeeds. Bill . . . I've got to go . . . I'll leave this matter in your capable hands . . . you've never failed me yet . . . or Orangeville Psychiatric for that matter.

(Bill makes a masturbation movement with his fist)

Bill I still view you as one of my 'king pins' why don't you take the rest of the week off . . . relax . . . play some golf . . . 'chase some skirt' as we used to say. I'm going to be late . . . <u>think it over Bill.</u>

(Dr Jonathon stands up and prepares to leave the office)

BILL WINTHROP:

Tom I can't compromise on this issue. I've gone too far in my commitment to Don Carmichael.

DR TOM JONATHON:

I've got to go

(walks briskly to the door and pauses to speak)

I know you'll see things clearly . . . take some time off and don't make any hasty decisions. <u>They have a habit of biting you in the ass.</u>

(laughs at his joke and walks out the door — Bill slumps his head on the desk covering it with his hands. General Stanley Morgan walks in and stands staring at Bill)

GENERAL STANLEY MORGAN:

Bill can I be of assistance? Having a bad morning Sport?

(Bill's head moves)

BILL WINTHROP:

Oh hi Stan . . . just taking a breather. Progressive deep muscle relaxation techniques . . . does it every time.

GENERAL STANLEY MORGAN:

Bill . . . you're talking to a diagnosed sexual psychopath. Don't try and con a crazy . . . what's wrong?

BILL WINTHROP:

Stan . . . it's been one of those days.

GENERAL STANLEY MORGAN:

Cut the crap Bill . . . I stopped by 'to say hi'

(states in a flippant manner for effect)

and see you sleeping on the job you slob . . . what's wrong amigo?

BILL WINTHROP:

No comment Stan.

GENERAL STANLEY MORGAN:

'Whoa' . . . looks like a cue to leave . . . if you need a 'third ear' give me a call.

III, ii, 88 | D.S. Hutcheon

(stands up from his chair stands to attention and gives a military salute)

BILL WINTHROP:

Stan I'm sorry for being brusque but I've got a meeting to go to . . .

(pregnant pause as Bill looks puzzled)

later maybe we can talk Stan. How 'bout tomorrow morning?

GENERAL STANLEY MORGAN:

As long as it doesn't interfere with the 'Wheel of Fortune'

(Bill laughs and Stan leaves the office barely missing Alice Mayfield who slides past Stan into Bill's office Stan makes an 'off the cuff' comment)

Alice . . . how pretty you look . . . we should do lunch sometime?

ALICE MAYFIELD:

I don't think so Stan.

(Stan makes a face and walks away)

Bill I just heard that 'snake in the grass' Dooley is trying to muscle Don Carmichael. Not that I mind . . . but it's all over the wards. The patients are laying odds on how long Carmichael lasts as a resident. Is it true?

BILL WINTHROP:

Alice you know I can't breech confidentiality.

ALICE MAYFIELD:

<u>So it's true.</u> Oh God . . . Dooley can be such a repulsive creep . . . even though Carmichael has it coming . . . I don't think he deserves that fate. Dooley is formidable when his credibility is challenged . . . he is so insecure.

BILL WINTHROP:
(Bill leans forward on his chair abruptly)

Alice how are

(phone rings and Bill answers)

'Dr Winthrop . . . hi Tom . . . later on today? Sure . . . what time? . . . 3:30 . . . in your office? O.K I'll be there . . . yah . . . goodbye

(hangs up and sits staring at Alice)

ALICE MAYFIELD:
(walks over from the door chooses a chair opposite Bill and sits down)

Who was that . . . Tom Jonathon? Oh God . . . the big boys are involved. Poor Carmichael . . . has he caught wind of this?

BILL WINTHROP:
Alice I can't really discuss

(cut off abruptly)

ALICE MAYFIELD:
I know I know . . . you can't breech confidentiality. I can't stand men under stress . . . they're so phony. Anyway . . . Nurse Mayfield must

leave before her patients 'beat the crap' out of each other. Bill . . . I'll be at the bar tonight . . . drop in for a drink . . . we can talk.

(Alice slowly stands up turns and leaves the office . . . Bill follows her with his eyes, stands up and stretches. Subsequently he turns around and walks over to look at the motto on his wall 'STO PRO VERITATE'. He turns around and standing at the doorway is Dr Carmichael smiling)

DON CARMICHAEL:

<u>Bill you are one gutsy sly dog.</u> I just got a call from Tom Jonathon... quite pleasant actually. He wants to see me at 3:30 in his office. And to think I was going to play dirty. But thanks to good old Bill the Personnel Director I didn't. Bill . . . I fossilized you . . . a company man from the old school . . . stiff upper lip and all that. <u>We will beat Dooley and this institution will be rid of a snake.</u>

BILL WINTHROP:

I heard that before somewhere

(cut off abruptly)

DON CARMICHAEL:

(walks to a chair opposite Bill's desk sits down and puts his feet on Bill's desk)

<u>I owe you Bill. I don't care . . . it's on me.</u>

BILL WINTHROP:

Yeh right . . . sex drugs and rock and roll.

(stands up from his desk and looks at his watch)

Don . . . I've got to meet someone in a few moments would you excuse me.

DON CARMICHAEL:
Bill is something wrong? You seem a little preoccupied . . . look if it's about this Dooley situation . . . <u>don't worry we've got him nailed.</u>

BILL WINTHROP:
Don you can be so idealistic

(cut off abruptly)

DON CARMICHAEL:
<u>C'mon don't talk like a 'wuse'.</u> We can beat this guy . . . like you said

(mimics Bill)

'Dooley doesn't deserve to be on staff'. Even if it means my residency I'm going through with this to the bitter end. Bill one thing . . . I gotta know you're with me?

BILL WINTHROP:
(Bill walks to the door turns and begins to speak)

Don I will be at the 3:30 meeting with you. I don't know how it will turn out but I will be with you. Now I must see someone.

(Bill motions Don to leave — Don gets up slowly walks to the door and offers Bill a handshake which is reciprocated)

DON CARMICHAEL:
I knew I could count on you Bill. I'll see yah at 3:30.

(Don walks out — Bill shuts the door and returns to his desk leans over picks up the phone and begins to dial)

BILL WINTHROP:
Could I speak with Dr Dooley please. Yes I'll wait.

STAGE LIGHTS DIM — END OF SCENE TWO

ACT THREE SCENE THREE

(The lights are raised Bill Winthrop and Don Carmichael are sitting in Tom Jonathon's office. Dr Jonathon is sitting behind a massive desk. Bill is sitting directly across from Tom and Don Carmichael is beside Bill staring intently at the diplomas on the wall behind Dr Jonathon's head)

DR TOM JONATHON:

I'll get right to the point gentlemen there have been serious allegations brought forward by Dr Dooley against you . . . Dr Carmichael.

> (Dr Carmichael leans forward to talk but is motioned to be quiet by Dr Jonathon)

Dr Carmichael to be more specific Alex Dooley contends that you have undermined his lab research. More specifically he states that over a protracted period of time you have spied on he and his staff . . . for what purposes? He contends you are trying to sully his reputation . . . that you phoned without authority or prior approval the University of Kansas in an effort to discredit him. We are here to listen to your side of the story. I hope his allegation is incorrect Dr Carmichael . . . for your sake.

> (Dr Jonathon waves a letter in the air and begins to quote from the letter)

Dr Dooley finds your conduct 'insubordinate and unacceptable' he feels you present a threat to he and his staff who have complained about your conduct on several occasions. Dr Dooley further states that quote 'Dr Carmichael's extracurricular activities in the evening hours in or near the lab are deleterious to the morale of the unit' . . . Dr Carmichael . . . I'm afraid he finds you a most contemptible young man and demands your residency be lifted. You will have lots of opportunity to defend yourself against these accusations . . . but first I wish to address Dr Winthrop. Bill I just received a rather alarming phone call from Alex Dooley about one hour ago. He claims that you wanted to make a 'deal' with him?

BILL WINTHROP:
I did no such thing.

DR TOM JONATHON:
He further contends that you threatened to have an inquiry launched against his research

(cut off abruptly)

BILL WINTHROP:
That part is true. I have received information from Dr Carmichael that will reveal the unethical nature of Dooley's research methodology. I will also

(cut off abruptly)

DR TOM JONATHON:
Bill you and I talked about Alex Dooley's situation at Orangeville. I believe I made myself perfectly clear on the matter. DID I NOT?

(Don Carmichael leaps up and steps forward aggressively to stand over Bill)

BILL WINTHOP:
His eminence as a researcher is a sham . . . a farce.

(Don Carmichael walks back to his chair smiling sits down comfortably)

He

(cut off by Dr Jonathon)

DR TOM JONATHON:

Dr Winthrop you're overstepping your authority with information that could jeopardize a man's career . . . let alone the reputation of this institution.

DON CARMICHAEL:

What the hell is going on here. I have proof that Alex Dooley biased his results in the double blind experiments during the past couple of years to match his 'B.S' prognostications. This man's reputation is a veneer . . . Alex Dooley is a fraud with a capital F. Like Bill said I've completed a statistical analysis on Dooley's double blind research results . . . they're bogus completely manufactured to meet his political agenda.

(Bill motions Don to stop)

BILL WINTHROP:

Tom it's

(Bill is abruptly cut off)

DR TOM JONATHON:

(controlled rage)

Bill would you ask this young man to leave my office. I don't wish to speak with him at this time . . . and if he's lucky he'll practice psychiatry someday. NOW GET HIM OUT.

(Don Carmichael startled maintains his composure slowly stands stares at Bill for a brief second and then leaves the office quietly closing the door behind him)

BILL WINTHROP:

Tom I've never

(abruptly cut off)

DR TOM JONATHON:

Bill I endorsed Dooley's research methodology and allowed him carte blanche authority to publish the results as he saw fit.

BILL WINTHROP:

(visibly stunned)

YOU DID WHAT? DO YOU KNOW WHAT YOU'VE DONE?

(Bill begins deep muscle relaxation exercises and then deep breathing before resuming to talk)

You've compromised the hospital's reputation <u>that's what. We're finished . . . doomed</u> . . . all those years struggling to change our B.S reputation from a 'custodial holding tank' to a viable research center . . . <u>wasted</u> . . . 'down the tube' . . . YOU BASTARD.

DR TOM JONATHON:

We were losing research money Bill. The powers to be were going to change our teaching mandate. I needed to find a way to gain notoriety . . . money to keep the talent the 'bright lights' <u>who helped build our reputation.</u> The Politicos talked about our track record . . . comparing our accomplishments with the urban centers. Bill I had no choice until Dooley came forward with his research discovery. I couldn't believe the coincidence and then his connections in Topeka called to say they were <u>extending our grant money</u>. Orangeville would continue as a research center for at least another five years. They believed Dooley's cock and bull B.S like I did . . . <u>fell for it hook line and sinker.</u>

BILL WINTHROP:

But why compromise your integrity Tom? Especially Dooley? He's so insidious . . . why didn't you dig deeper? This guy's an 'open book' of guile and deception . . . a real slime ball.

DR TOM JONATHON:

<u>Bill I didn't give a damn.</u> Our organization . . . the hard work to change our reputation from a back woods psychiatric joke steeped in mediocrity . . . to a viable teaching research center with a solid reputation . . . took almost ten years of my life Bill. Anyway that's water under the bridge. Dooley wants you and Carmichael off the premises by the end of the week. If I don't comply he'll bring me down as his accomplice when you expose him.

BILL WINTHROP:

Tom does it really matter? Do you think Carmichael and I will let this sham continue? Did you really think you could get off untarnished? The gig's up Tom . . . <u>you're finished and so is Dooley.</u>

DR TOM JONATHON:

Don't be self-righteous Bill. I'll make sure you and Carmichael get good jobs. I still have contacts who owe me

(cut off abruptly)

BILL WINTHROP:

You're in no position to make deals Tom <u>see you in court.</u>

(Bill walks to the door and turns to face Tom)

DR TOM JONATHON:

Bill leave this thing alone . . . let Carmichael play hero . . . for your sake leave quietly

(cut off abruptly)

BILL WINTHROP:

I trusted your judgement you were my friend and I thought a good mentor.

(Bill opens the door)

DR TOM JONATHON:

Bill just leave . . . remember the good times at Orangeville.

(Bill leaves shutting the door behind him Dr Jonathon walks to his desk and begins to write a letter).

STAGE LIGHTS DIM — END OF SCENE THREE

ACT THREE SCENE FOUR

(The lights are raised. Bill is reading a memo at his desk. His door is wide open and as usual the patients are strolling in the corridor outside his office. The occasional 'Hi' provokes a smile from Bill. General Stanley Morgan enters Bill's office. Stan is wearing a brightly colored Hawaiian shirt red running shoes and a New York Mets baseball cap. Bill remains intent on reading and then becomes aware that someone is staring at him. Bill slowly raises his eyes)

BILL WINTHROP:
Hi Stan how are we doing today?

GENERAL STANLEY MORGAN:
Bill cut the crap . . . What d'ya think of Tom Jonathon resigning? I also hear he could end up on one of our wards . . . as in having a nervous breakdown. Or in Shrink rhetoric a severe case of agitated

   (affected speech)

depression.

   (Stan sits down on the chair opposite Bill's desk puts his feet on the
   desk and his arms behind his head — he tilts the chair and begins
   to rock back and forth)

BILL WINTHROP:
Stan . . . Dr Jonathon needs a rest away from Orangeville. He's been Chief of General Staff for almost ten years fought a lot of battles and won most of them . . . but he has the scars mental and otherwise . . . yah know.

GENERAL STANLEY MORGAN:
(plays the invisible violin in an exaggerated fashion)

Tell me a story why don't yah. Alex Dooley set him up for a fall. You and I and the rest of the hospital know it.

BILL WINTHROP:
Stan I can't possibly comment

(abruptly cut off)

GENERAL STANLEY MORGAN:
Bill . . . don't con a con. He was compromised when Dooley felt some heat he leaned on the 'Old Man' and Jonathon caved in. I remember once on 'Wheel of Fortune' Vanna

(abruptly cut off)

BILL WINTHROP:
Stan could you pop by later on I'm afraid I've got some pressing business.

GENERAL STANLEY MORGAN:
(stops rocking the chair and slowly stands up stretching as he reaches full height)

Bill I can take a hint. Sorry if I was a little brusque . . . tact is not my forte. However I've been known to 'trip the light fantastic' with the occasional femme fatale . . . you know what happens when you've got that animal magnetism.

(smiles turns and walks to the door and then stops abruptly)

I think I'm going to apply to 'Wheel of Fortune' as a contestant.

(shrugs and walks out the door passing Don Carmichael who enters Bill's office. A loud gaffaw is heard 'off stage' and the word SICK spoken loudly. Don swings around and looks out the doorway of Bill's office down the corridor. He laughs and walks back inside Bill's office and sits down swinging his feet onto Bill's desk with a thump)

BILL WINTHROP:

Don how's your day going?

DON CARMICHAEL:
(Don hits his head with his hand)

Bill . . . Dooley has knocked off the old man. I can't believe it. Jonathon had a state wide reputation for being a tough no nonsense S.O.B. What gives . . . c'mon I'm all ears . . . what did he say when I left yesterday?

BILL WINTHROP:

You read his memo Don. He wants a break from all the B.S. I can't say that I blame him. Besides you know I can't breech confidentiality.

DON CARMICHAEL:
(hits his head with his hand)

Bill . . . Dooley levered the old man out. He parlayed a coup and you know the reason why. C'mon . . . what happened?

BILL WINTHROP:
(leans forward pointing his finger)

Don whatever decision Tom Jonathon made . . . he made on his own volition. He's a man of strong

(Don begins to laugh Bill stands frozen and chooses his words carefully)

nine plus years is a long time in that position . . . he needed a break.

DON CARMICHAEL:
(stands up abruptly turning to leave)

Loyal to the end huh. Bill I find your sanctimonious behavior <u>nau-seating.</u> You know the risks I took in coming to you with the Dooley crap. Yes I'm curious and I feel I've earned a disclosure from you. Maybe someday you'll tell me . . . look . . . all I want to do is finish my residency be a good Shrink and get out of this place. Well I've got to go . . . but one minor update . . . Dooley hasn't been on my case in over a week. Should I breathe a sigh of relief or vomit with fear. Have a good day Bill.

(leaves the office — Bill returns to reading and Susan Crawford enters)

BILL WINTHROP:
Susan long time no see . . . what gives?

SUSAN CRAWFORD:
I've just been appointed Acting Chief of General Staff until they can find a replacement for Tom. God that aggravates me . . . <u>I'm not ready to inherit this mess.</u>

BILL WINTHROP:
Susan you'll do a great job I'm really happy to hear the Board appointed you. What about your clinical casework and supervisory duties with the residents?

SUSAN CRAWFORD:

Super woman will have to cope according to the Chairman or should I say Chairperson of the Board

(sarcastic tone)

'but don't worry it's only for a short period of time until we find a replacement'. The whole thing stinks . . . Jonathon 'bails' just before the cutbacks and I'm left holding the proverbial bag. Bill they say I'm the only one that can do the job. Believe me I racked my brains trying to think of a better replacement . . . and drew a blank.

(both laugh)

BILL WINTHROP:

Susan opportunity's knocking thrusting its fecal matter in your direction and the fan's turned on high.

(both laugh)

SUSAN CRAWFORD:

Bill I need your help win lose or draw. According to the gossip Dooley's behind Tom's resignation . . . nothing like a scandal to start things off huh.

BILL WINTHROP:

Susan 'get outta here' you'll do great . . . Why don't we meet for coffee next week? You can spill your guts all you want.

(both laugh Susan stands up smiles radiantly and leaves the office. Bill returns reading the phone rings and Bill answers)

'Hello Dr Winthrop . . . O.K how 'bout talking with Susan Crawford? Yes . . . she's the new Acting chief of General Staff . . . she can arrange the meeting and 'chair it'. No don't worry she's competent' . . . Don calm down Alex is probably using this opportunity to test his wits against Susan . . . no no maybe . . . could be . . . no. Don I've got to go I'll see yah at the meeting.

(hangs up phone and returns to reading. Bill looks up and standing in his doorway is Alice Mayfield. Alice is wearing tailored clothing looking very professional. Her hair is back in a 'bun' she is obviously stressed)

BILL WINTHROP:

Hi Alice c'mon in.

ALICE MAYFIELD:

Bill did you hear that Susan Crawford is Acting Chief of Staff?

BILL WINTHROP:

Yeh she was just here. I think it was a good choice considering the Board's options.

ALICE MAYFIELD:

Are you demented? She can be a <u>Grade A Bitch on Wheels.</u>

(Bill laughs)

BILL WINTHROP:

Alice . . . she's not that bad.

ALICE MAYFIELD:

Bill you know she hates me with a passion. You watch she'll start tightening the screws in a few weeks . . . <u>Bitch.</u>

BILL WINTHROP:

Alice I'm sure she'll be a fair boss.

ALICE MAYFIELD:

Bill will you do me a favor we've been friends for almost three years. Just tell me anything if you hear anything through the 'grapevine'.

(Bill begins to talk but is interrupted)

<u>I mean it.</u> Everybody trusts you you know everything that goes on in this place. I'm not saying to betray confidentiality but please promise that you'll let me know of any gossip about me. The job is hard enough without Susan Crawford down my back.

(Alice begins to cry and Bill gives her a tissue)

BILL WINTHROP:

Hey hey don't cry. I promise I'll let you know if I hear anything . . . everything is going to be fine.

ALICE MAYFIELD:

(stands up from her chair and gains composure)

Thanks bill I appreciate your support.

(Alice leaves Bill's office Bill stands up and walks to his door shuts it behind him and returns to his desk, sits down and begins to read, the phone rings Bill answers with a 'matter of fact' tone)

BILL WINTHROP:

'Hi Dr Winthrop here . . . Susan . . . yeh what time? Tomorrow afternoon hmm let me check my day calendar . . . 2:00 P.M sounds fine. What's up? A council of war . . . who's coming? Hmm sounds good. Let me think . . . Alex will probably raise some flak but lets find out. You're pretty quick on your feet . . . don't worry. O.K bye.

(Bill hangs up the phone leans back in his chair and pauses before standing up facing the motto on the wall STO PRO VERITATE.

STAGE LIGHTS DIM — END OF SCENE FOUR

ACT THREE SCENE FIVE

(The lights are raised. A Board table is at center stage. Susan Crawford sits at the head of the table. Bill Winthrop sits to her immediate right. Alice Mayfield beside Bill, Alex Dooley sits to the immediate left of Susan Crawford directly opposite Bill Winthrop, it is 9:00 A.M)

SUSAN CRAWFORD:
(talks with deliberation and confidence)

Thank you for attending this meeting I'll make it short and sweet. I wish first to talk about my appointment as Acting Chief of General Staff at Orangeville Psychiatric. As you know Tom Jonathon's resignation two days ago came as quite a shock . . . to most of us.

(all eyes are focused on Alex Dooley who looks down)

I must say I will miss Tom he was a tower of strength. His leadership skills will be a hard act to follow. However I am also here to tell you that we will not falter in his absence and that no one is indispensable. But . . . before I continue I wish to complete some 'house cleaning' chores.

(staff look at each other)

More specifically I want to state categorically that I will not tolerate anymore collegial 'back stabbing'. This has been going on far too long. Alex you are 'persona non grata' from this day on

(Alex begins to speak and is cut off)

STOP LOOK AND LISTEN . . . to Susan.

(staff laugh except Alex Susan silences them with her hand)

We are a big family here unfortunately over the past two years or so we've become a dysfunctional family . . . <u>that ends today.</u> I want a functional and supportive team.

(Alex looks visibly enraged but remains passive)

I'm also here to state categorically my decision to place you

(looks directly at Alex who looks down at desk)

on suspension for a three month period . . . this will allow you enough time to negotiate another job <u>hopefully out of State.</u>

(staff cheer and then are silenced by Susan's hand motion)

Alex I want you and Dr Winthrop in my office tomorrow morning at 9:00 A.M . . .

(looks directly at Alex before continuing with a measured voice)

if I hear even a whisper of gossip that you're provoking the staff . . . <u>any staff</u> I'll personally phone the police and have you escorted off the premises . . . use your three months wisely NOW GET OUT.

(staff are subdued as Alex gets up from the desk and leaves the office)

I always wondered why Alex thought he was above retribution?

(Susan looks around the room and smiles)

A little bird flew into my office yesterday and opened my eyes

(staff clap and begin to laugh which increases in intensity, Susan frowns and they stop in unison)

<u>Now if I hear of anyone pulling a stunt like Dooley's you'll get the same treatment.</u> AM I UNDERSTOOD?

(staff nod in unison)

The second piece of agenda is also alarming but has a positive twist. Dr Carmichael has decided to end his residency at Orangeville

(staff begin to talk and are once again silenced by Susan's hand motion)

and will be transferring to our colleagues across the State at Williamsburg Hospital.

(staff groan in unison as Susan raises her hand for silence)

Remember we are professionals at Orangeville however as an aside and strictly confidential that means 'off the record' folks. I I. . . I mean we owe Dr Carmichael a debt of gratitude. I wish him the best of luck. I think he'd appreciate you stopping in to say goodbye this afternoon . . . as he's leaving our little family at 5:00 P.M.

(staff groan in unison Susan lifts her hand for silence)

Bill . . . Alice you must be wondering about today's agenda with our former colleague Dr Dooley? Tom Jonathon phoned me last night and talked for two hours . . . before putting a gun into his mouth.

(the group cry out Alice begins to shriek. Susan comforts Alice with her hand on her shoulder and waits for the group to calm down before continuing her dialogue)

Luckily I taped the entire conversation as I have done in the past with depressed patients who phone me. Tom's phone call and disclosure about Dooley's bogus research came as quite a shock.

(visibly shaken Susan's voice trails off)

It appears Tom decided to end his life rather than face anymore disgrace.

BILL WINTHROP:

(crying)

Tom is dead . . . <u>I just talked with him a couple of days ago.</u>

ALICE MAYFIELD:

(crying)

<u>I can't believe it.</u>

SUSAN CRAWFORD:

Alice I always pegged you as a tough rigid little number. Thank God you proved me wrong.

(Susan smiles reassuringly at Alice and provides her with a tissue)

Bill I'll need you present tomorrow morning as you're the Personnel Director and I'll be giving Alex his Notice of Termination. I wouldn't be surprised if he brings a lawyer and I want a reliable witness.

(Bill nods in agreement)

BILL WINTHROP:

Susan how does Don Carmichael feel about everything?

SUSAN CRAWFORD:

Bill don't you have a motto hanging in your office wall?

(Bill nods slowly)

What does it say?

BILL WINTHROP:

'Sto Pro Veritate'.

SUSAN CRAWFORD:

What's that in English?

BILL WINTHROP:

I stand for truth.

SUSAN CRAWFORD:

I think Don Carmichael took it to heart. Now I would appreciate you and Alice leaving me alone. I have some documentation I have to complete in preparation for tomorrow's meeting.

(Bill and Alice stand up and leave the office as Susan begins to work at the Board table).

STAGE LIGHTS DIM — END OF SCENE FIVE

ACT THREE SCENE SIX

(The lights are raised and highlight the interior of a sophisticated and very expensive restaurant. Bill and Alice are seated across from one another dressed in evening clothes. Alice has on a low cut evening gown. Bill is wearing a black tuxedo. The food has been served the wine is flowing and the couple is enjoying each other's company)

BILL WINTHROP:
Alice would you like some more wine?

ALICE MAYFIELD:
(mockingly)

Bill that's the fourth refill . . . are you trying to get me drunk?

BILL WINTHROP:
The thought never crossed my mind.

(both laugh)

ALICE MAYFIELD:
(slightly intoxicated)

Bill you are a pistol . . . when you want to be I think you look so sexy tonight.

BILL WINTHROP:

Alice I thank you my mother thanks you and the place I rented the tuxedo from thanks you.

(toasts Alice with his glass)

ALICE MAYFIELD:

(drinking copious wine)

Bill how much did you know about Dooley and Jonathon? C'mon everybody tells you their life story . . . I bet Carmichael had a ball spilling his guts to Susan Crawford <u>he despised Dooley.</u>

BILL DOOLEY:

Alice you can be a coquette.

(Alice roars with laughter)

You know I'm not at liberty to say anything.

ALICE MAYFIELD:

Winthrop you creep tell me. I didn't buy this dress only to have you ogle at me. It was also supposed to loosen your tongue.

(he roars with laughter at the same time Alice locks his leg under the table)

BILL WINTHROP:

Alice what are you planning . . .

(Alice roars with laughter)

in the hospital?

ALICE MAYFIELD:

Bill for God's sake do you have to be so serious? To answer your nosy question how the hell do I know? I barely know what I'm doing tomorrow let alone one year from now.

(Alice leans forward Bill looks down her cleavage)

Why do you ask?

BILL WINTHROP:

Alice we've worked together

(cut off)

ALICE MAYFIELD:

(leans forward seductively Bill tries to avert his stare from her cleavage)

Bill shush. Why don't you pay the bill and we can finish this conversation over a liqueur at my place.

(Alice purses her lips and lifts her eyebrows)

BILL WINTHROP:

Alice I was enjoying my meal but if you want to.

(cut off)

ALICE MAYFIELD:

Bill sometimes you're so stupid.

(Bill looks at her heaving cleavage moves his head in unison)

Can't you see I'm totally in love with you?

(Bill looks down suddenly and blushes Alice throws back her head and laughs)

BILL WINTHROP:

(Bill throws his shoulders back and nods his head and returns his gaze at her cleavage)

Alice . . . I'm still feeling a little fragmented from Tom's . . . maybe we should think about.

(cut off abruptly)

ALICE MAYFIELD:

Bill I want you . . . you must know that by now.

(Alice leans forward exposing an ever increasing cleavage)

I. . . want . . . you.

(Alice points her finger at Bill and then grabs for his tie)

BILL WINTHROP:

(Bill tries to avoid being grabbed and holds onto the dinner table with both hands)

Alice sometimes when we ingest alcohol too quickly our emotions spring to attention

(Bill looks down and Alice roars with laughter)

You are such a full figured woman I hadn't

(Alice leans forwards holding the table mimicking Bill)

ALICE MAYFIELD:

Winthrop 'time is ...awaiting' and my place is awaiting.

(Bill nods)

C'mon you stallion . . . onwards and upwards

(Bill looks at Alice's cleavage and nods)

Bill I'll count to three and then we'll both get up.

(Alex Dooley enters the restaurant spies Bill and Alice and approaches the table. Alex is intoxicated and staggers as he walks)

ALEX DOOLEY:
(weaving as he stands over Bill and Alice)

So the two love birds have made a nest.

BILL WINTHROP:
(Bill clenches his fists but remains seated)

Alex please leave for your own

(abruptly cut off by Alex)

ALEX DOOLEY:

You scumbag . . . you cost me my job my reputation and paycheck.
GET UP

(almost falls over backwards but catches his balance at the last moment)

BILL WINTHROP:
(remains seated as the Maitre de starts across the floor to intervene)

Alex you destroyed yourself and Tom Jonathon . . . get out or I'll phone the police and lay a charge of harassment.

ALEX DOOLEY:

(begins to pace around the table enraged)

WINTHROP I HATE YOUR GUTS. ALONG WITH YOUR HALF WIT GIRLFRIEND.

(Bill leaps to his feet and throws an uppercut punch knocking Alex to the floor, the Maitre de arrives and slowly helps the dazed Alex to a sitting position and then to his feet. The Maitre de puts his arm around Alex and helps him make his way to the door at which point Alex is pushed outside)

BILL WINTHROP:

(smiling as he rubs his knuckles)

I've wanted to do that for a long time. I hope Alex remembers what happened tomorrow morning . . . he was really loaded.

ALICE MAYFIELD:

(leans forward and kisses Bill's hand and begins to lick his forefinger)

Bill you're my hero. Now for the last time from the top

(slowly enunciates)

I. . . would . . . like . . . you . . . to . . . take . . . me . . . home . . . immediately . . . I would then like you to help me off with my clothing which is too damn tight anyway. You will then reciprocate Winthrop. Do you copy Doctor?

BILL WINTHROP:

(motions Alice to stop)

Alice you are a fox . . .let's get outta here.

(They stand up and Bill helps a slightly drunk Alice on with her coat. They turn and walk to the entrance of the restaurant at which point Bill looks over his shoulder at the audience)

YOU DIDN'T THINK IT WAS GOING TO END ANY OTHER WAY DID YOU?

**STAGE LIGHTS DIM AS CURTAIN
CLOSES TO END THE PLAY**

LORD OF THE PLANET

A THREE ACT PLAY

TIME:

The late 1980's New York City, afternoon

PLACE:

The office of Dr Simon Shorter who specializes in the assessment and treatment of psychotic illness. Dr Shorter's office has a desk and bookcases filled with volumes of psychology textbooks, including one wall with his diplomas hanging in neat rows. There is conveyed a 'no nonsense' atmosphere in this work setting.

CHARACTERS

DR SIMON SHORTER (38) ... PSYCHOTHERAPIST

NATHAN PIERCE (25) . . . OUT-PATIENT

ALANA (22) . . . RECEPTIONIST

ACT ONE SCENE ONE

(The lights are raised revealing an office used for the purpose of psychotherapy. Sitting at a desk is a middle aged man approximately six feet in height and muscular build. He is reading a text as the phone rings)

DR SIMON SHORTER:

Oh hi Alana tell him I'll be right out.

(hangs up and leaves the office returning with a young man in his mid twenties)

Mr Pierce take a seat.

(motions towards a comfortable chair opposite the chair and beside the couch)

NATHAN PIERCE:

Thank you Doctor I feel a bit uncomfortable I've never been to a Shrink's office. You may call me Lord of the Planet if you don't mind.

DR SIMON SHORTER:

O.K but could I suggest some ground rules before we start? First . . . please try to tell me everything during our meetings this should become easier as trust increases between us. Second try and be punctual M' Lord.

NATHAN PIERCE:

I must first begin by challenging my employer's request for seeing a person such as yourself. I am a research engineer of some repute in the chemical industry and could snag employment anywhere.

DR SIMON SHORTER:

What have been your shortcomings from their perspective? What precipitated them sending you to a therapist?

NATHAN PIERCE:

I dunno . . . one moment I was checking data the next I became connected with a galaxy from beyond and told to wear a robe to work which I did until senior management complained. I have since travelled psychically to other Planets and when I expound on my visits to various colleagues they become disgruntled. Lame narrow intellects . . . recently I changed my name to something more in line with my status . . . are you with me Doctor?

DR SIMON SHORTER:

Lord of the Planet is life comfortable now that you've changed your name?

NATHAN PIERCE:

Yes and no . . . you see I imagined people would sacrifice for my sake as I have sacrificed for theirs and to a degree this has happened. But recently I became deadlocked with the dilemma of retaining the old me or progressing ahead with the new me . . . to start anew you might say.

DR SIMON SHORTER:

M'Lord who told you to wear a magic cloak to work and for what purpose was this done?

NATHAN PIERCE:

I see they told you. O.K one moment I was examining data from a chemical experiment in the lab . . . the next I felt inclined to develop a map of the Planet Zachreb's terrain. Subsequently as I thought of the the terrain I was there . . . standing on the Planet feeling the softness of the sand between my toes. The next day I came to work with a magic cloak befitting a person of rank and privilege.

DR SIMON SHORTER:

Can you tell me the importance of wearing the cloak M'Lord?

NATHAN PIERCE:

That's easy the psychic transportation system from earth to Planet Zachreb requires a uniform of dignity and in order to visit my people I must wear the cloak. As you get to know me you will realize the simplicity of something so obvious.

DR SIMON SHORTER:

M'Lord am I able to join you when you visit the Planet Zachreb?

NATHAN PIERCE:

You're not serious . . . this is dangerous work Bub.

DR SIMON SHORTER:

Have you made any calculations of the distance and travel time to Planet Zachreb?

NATHAN PIERCE

Plenty but the complexity of the calculations are beyond your level of comprehension Doctor.

DR SIMON SHORTER:

I see

(cut off)

NATHAN PIERCE:

I can only surmise that your interest in my job and status are professionally motivated . . . am I correct Doctor?

DR SIMON SHORTER:

You were referred to me by your company doctor . . . my job is to get to know you. Are you on any medication currently?

NATHAN PIERCE:

Are you sure of being up to the task Doctor? My travel itinerary most days precludes interruptions from earthlings and no I do not require drugs currently or anytime in the future.

DR SIMON SHORTER:

That's why I asked if I could arrange to travel and assist you with your duties

(cut off vociferously)

NATHAN PIERCE

Your brain is flaccid Doctor . . . no means no . . . does idiocy run in your family?

DR SIMON SHORTER:

I'm sory for mentioning it again M'Lord

(cut off)

NATHAN PIERCE:

You better be . . . I have to catch the next projection and my brain must be aligned with the astrophysical calculation to Zachreb.

(closes eyes and yawns Nathan stays in an upright position and begins a monotone hum that does not stop)

DR SIMON SHORTER:

M'Lord

(five seconds pass)

M'Lord

(another five seconds pass — Dr Shorter begins to mimic Nathan's sitting posture and the same monotone hum but at a different pitch and decibel level. They both begin to compete with each other until Nathan suddenly stops)

NATHAN PIERCE:

(jumps up and races towards Dr Shorter stopping suddenly in front of him)

<u>What the hell d'ya think you're doing we could have been killed.</u>

(Nathan wheels around and walks towards the chair sits down and crosses his legs)

DR SIMON SHORTER:

Lord of the Planet your calculations are too easily accessed and I'm sorry but I was worried about your flight plan to Planet Zachreb and tagged along.

NATHAN PIERCE:

What the hell gives you the right to encroach on my mental health?

DR SIMON SHORTER:

You could complain to my College and have my license revoked but that wouldn't stop me from trailing you on your flights to Zachreb.

NATHAN PIERCE:

Doctor I'm doing this for your own good. Do you know how many ships have been lost travelling to Zachreb?

DR SIMON SHORTER:

I'll take my chances M'Lord now I want to ask a few more questions before we stop for today

(cut off)

NATHAN PIERCE:

You're very sure of yourself Doctor. But go ahead my travel arrangements are being processed as we talk . . . please . . . continue.

DR SIMON SHORTER:

I must ask a favor M'Lord . . . could you bring a sample of your astrophysical calculations next time we meet so as to compare our travel routes. I wouldn't want to cause an accident by travelling in your orbit. Secondly could you draw me a picture of the inhabitants of the Planet Zachreb to help me identify them and lastly what is the travel time to Zachreb? I need to know this to allow for provisions and what not.

NATHAN PIERCE:

<u>Doctor you're drifting into dangerous waters.</u> But your interest in travel has sparked my curiosity. To answer your first question my intellect 'free associates' to use your vernacular. It improvises the calculations to meet the need thereby reducing your fears of collision during space travel. Secondly I will draw a picture of Zachreb inhabitants.

(begins to pace while thinking aloud)

On one condition that you follow my directions as to action/reaction protocol when in their presence. You can imagine the catastrophic results of your bungling if you met one without my instruction and proximity. Lastly the travel time to Zachreb is my business and dependent on my state of mind to calculate the flight path accurately. <u>There you have it lock stock and what not.</u>

DR SIMON SHORTER:

Thank you M'Lord I think we have made a positive beginning and I look forward to future discussions with you why don't we call it a day?

(Simon gets up from his chair and crosses the room to shake Nathan's hand. He then follows Nathan to the door and lets him out closing the door behind him)

STAGE LIGHTS DIM — END OF SCENE ONE

ACT ONE SCENE TWO

(One week later — Dr Shorter is sitting at his desk and the phone rings he responds politely requesting that his receptionist show Nathan Pierce into his office)

NATHAN PIERCE:
(the door is opened by the receptionist at which point Nathan enters the room wearing a 'house coat' with multiple stars and figures sown onto the garment. He heads directly to the same chair he was sitting on the previous week sits down suddenly shuts his eyes crosses his arms and begins a monotonous hum)

DR SIMON SHORTER:
M'Lord welcome.

(no response — a pause of five seconds)

M'Lord.

(a further extended pause Dr Shorter closes his eyes folds his arms and begins a monotonous hum at a different pitch and decibel range)

NATHAN PIERCE:
(opens his eyes shuts them again and changes the rhythm of the monotonous hum. Dr shorter competes with him until Nathan abruptly stops uncrosses his arms and opens his eyes. This is repeated by Dr Shorter)

<u>What the hell d'ya think you're doing . . . this is my orbit Bub.</u>

DR SIMON SHORTER:

M'Lord how was your intergalactic travel this past week?

NATHAN PIERCE:

My astronomical projections were more than satisfactory if that's what you mean?

DR SIMON SHORTER:

Could I talk to you about other issues M'Lord?

NATHAN PIERCE:

That depends Doctor I find your interest in my interplanetary travel a touch obsessional so maybe a change in topic might do us both some good.

DR SIMON SHORTER:

How would you describe your past life M'Lord?

NATHAN PIERCE:

O.K if it makes you happy I prided myself as a tough, no nonsense guy . . . able to take anything from anybody. I was a clean cut guy didn't drink smoke pot or swear. I learned undergraduate chemistry because of its precision and detail. It allowed the opportunity to work independently but also as a member of a team . . . if I wanted.

DR SIMON SHORTER:

How did you deal with frustration in your former life M'Lord?

NATHAN PIERCE:

Easy . . . continuity and sameness day in and day out when that was lost . . . well.

DR SIMON SHORTER:

Well what M'Lord?

NATHAN PIERCE:

Well look I'm getting sick of this game Doctor. Can't we play another one . . . <u>this is my hour Bub.</u>

DR SIMON SHORTER:

One further question M'Lord how was your boss in your former life?

NATHAN PIERCE:

(immediately closes eyes crosses his arms and begins the monotonous humming sound. Dr Shorter imitates Nathan's actions who suddenly opens his eyes and uncrosses his arms)

DR SIMON SHORTER:

I believe we have hit on something Milord what do you think?

NATHAN PIERCE:

In my former life a list of annoyances would have begun with bosses petty politics and subterfuge . . . with the sub total result of the square root of sweet

(cut off abruptly)

DR SIMON SHORTER:

M'Lord could we delve a little deeper into your past life this session?

NATHAN PIERCE:

For what purpose Doctor? To open the flood gate of infantile urges? Really . . . for what purpose?

DR SIMON SHORTER:

Your past life appears to involve logic and precision whereas your current life is 'free wheeling' and spontaneous. I need a bridge Milord a bridge to understand what connects your mind from past to present.

NATHAN PIERCE:

Honesty opens the bottle with the genie Doctor. Your wish is my command. Please begin your travels . . . my oasis awaits you with cunning mind and savage wit.

DR SIMON SHORTER:

In my experience it's not the weak and the unstable that lack resistance to fearful situations but generally the timid and passive who can't mobilize resources and externalize anger to discharge tension that falters in these

(cut off)

NATHAN PIERCE:

What the hell are you getting at?

DR SIMON SHORTER:

Milord in your former life were you disillusioned with the leadership of your organization?

NATHAN PIERCE:

That's better . . . in what regard Doctor?

DR SIMON SHORTER:

Did you have confidence in their ability to provide a vision a realistic assessment of talent . . a

(cut off)

NATHAN PIERCE:

Unfortunately in my former life leaders as 'Den mothers' were as controversial as penis envy in your field Doctor.

DR SIMON SHORTER:

Milord . . . by your answer you suggest . . . you insinuate that leadership or lack of appropriate direction was disillusioning.

NATHAN PIERCE:

Let's put it this way . . . the concept of leadership ego strength and resilience of character were not highly cultivated with the Directors of the Clinic from whence I survived in my former life.

DR SIMON SHORTER:

Survived . . . that is the operative word Milord survived. To reiterate I'm wondering . . . in your former life did some of your disillusionment with the leadership increase your anxiety and did your colleagues feel the same way you did?

NATHAN PIERCE:

I'm wondering why psychoanalysis has been repudiated for so many years Doctor? I believe my next intergalactic mission is about to disembark. Please . . . with your permission I must take my leave.

(shuts his eyes crosses his arms and begins to hum)

DR SIMON SHORTER:

(attempts to imitate Nathan's behavior. Gets up from his chair and approaches the other man. At a distance of two feet mimics Nathan perfectly. For a period of ten seconds both men hum in unison never faltering in intensity, pitch or range. Finally Nathan stops and falls to the floor where he assumes a fetal position)

M'Lord

(pauses for five seconds)

M'Lord may I lay with

(abruptly cut off)

NATHAN PIERCE:
(leaps up suddenly and faces the Doctor aggressively)

Not friggin likely Bub.

DR SIMON SHORTER:

M'Lord please sit down

(motions Nathan to sit down on the chair)

NATHAN PIERCE:

On one occasion Doctor . . . in the future when you decide to tag along on my missions <u>let me do the calculations.</u>

DR SIMON SHORTER:

M'Lord you are displeased with my behavior . . . would you have been able to state this to me in your former life?

NATHAN PIERCE:

That's for me to know and you to find out Doctor.

DR SIMON SHORTER:

Look . . . what if other people find your behavior enviable. How are you going to cope when everyone lines up to go on intergalactic missions and you're their only connection. Will you have the energy and resources to help them?

NATHAN PIERCE:

Nice try Doctor but high and outside . . . <u>batters up.</u>

DR SIMON SHORTER:

M'Lord could you help me learn about the computations to the Planet Zachreb?

NATHAN PIERCE:

You are travelling in circles Doctor and the oasis is a glimmer in the distance. However my capabilities are such that forgiveness is provided those who appreciate logic brilliance and the guts to make a difference. Please . . . let me help you.

(stands up from the chair and walks to the Doctor's desk)

Doctor I need a pen and paper . . . May I?

(requests to sit by the Doctor's chair the request is granted)

DR SIMON SHORTER:
Please begin and be as complex as you like Milord.

NATHAN PIERCE:
(begins to talk as he writes and subsequently draws)

Planet Zachreb requires a glossary of sixty pages or so to really understand its makeup. The people my subjects and a host of other maps architectural drawings and of course the transportation system. I believe if you learn this information each week within lets say six months or so you should be ready to assist me in training other Earthlings. There . . . how's that?

(hands two to three pages of rough drawings to the Doctor)

DR SIMON SHORTER:
Milord thank you for this disclosure about your new life. Our time is just about over today . . . could I keep this information to study for our next session?

NATHAN PIERCE:
On one condition Doctor . . . appraise this material as a means of joining me in my new life. I have jettisoned my old destructive life and if you engage me at a scientific level we will be parallel. That bond would provide solace and comfort . . . can you dig?

DR SIMON SHORTER:
Thank you Milord I look forward to our next meeting.

(both men shake hands and then Nathan is led to the door and leaves the office)

STAGE LIGHTS DIM — END OF SCENE TWO

ACT ONE SCENE THREE

(Dr Shorter is sitting at his desk one week later. The telephone rings informing him that Nathan Pierce has arrived. Dr Shorter tells his receptionist to send him in)

NATHAN PIERCE:

(wearing the same magic cloak as the previous week Nathan enters the room and strides to the chair opposite Dr Shorter. Underneath Nathan's arm is a roll of paper tied together with a yellow ribbon. Upon sitting down in the chair he places the roll of paper gently beside him on the floor)

DR SIMON SHORTER:

Milord I see you have come prepared for dialogue and

(cut off)

NATHAN PIERCE:

I have simply followed your instructions and do hope you had a good night's sleep because today we work . . . <u>enough pap.</u>

DR SIMON SHORTER:

Thank you Milord let us begin.

(he motions Nathan to come to his desk. Nathan leans over gingerly and picks up the roll of paper. He slips the ribbon off the end of the paper and walks over to the desk. He sits down quickly unrolls the paper and straightens it several times with his arm simultaneously)

NATHAN PIERCE:

Doctor pull up a chair. I will share my calculations with you on one condition. <u>Never touch the documents</u> . . . is that understood?

DR SIMON SHORTER:

I understand and will comply Milord.

NATHAN PIERCE:

Now let us begin . . . a permutation is the number of different outcomes regardless of the order of occurrence. To travel safely in orbit to Zachreb factorials are used to quickly calculate the number of possible ways that flight outcomes can occur given the number of factors involved and the number of arrangements. For example . . . even for you this will be simple. If the first region of orbit ends with lets say a five outcome and the second orbit with a six outcome this is called a five dash six. If the order of orbit is reversed so that the first region has a six outcome and the second has a five this results in a different orbit outcome. Another rule of permanence states . . . the same result in different groupings is not counted.

DR SIMON SHORTER:

For example a five dash five or a six dash orbit outcome would not be considered a permutation.

NATHAN PIERCE:

<u>Full marks Doctor . . . I am impressed.</u>

DR SIMON SHORTER:

Obviously with these considerations to think about the orbit formula is continuously adjusted to suit the flight path you are improvising on a given day Milord.

NATHAN PIERCE:

By jove I think he has it.

DR SIMON SHORTER:

Pray continue Milord.

NATHAN PIERCE:

The permutation formula for the orbits I fly is as follows: The number of factors (n) for a given number of arrangements (r) is equal to the factorial of n divided by the factorial for the difference between n and r. Doctor . . . this is not as confusing as you might think. When applied to the frame of mind I am feeling at a specific time on a specific day the probability of orbit analysis is based on the number of factors or n and number of arrangements of my mind set or r. Now . . . what do you think good Doctor?

DR SIMON SHORTER:

N P R is equal to N divided by N minus R.

NATHAN PIERCE:

(falls to the ground at the same time grabbing Dr Shorter's legs and begins to hum in monotone)

DR SIMON SHORTER:

Milord I don't think I'm ready for my first solo . . . Milord?

(cut off vociferously)

NATHAN PIERCE:
(jumps up suddenly and sits down again poring over the papers)

Doctor let me be the judge of your progress. To date you score 100 and bat 1000 . . . <u>I am impressed.</u>

DR SIMON SHORTER:
But what about combinations Milord as in permutations and

(cut off)

NATHAN PIERCE:
Combinations?

DR SIMON SHORTER:
Too quick M'Lord?

NATHAN PIERCE:
A keen mind and what have you make for strange bedfellows Doctor. <u>Back off</u> and yes . . . I will discuss combinations . . . pray be silent.

DR SIMON SHORTER:
My apologies . . . and I will be patient Milord.

NATHAN PIERCE:
A mathematical combination is the number of different arrangements of outcomes when the order of occurrence is not interchangeable . . . there you have it. Unfortunately from day to day I make rapid changes in logic mood and inclination for interplanetary

travel. Hence the need to interject the formula for combinations to orbit successfully is not often required. <u>However for you I will continue.</u>

DR SIMON SHORTER:

My brain if flaccid Milord I must learn to be parallel once again I apologize.

NATHAN PIERCE:

When I become aroused I'll let you know good Doctor . . . let us continue. I am attempting to impart greatness and have found a willing participant to learn that is all. Remember our scientific minds in order to coincide must remain parallel both in tempo and integration. <u>When you race it creates waves do you understand?</u>

DR SIMON SHORTER:

I do M'Lord and will comply.

NATHAN PIERCE:

Now listen to my definition of combinations Doctor. C equals N divided by R times N minus R. Obviously N equals the number of factors C equals the combinations R equals the number of arrangements and the exclamation mark which I forgot to include earlier equals a factorial. There you have it . . . any questions?

DR SIMON SHORTER:

Basically the combination's formula works in many applications including calculating interplanetary travel. I would presume you need to remember the exact combination you are measuring the possible combinations of orbits without reverse orders and of course I nearly forgot . . . no duplicating the outcomes like five dash fives or six dash sixes.

NATHAN PIERCE:

You are a very capable and clever man Doctor. Obviously you were well chosen to meet your task or cause celebre. Permutations and combinations can be used ad nauseum. Probabilities are always a factor to be factored correctly when I travel to Zachreb . . . you can well imagine any mental screw ups <u>and I'd never return to earth.</u>

Dr SIMON SHORTER

Broad based analysis improves dependability of mental calculation in probability analysis Milord. But what became of your abilities at your former job? Could not this facility of flexibility and improvisation be used at your old job?

NATHAN PIERCE:

Doctor . . . when you leave a job you never return . . . or I haven't to my recollection. When I forecast my travel arrangements to Zachreb I don't just face the question of orbit accuracy . . . rate of acceleration and what not to use your plebeian phrase. Success requires the facility of agile thought and determination of a series of events taking place exactly the way I calculate them to take place. The accuracy of the forecast namely the decision to travel inter galacticly rests on the accuracy of assumptions about timing . . . can't you see this? <u>We've met three times Stupe.</u>

DR SIMON SHORTER:

Our alliance in these sessions rests on the mutual respect and an understanding of why we are meeting Milord. There is a matched equality of logic and spirit working in parallel not at crossed purposes. People whose talk appears different . . . much different become alienated from their peers who by reason of helplessness in understanding their colleague remove themselves from that person. It makes the person feel as if talking to extraterrestrials would be a better choice. What do you think Milord?

NATHAN PIERCE:
I think its been a long session Doctor . . . may we end in truce?

DR SIMON SHORTER:
Until next week Milord same time same place and feel free to bring back your notes I am fascinated by your inner force.

STAGE LIGHTS DIM — END OF SCENE THREE

ACT ONE SCENE FOUR

(The lights are raised and Dr Shorter is seen reading and then writing in earnest at his desk. The phone rings and he responds, nodding his head, smiling and getting up. Dr Shorter strides to the door and leaves for a moment returning with Nathan Pierce. Once again Nathan is wearing a house coat adorned with space drawings, an armful of papers and a serious expression on his face)

DR SIMON SHORTER:

Milord I see you came prepared . . . thank you.

NATHAN PIERCE:

After last session I changed my mind about you. I embrace you as a willing follower . . . now may we begin?

DR SIMON SHORTER:

Milord before engaging in this work could I make a request?

NATHAN PIERCE:

You may . . . what is it pray tell?

DR SIMON SHORTER:

Unfortunately the training from my profession . . . my Shrinkery ways has peaked my curiosity regarding our discussions last week and I wish to chat for awhile with your permission of course.

NATHAN PIERCE:

Of course . . . proceed . . . full speed ahead dazzle me with your

(cut off)

DR SIMON SHORTER:

Without sounding pretentious I believe there is a 'reality of replication' in your life Milord . . . people tend to repeat co-dependent destructive behaviors in organizations that they have become habituated to in their family of origin

(cut off)

NATHAN PIERCE:

Get to the point Wise One . . . we've got work to do Bub.

DR SIMON SHORTER:

I believe co-dependency developed with certain colleagues . . . not excluding some of your bosses. We've had subversive behavior in the work force since the beginning of time. These people need the Lords of the Planet to

(cut off)

NATHAN PIERCE:

(begins to sit cross-legged humming monotonously and bowing his head. Dr Shorter immediately imitates the behavior but at a different pitch and decibel range . . . Nathan stops humming)

Doctor . . . to coin a phrase from your profession are you trying to <u>crack my autistic shell?</u>

DR SIMON SHORTER:

I am simply trying to get to

(cut off)

NATHAN PIERCE:

I thought we were developing a healthy symbiosis Doctor . . . <u>let's keep it that way.</u>

DR SIMON SHORTER:

No malice intended Milord.

NATHAN PIERCE:

Humoring Lord of the Planet does not win brownie points Bub . . . but if you must.

DR SIMON SHORTER:

I believe part of the problem lies in the co-dependency at your Work Site. Your colleagues blamed you for their own misgivings and

(cut off)

NATHAN PIERCE:

You do go on Doctor . . . please . . . develop the therapeutic alliance before you attempt any diagnostics . . . <u>come on</u> . . .

DR SIMON SHORTER:

Excuse me M' Lord.

NATHAN PIERCE:

Getting back to logic and general truisms . . . take my former life for instance. The amount of deviance I got away with at my job was an obtained mean if you can believe it. Those 'two-bit' no accounts lived off my brilliance and then . . . well screw that crap can you dig it or what?

DR SIMON SHORTER:

You do agree there was conflict in your job from your previous life.

NATHAN PIERCE:

Doctor if you want to be my sidekick 'Jingles' get with the program. The confidence interval and level of confidence is proportional quantitatively in statistics. I measure your responses and determine how much or how little I must calibrate the next orbit to Zachreb. To put it bluntly the more you investigate my existence the less I equate your 'Being' as quantitatively significant. Can you dig it?

DR SIMON SHORTER:

Can you give me an example mathematically?

NATHAN PIERCE:

(jumps up from the chair with his role of papers and strides confidently to Dr Shorter's desk. He pushes Dr Shorter aside and sits down aggressively spreading out the papers with his forearm and placing two books on either side of the papers to keep them flush. He subsequently begins to draw a diagram with numerous calculations at the same time explaining his example to Dr Shorter who is standing over Nathan's left shoulder)

You will recall from past statistic classes that there is a variance in the means of random samples from the same population. That being the case . . . let's say the population mean of 'Head Doctors' trying to screw up. I mean if the population mean were . . . say . . . 0.2 below the obtained sample mean of 'Head Doctors' . . . how many of a thousand sample means would be as high as the one we got . . . can you see?

(shows his diagram and math to Dr Shorter)

DR SIMON SHORTER:

I can see in the drawing that approximately

(cut off)

NATHAN PIERCE:

I never approximate Bub.

(begins to close his eyes cross his arms and hum. Dr Shorter imitates Nathan's behavior which causes Nathan to stop his behavior and resume his calculations)

DR SIMON SHORTER:

I'm sorry Milord let me try again . . . your calculations accurately depict 25 out of every thousand 'Head Doctor' sample means would be that high. From your calculations one could state that the population mean of all 'Head Doctors' is not lower than 115.3 and we can state it with a level of confidence of 1.000 less .025 equals .975. Yes . . . I think that's it.

NATHAN PIERCE:

I must say I am impressed Doctor . . . pray continue.

(Dr Shorter makes a frustrated face and continues)

DR SIMON SHORTER
I think one asks if the population mean of 'Head Doctors' were 0.2 of a point above the obtained sample mean of 'Head Doctors' that the probability would be .25.

NATHAN PIERCE:
<u>By jove I think he has it . . . I am impressed.</u>

DR SIMON SHORTER:
Hmm our next course

(cut off)

NATHAN PIERCE:
Doctor you must realize that I already know the answer . . . <u>come on.</u>

DR SIMON SHORTER:
Milord . . . if I'm to continue with this exercise I need your respectful indulgence can you dig it?

NATHAN PIERCE:
(quickly crosses his arms and leans forward examining his calculations as Dr Shorter begins to walk around the office talking)

DR SIMON SHORTER:
What is the probability that the population mean of 'Head Doctors' is outside the interval you've described in your calculations?

If I remember correctly . . . the answer is . . . that's it the answer is .025 plus .025 which equals .05. So if the population mean of 'Head Doctors' is somewhere within the interval we can say at a confidence level of 1.0 less .05 or .95 which means at the 95 percent confidence interval M' Lord.

NATHAN PIERCE:

(claps his hands and screams hysterically falls off the chair to the ground and rolls into a fetal position at which point he begins to hum monotonously. Dr Shorter falls to the floor and imitates the behavior but at the same pitch and decibel level. Abruptly Nathan stops humming jumps up and returns to his original seat in the chair opposite Dr Shorter's desk. Dr Shorter gets up slowly and returns to his chair)

DR SIMON SHORTER:

May I say one thing before we continue Milord.

NATHAN PIERCE:

Doctor Perfection . . . pray continue.

DR SIMON SHORTER:

I only wish to say that the amount of deviation of an obtained mean from a hypothetical population is somewhat arbitrary.

NATHAN PIERCE:

I beg your pardon.

DR SIMON SHORTER:

It depends on where you imagine the true mean to be Milord.

NATHAN PIERCE:

Rats.

DR SIMON SHORTER:

I beg your pardon.

NATHAN PIERCE:

Double rats.

DR SIMON SHORTER:

Have I passed another test Lord of the Planet? Your tests of intellectual vanity? What about your family in your past life M'Lord?

NATHAN PIERCE:

My father was a drunk my mother a doting rube . . . my life a ceaseless circle of crap. So . . . now we begin . . . now we begin is that it?

DR SIMON SHORTER:

To touch on my observations about you . . . yes I believe I've earned the right Milord. It seems to be the same order in all depressed states. Frustration arouses rage which leads to hostile attempts to gain desirable gratification. I believe a lot of the isolation you felt in your previous life was the effect of the underlying hostility related to your formative years growing up.

NATHAN PIERCE:

It should be duly noted that the concept of making a lot of money is not the purpose of workaholism . . . but rather the process of working which is the fix not the crappy outcome Bub.

DR SIMON SHORTER:
Can we be honest? Please . . . let's be honest.

NATHAN PIERCE:
OK . . . work work and more work makes Nate the dull boy. Get out there and get laid kid . . . you're almost twenty and haven't dated, what gives? But dad I live by studying chemistry. Nate Nate Nate get out there and get laid . . . book knowledge is for rubes.

DR SIMON SHORTER:
I believe the efforts at your job was a smoke screen . . . to take the attention away from your life outside of work. Work acted as a crutch allowing your denial to remain intact.

NATHAN PIERCE:
Doctor

(fading in concentration)

DR SIMON SHORTER:
Just a little more for today Nathan . . . please . . . I've earned this.

NATHAN PIERCE:
Pray continue oh wise one.

DR SIMON SHORTER:
The work as a smoke screen kept you from focusing or more accurately dealing with the main problem

(cut off)

NATHAN PIERCE:
Which was?

DR SIMON SHORTER:

Work allowed you to avoid facing your inner turmoil. Your conflict about the past and over time you began to fantasize about . . . well about a better lifestyle. But by Monday you were back at the Lab with your quote 'two bit second rate cronies' who lived vicariously off your success. Gee . . . I wonder if this happened growing up Nathan?

NATHAN PIERCE:

You have parried my thrusts crossed my t's and dotted my I's what next good Doctor?

DR SIMON SHORTER:

Your primary addiction to work and consequent success kept the 'higher ups' and less competents from looking behind your 'smoke screen' personality. Man requires love and nurturance Nathan . . . no 'slight of hand'.

NATHAN PIERCE:

I must say . . . I must say nothing. Can we stop for the day the ability to process intergalactic travel has

(Nathan collapses to the floor as Dr Shorter rushes to his side the stage lights darken)

STAGE LIGHTS DIM — END OF SCENE FOUR

ACT TWO SCENE ONE

(The lights are raised and Dr Shorter is sitting quietly at his desk reading a psychology text. The telephone rings announcing that Nathan Pierce has arrived. Dr Shorter requests his presence and swings his chair around to meet his patient. Nathan dressed in his 'magic cloak' strides into the room and stands over Dr Shorter)

DR SIMON SHORTER:

Milord nice to see you again.

NATHAN PIERCE:

Thank you thank you . . . as I recall the last time I was here our session ended by . . . kissing your hardwood floor. The intensity of the session precipitated my physical demise you might say.

DR SIMON SHORTER:

Milord I must be honest I wasn't sure you would return for today's session. Yes it was a very intense diatribe between two very competitive men.

NATHAN PIERCE:

Uncompromising honesty . . . keeping promises and from your perspective checking reality . . . testing your patient's fixed delusion. Simon you're a band of steel . . . consistent non punitive and unexploitable. What next oh relentless one . . . <u>what next?</u>

(lays down and wraps the cloak around his neck and rolls into a fetal position)

DR SIMON SHORTER:

Milord first of all may I begin the session by calling you by your first name?

NATHAN PIERCE:

(rolls back into a rigid 'attention position' and begins to use his stomach as a drum beating a rhythm while talking)

I suppose after last session's disclosures you have earned the right big guy. But first . . . one last test . . . for old time's sake.

DR SIMON SHORTER:

What's that?

NATHAN PIERCE:

Have my needs been exposed . . . you know . . . from you're perspective?

DR SIMON SHORTER:

Frankly I think you've run from your mistakes. There is only so much a person can take before they attempt to hide from those who they feel could find them out. I hope my office my personality and clinical experience can make a difference. But time will tell . . . how's that for an answer?

NATHAN PIERCE:

Why did my upbringing impact on me now? That's all . . . why now?

DR SIMON SHORTER:

Feelings of shame and being shamed by our parents often haunt us later in life. In your case I believe the stress you imposed on yourself to be the ideal worker led to your belief that life might be happier on another Planet. Less stress more control increased self esteem . . . what do you think?

NATHAN PIERCE:

Shame is a sense of being seen as bad . . . your ability to challenge me without resorting to dirty tricks reflects strength of will and honest acceptance of my situation. Not an agreement but an honest acceptance.

DR SIMON SHORTER:

I believe the only time that was invested in your upbringing was when you were being 'put down' and I don't want to replicate that during our sessions. However after making such a statement I must also say that we will take a long time . . . as much as it takes to develop a strong healthy relationship during these sessions.

NATHAN PIERCE:

My mother loved me but as a boy wonder who could be bragged about talked at and made to feel important. But only with those cans tied to my tail. Signal flares of acceptance vicarious signal flares lifting mother's skirts in a boring mundane marriage.

DR SIMON SHORTER:

We have to begin to challenge your concept of what happened at home and give it proper perspective as it relates to now. Not to dwell on it but give it its proper weighting.

NATHAN PIERCE:

No games or I will journey far away without you or anyone else for that matter.

DR SIMON SHORTER:

I promise you . . . there will be no games.

NATHAN PIERCE:

I have an obsession with manipulation . . . to maintain a sense of self, an abstract sense of position control and self esteem. Why the con game to 'get the boost'?

DR SIMON SHORTER:

Nathan you placed yourself in milieus where the potential to be powerful was at a premium. Manipulation of your peers kept you from dealing with your anxiety about risking . . . taking real risks like the rest of us.

NATHAN PIERCE:

My parents made me dependent on their jazz their game of 'play the fool Nate'. The clever resourceful A-1 achiever . . . so we can feel better. Right Mom right Dad . . . no matter the dynamics of how it manifested itself this is the outcome . . . how I feel today about surviving in this Jesus Christ world.

DR SIMON SHORTER:

The more dependent one is the more they need to idealize. Your parents used your brilliance to upgrade and 'kick start' their mundane lives. At your expense they idealized you and molded the character you have become. That doesn't mean you can't change . . .

only that it will take time energy and guts to conquer this tendency to escape, avoiding the anxiety of uncertainty doesn't work Nathan . . . it doesn't work.

NATHAN PIERCE:

Simon a quid pro quo . . . a Ted Hughes poem and I believe post Silvia Plath 'All day he stares at his furnace with eyes red raw. But when she comes they close. Polly pretty Poll she cajoles and rocks him gently. **She caresses whispers kisses the blue lids stay shut'**.

DR SIMON SHORTER:

Nathan do you see yourself . . . your problems as intransigent? They aren't . . . in just a few sessions we have begun

(cut off)

NATHAN PIERCE

(rolls into a ball and begins a mantra. Dr Shorter also begins to replicate the mantra at a different pitch but cannot break Nathan's concentration. After 15 seconds Nathan abruptly stops gets up walks to the door)

See yah next week Simon . . . good workout.

(exits through the door flamboyantly)

STAGE LIGHT DIMS — END OF SCENE ONE

ACT TWO SCENE TWO

(Lights are raised — Dr Shorter is sitting across from Nathan Pierce who as usual is wearing the magic cloak. He is subdued with frequent yawns. Nathan is uncomfortable with the therapeutic process)

DR SIMON SHORTER:

I want to reflect back on our last session when you left so

(cut off)

NATHAN PIERCE:

The issue as I recall from the last 'friggin' session was one of degree and balance. Your persistence regarding my upbringing . . . its quality or lack thereof causing my current state of imbalance. Do I bat one thousand or am I high and outside?

DR SIMON SHORTER:

Nathan . . . may I call you Nathan?

(Nathan shrugs and then nods slowly)

From my perspective you have achieved and achieved and achieved . . . for what purpose? To reduce a sense of inferiority? An ugliness? I think you know you are incredibly vulnerable and quite

(cut off)

NATHAN PIERCE:

OK OK enough said about my hang-ups . . . but how are we going to fix me up Doctor I.Q?

DR SIMON SHORTER:

I think you feel 'subjectively empty' . . . in lay terms . . . devoid of a sense of self. I'm going to clarify your parent's behavior as a contributing influence and hope to encourage honest disclosure throughout the course of therapy.

NATHAN PIERCE:

Simon the operative word in this gobblygook' is appropriate. I think I'm going to

   (cut off)

DR SIMON SHORTER:

Is facing the reality about ourselves so devastating?

NATHAN PIERCE:

That's a stupid question Doctor . . . obviously for me it has been. How many people do you know blast off to the Planet Zachreb?

DR SIMON SHORTER:

I believe your excursions to Zachreb are incited by some precipitating factor. Someone or something causes stress and you play your Zachreb fantasy. Unfortunately this method of coping has landed you in my office and jeopardized your ability to make a living.

NATHAN PIERCE:

Stress mediates reality Simon . . . Zachreb comforts and reinforces who I am and what I am to me.

DR SIMON SHORTER:

I believe Zachreb is a big 'cop out' . . . a method you use to compensate for the stress you face and have become incapable of handling. Am I being too confrontational or is it mantra time Nathan?

NATHAN PIERCE:

<u>What do you want me to say?</u> That I'm hungry for a relationship that is meaningful . . . appreciative of the care you provide me. <u>Come on</u> . . . <u>get with the program Doctor</u> . I'm nuts . . . very close to being certifiable. I feel a delusion coming on.

(Nathan begins to hum)

DR SIMON SHORTER:

Nathan have I abused you like your colleagues? Your parents? We've just begun this treatment process give it a chance.

NATHAN PIERCE:

Doctor . . . I believe you care about how bad I feel and want to . . . in your own terms of reference 'give it a chance'. But I'm not willing to give up Zachreb. It's a bit of a dilemma . . . the fringe benefits are the boost and I <u>dig the jazz.</u>

DR SIMON SHORTER:

You like the attention?

NATHAN PIERCE:

It's real and in the past I was comforted with phony platitudes . . . real requires I maintain the status quo Doctor. I don't want to go back to phony platitudes . . . would you?

DR SIMON SHORTER:

You are comfortable when you provoke I can feel this Nathan, but why the cruelty to yourself and other people?

NATHAN PIERCE:

Doctor you have a self righteousness that makes me 'ring a ding ding' and here I thought you were a peer.

(Nathan begins to hum)

DR SIMON SHORTER:

Nathan

(humming continues)

<u>Nathan</u>

(humming stops)

It's OK to be fallible . . . it's OK to be dependent on others and to challenge the past as it effects your present.

NATHAN PIERCE:

I believe you have me pegged as an inferior being and I wish to travel to the Planet Zachreb. When I return or not is dependent on the next few moments Doctor . . . comprenez vous?

DR SIMON SHORTER:

Mon français n'est pas le meilleur si tu parles lentement et je pourais comprendre.

NATHAN PIERCE:

Very good Doctor . . . you're back in the good books of this lone-some cowboy. Now one quick disclosure and then I must go.

DR SIMON SHORTER:

What's that Nathan?

NATHAN PIERCE:

Conscious manipulation of my environment turns me on right? As you implied it has allowed me to avoid anxiety and maintain my sanity.

(cut off)

DR SIMON SHORTER:

Self esteem Nathan . . . <u>self esteem.</u>

NATHAN PIERCE:

OK OK . . . . how 'bout I stir the brew with a 'throw away' state-ment that you can interpret anyway you want?

DR SIMON SHORTER:

Nathan

(cut off)

NATHAN PIERCE:

Aberrant infantile development . . . there I've said it and you don't have to play Otto Kernberg to get that one Simon.

DR SIMON SHORTER:

There is a spectrum of disclosure that you state again and again that
I was waiting for the right moment to bring up

(cut off)

NATHAN PIERCE:

Out with it . . . on a continuum of one to ten I'm an eleven plus
right Simon. Nate the snake Mr Pierce is fierce . . . right Otto?

DR SIMON SHORTER:

Your frame of reference . . . your past continues to interfere with
your ability to function appropriately.

NATHAN PIERCE:

If I was to marry . . . conceive a child and then misuse the parenting
role . . . what would that mean to you Doctor?

DR SIMON SHORTER:

I believe your past abuse was not strictly emotional Nathan can we
go there next session?

NATHAN PIERCE:

Can I bring my cloak Simon?

DR SIMON SHORTER:
If it makes you feel comfortable Nathan.

STAGE LIGHTS DIM — END OF SCENE TWO

ACT TWO SCENE THREE

(Lights are raised — Dr Shorter is reading a Journal article when the phone rings signalling the arrival of his next therapy patient. Nathan Pierce is let into the office still wearing the 'magic cloak'. He takes a chair from the far side of the office and carries it to a position directly across from Dr Shorter — the session commences)

DR SIMON SHORTER:

Nathan have you any comments about how we left the last session?

NATHAN PIERCE:

No Doctor . . . I see you are primed for today's session. As you see I decided to return despite

(Nathan mimics Dr Shorter's accent)

'a lot of intrapsychic conflict'. Proceed Doctor . . . proceed.

DR SIMON SHORTER:

A delicate question Nathan but one I must ask . . . have you ever been molested . . . in your past life time I mean?

NATHAN PIERCE:

Quick and to the point how should I answer the question good Doctor?

DR SIMON SHORTER:

I would hope honestly Nathan . . . honestly.

NATHAN PIERCE:

In the past you have alluded to emotional nurturance . . . emotional interaction is what people most deeply yearn for and what fundamentally gives the boost for living . . . am I right?

DR SIMON SHORTER:

Yes and

(cut off)

NATHAN PIERCE:

Interpretation of parental models is not my strong suit Doctor.

DR SIMON SHORTER:

Nathan can you think of any important figures that you had outside of the immediate family when you were growing up?

NATHAN PIERCE:

Good Lord . . . role models heroes etcetera?

DR SIMON SHORTER:

If you put it that way . . . yes . . . role models . . . heroes.

NATHAN PIERCE:

My feelings are truly amorphous . . . however to make you happy why don't we say all inquisitive psychologists who represent truth and honesty.

DR SIMON SHORTER:

Nathan lets discuss this process . . . the development of our relationship as a

(cut off)

NATHAN PIERCE:

(Nathan begins to hum while swaying in his chair with his eyes closed)

DR SIMON SHORTER:

Nathan

(cut off)

Nathan

(no response — Dr Shorter gets up from his chair walks to the center of the room and lays down. He begins to hum in a different key. Nathan immediately stops his humming)

NATHAN PIERCE:

Simon lets get on with it . . . <u>come on.</u>

(Dr Shorter gets up and resumes his seat in the chair opposite Nathan)

DR SIMON SHORTER:

I think in your family the outside world was considered hostile am I right?

NATHAN PIERCE:

Outsiders were probably a threat to my parents . . . yes.

DR SIMON SHORTER:

Probably?

NATHAN PIERCE:

OK OK . . . yes.

DR SIMON SHORTER:

Would you say that attempts to mingle were viewed as intrusive . . .
a threat to your parents and subsequently you?

NATHAN PIERCE:

Look from your point of view I'm sure their behavior was ambiva-
lent and yes . . . if I was too friendly there were

> (pauses and begins to flick imaginary dust off the 'magic cloak' — Dr
> Shorter nods encouragement for Nathan to continue whose response
> is stated in a 'stage whisper')

reprisals.

DR SIMON SHORTER:

They encroached on your boundaries?

NATHAN PIERCE:

I beg your pardon?

DR SIMON SHORTER:

You were violated?

NATHAN PIERCE:

I BEG YOUR PARDON.

DR SIMON SHORTER:

Look Nathan . . . I believe abuse sexual or otherwise is profoundly destructive for everyone involved. But most importantly the child's rights are violated

(cut off)

NATHAN PIERCE:

'Oh lady when the sea caressed you you were a marble of foam but dumb. When will the stone open its tomb'? Ted Hughes do you like it?

DR SIMON SHORTER:

Nathan are we back to 'game playing'?

NATHAN PIERCE:

'Though deeper within darkness is entering the loneliness' Ted Hughes again do you like it? I think this one was pre Silvia Plath but I could be wrong.

DR SIMON SHORTER:

Lets continue Nathan

(cut off)

NATHAN PIERCE:

Doesn't your rhetoric call it 'interdependent dysfunctional behavior'? I dunno . . I read the phrase somewhere at some point when I gave a damn.

DR SIMON SHORTER:

Nathan I feel we've made headway in our sessions the past month or so. Unfortunately in my field as soon as one problem has been solved it becomes the starting point for a new one . . . Wilfred Bion do you like it?

NATHAN PIERCE:

Is this demonstrating counter transference good Doctor?

DR SIMON SHORTER:

I'm merely trying to reflect or should I say mirror some of your behavior to allow . . . look . . . riddles can be fun at the appropriate time Nathan that's the only point I was trying to make. I see I should be a little more careful about exploring your fears.

NATHAN PIERCE:

Fears . . . I have no fears per se. I chose to live my life on the edge . . . is it my fault the masses are offended?

DR SIMON SHORTER:

Nathan your behavior precipitated a referral to a mental health expert that should ring some bells.

NATHAN PIERCE:

Do you believe me as a functional crazy? If so take the time to LIS-TEN good Doctor.

DR SIMON SHORTER:

I believe you have been victimized as a child and I want to help you.

NATHAN PIERCE:

I had no one . . . <u>no one to talk to</u> is that what you want to hear Simon?

DR SIMON SHORTER:

You have someone now.

NATHAN PIERCE:

Nathan a bright precocious child who had done well academically was age 16 when he was referred to the School Counselor because his grades were abysmal. Counseling was initiated and after awhile a trusting relationship formed with a man who filled the emotional void of having default parents. Several months went by before Nathan told his Counselor about the situation at which time Nathan's quote unquote <u>Counselor who was not a skilled clinician rated me out to my parents.</u> There . . . is that what you wanted to hear good Doctor.

DR SIMON SHORTER:

How did your parents react?

NATHAN PIERCE:

<u>I was kicked out of my friggin house</u>

(glaring intense stare — soft voice)

What d'ya think?

DR SIMON SHORTER:
Then what transpired?

NATHAN PIERCE:
Basically over the next few years I hung out . . . mostly with 'older friends' if you 'catch my drift'. Subsequently I upgraded and finished High School with a 3.8 grade point average and twin 700's on my SAT's. That allowed me to enrol in engineering at a good College. The tuition was paid by my 'older friends' and the rest they say is histoire docteur . . . histoire.

DR SIMON SHORTER:
Let's talk about the abusive situation with your parents can we?

NATHAN PIERCE:
Possibly maybe good Doctor. 'Polly pretty Poll she cajoles and rocks him gently she caresses whispers kisses. The blue lids <u>stay shut.</u>

DR SIMON SHORTER:
Ted Hughes post Silvia Plath?

NATHAN PIERCE:
Your guess is as good as mine Si.

DR SIMON SHORTER:

Was your father

(cut off)

NATHAN PIERCE:

Please show some restraint you make hasty assumptions.

DR SIMON SHORTER:

Was your mother

(cut off)

NATHAN PIERCE:

Unassertive . . . quiet . . . disconnected until the booze brought out the ugly cruelty . . . contempt for life <u>and its stressors.</u> Namely a child called Nathan Pierce who was the 'showpiece' of the family. Unflappable instrumental <u>and a friggin enabler.</u>

DR SIMON SHORTER:

Nathan I want to discuss the dynamics

(cut off abruptly)

NATHAN PIERCE:

<u>What the hell kind of lead was that Simon?</u>

DR SIMON SHORTER:

You're right not much.

NATHAN PIERCE:

I mean this is gut wrenching stuff Si.

DR SIMON SHORTER:

Nathan did you ever confront your parents?

NATHAN PIERCE:

'And their eyes were screwed so tight while their grand bellies shook.
Oh their flesh would drop to dust at the first sober look'.

DR SIMON SHORTER:

I know Ted Hughes.

   (Nathan responds with a stage whisper)

NATHAN PIERCE:

Pre or post?

DR SIMON SHORTER:

Nathan does it matter?

NATHAN PIERCE:

It does to me Bub.

DR SIMON SHORTER:

OK wasn't Ted Hughes blamed for Silvia Plath's suicide?

NATHAN PIERCE:

Year please?

DR SIMON SHORTER:

Nathan for God's Sake

(interrupted in mid sentence by Nathan cocking his head)

OK . . . if my mind serves correctly

(cut off)

NATHAN PIERCE:

<u>It better.</u>

DR SIMON SHORTER:

1962 or 63 . . . so?

NATHAN PIERCE:

(softly spoken)

<u>Did she appreciate her self worth stupid?</u>

DR SIMON SHORTER:

Nathan . . . have I once denigrated you? <u>Have I once denigrated you?</u>

NATHAN PIERCE:

No.

DR SIMON SHORTER:

I'm neither stupid nor incompetent

(cut off)

NATHAN PIERCE:

See how it feels good Doctor

(laughs which becomes hysterical and monotonous)

DR SIMON SHORTER:

You baited me.

NATHAN PIERCE:

That I did good Doctor . . . <u>and that's the crap I took growing up</u>.

DR SIMON SHORTER:

Can we continue?

NATHAN PIERCE:

I believe we can . . . a person like me needs external affirmation to feel internal validity Simon . . . I read that somewhere.

DR SIMON SHORTER:

You worry about how good you are.

NATHAN PIERCE:

I envy your ability to proselytize your friggin religion

(sarcastically)

Good Doctor.

DR SIMON SHORTER:

I only wish to gain disclosure through truth Nathan . . . no one said change is easy it can be a bitch.

NATHAN PIERCE:

And a bastard Simon . . . and a bastard. Why don't we talk to Silvia next session . . . she'll tell you.

DR SIMON SHORTER:

I'm sure there have been tons of dissertations written about the Hughes-Plath demise. He certainly never lived it down

(cut off abruptly)

NATHAN PIERCE:

And why should he?

DR SIMON SHORTER:

Forgiveness.

NATHAN PIERCE:

Forgiveness? Have you ever been compromised good Doctor? Lovely friggin word 'forgiveness' . . . <u>an esoteric vacuous word.</u> Are you a Ted Hughes fan by the way?

DR SIMON SHORTER:

I can't say one way or another Nathan. He was made Poet Laureate of England I think.

NATHAN PIERCE:

And I bowled 172 ten pin Simon. C'mon, COME ON.

DR SIMON SHORTER:

One last question before we end the session today.

NATHAN PIERCE:

As long as it's entertaining.

DR SIMON SHORTER:

Courage . . . not entertainment is essential to work . . . through your problems Nathan.

NATHAN PIERCE:

The game is a long intense struggle Simon . . . and in order to earn points <u>you've got to work Bub.</u>

DR SIMON SHORTER:

Lets talk about it next session Nathan.

LIGHTS ARE DIMMED END OF SCENE THREE

INTERMISSION

ACT THREE SCENE ONE

(Dr Shorter is reading quietly at his desk when a phone call announces that Nathan Pierce has arrived. Prior to leaving his office Dr Shorter drops down to the floor and completes five pushups. He subsequently leaves his office and returns with Nathan Pierce dressed in his 'magic cloak'. Nathan sits directly across from Dr Shorter and stares intently at the therapist)

DR SIMON SHORTER:

How was your week Nathan?

NATHAN PIERCE:

I traveled to Zachreb and ruminated . . . and you?

DR SIMON SHORTER:

I thought about our last session and would like to return to where we left off if that's OK?

NATHAN PIERCE:

The term erotic comes from sublimated sexual energy is that right Doctor.

DR SIMON SHORTER:

Could we first discuss the molestation that occurred in your childhood Nathan?

NATHAN PIERCE:
Please . . . my question must be answered before the game continues.

DR SIMON SHORTER:
I believe eroticism can be a product of shame. The individual feels overwhelmed with passion and often tries to fight those feelings.

NATHAN PIERCE:
But what if he has difficulty discriminating between passion and the fear of passionate consequences?

DR SIMON SHORTER:
How did you deal with being victimized?

NATHAN PIERCE:
In your vernacular . . . old fashioned sublimation denial and rationalization . . . with a twist of suppression thrown in for good measure.

DR SIMON SHORTER:
Nathan all victims of abuse can be expected to fear the consequences of disclosure

   (cut off)

NATHAN PIERCE:
<u>What d'ya know about the consequences of disclosure Bub?</u>

DR SIMON SHORTER:
Nathan can we discuss your parent's relationship as you remember it?

NATHAN PIERCE:

The old man was a frustrated loser . . . unsupported neglected generally 'put down' by his demeaning wife of twenty years. Mother
had put up with the old man's crap . . . his drinking his instability
and 'mootching ways' . . . anything else?

DR SIMON SHORTER:

How old were you when the molestation began?

NATHAN PIERCE:

I can't remember.

DR SIMON SHORTER:

Can you describe the nature of the abuse by your parents?

NATHAN PIERCE:

It mostly occurred when they drank . . . a game of 'hide n seek' I hid
they mostly sought.

DR SIMON SHORTER:

Please . . . continue.

NATHAN PIERCE:

It always ended in the bathroom. The 'boudoire of impropriety' I
did most things but drew the line at oral . . . well . . . you know.

DR SIMON SHORTER:

Did you ever disclose these 'goings on' to authorities . . . a friend

(cut off)

NATHAN PIERCE:

No and to answer your next question I wasn't threatened to 'keep a secret'.

DR SIMON SHORTER:

Nathan I believe you and I'm here to help you sort out the past.

NATHAN PIERCE:

How d'ya do that? Talk talk and then some more talk? <u>What kind of bull</u>

(cut off)

DR SIMON SHORTER:

Resolution requires confrontation Nathan.

NATHAN PIERCE:

Says who which authority?

DR SIMON SHORTER:

Mental health to my way of thinking concerns quality of life. Your life at home was just 'bare bones' survival Nathan.

NATHAN PIERCE:

I was in bondage to my parent's whims and became dependent on the degragation. So what . . . if I lived in Hollywood I could 'hang out' with other molested 'wanna be's' it's all relative.

DR SIMON SHORTER:

The abuse of power at your expense lets' talk about it.

NATHAN PIERCE:

OK failure failure failure. Failure to protect . . . failure to set boundaries and abuse of power equals what?

DR SIMON SHORTER:

How often did the abuse occur Nathan?

NATHAN PIERCE:

Too often to remember . . . let's see . . . the 'old man' drank and
drank mother abused the 'old man' . . . this 'quid pro quo' B.S went
on for awhile and then the game began.

DR SIMON SHORTER:

Can you describe the game Nathan?

NATHAN PIERCE:

I believe boundaries were crossed Simon can we leave it at that.

DR SIMON SHORTER:

What were the boundaries Nathan?

NATHAN PIERCE:

Do I have to draw a friggin roadmap?

DR SIMON SHORTER:

What were the specifics of the game Nathan?

NATHAN PIERCE:

I read somewhere that survivors of long term abuse can require therapy for two years or more . . . is that right good Doctor?

DR SIMON SHORTER:

What were the specifics of the game Nathan?

NATHAN PIERCE:

Long term therapy is required to work through violations of trust is that right Simon?

DR SIMON SHORTER:

What were the specifics of the game Nathan?

NATHAN PIERCE:

Nurturance as in need for control . . . <u>Do I have to draw a friggin roadmap?</u>

DR SIMON SHORTER:

Sexual exploitation involves both variables Nathan . . . please we're almost there.

NATHAN PIERCE:

The alcohol . . . my parent's relationship and their number one son . . . <u>fill in the blanks.</u>

DR SIMON SHORTER:

What were the specifics of the game Nathan?

NATHAN PIERCE:

They concealed their life with guile and wit no one knew the wiser. When they drank I hid . . . they sought . . . their prey.

DR SIMON SHORTER:

Please expand Nathan.

NATHAN PIERCE:

(falls to the floor dramatically and sits on the 'magic cloak'. Dr Shorter quietly sits across from Nathan who places both hands outstretched on Dr Shorter's respective shoulders. Nathan begins to recite poetry)

'Now is the globe shrunk tight round the mouse's dulled wintering heart. Weasel and crow as if moulded in brass move through an outer darkness. Not in their right minds with the other deaths. She too pursues her ends brutal as the stars of this month her pale head heavy as metal'.

DR SIMON SHORTER:

Your mother?

NATHAN PIERCE:

No I believe it was Ted Hughes . . . pre or post . . . I'm not sure.

DR SIMON SHORTER:

Did your father

(cut off abruptly)

III, i, 192 | D.S. Hutcheon

NATHAN PIERCE:

The 'old man' was passed out on the couch. The little munchin running the bath upstairs and the rest is history.

DR SIMON SHORTER:

How long did the abuse last?

NATHAN PIERCE:

Long enough that I decided my designated role in the good ship Pierce was survival whatever the cost. Suppression denial and rationalization spent their force . . . what

(Nathan looks at his watch)

three months ago? Not bad . . . roughly twenty years . . . what d'ya think?

DR SIMON SHORTER:

Guilt and shame

(cut off)

NATHAN PIERCE:

Simon I felt dirty and unworthy of anything positive and I said School not disclosure was my ticket out of insanity . . . 'can you dig'?

DR SIMON SHORTER:

Suppression denial rationalization the words you mentioned earlier masked the pain you felt. These feelings don't just go away Nathan.

NATHAN PIERCE:

And Planet Zachreb looks better and better Doctor. What do you want to play B.S 'quid pro quo' games. I thought we agreed on a truce a month ago Simon.

DR SIMON SHORTER:

Can we return to our discussion Nathan?

NATHAN PIERCE:

What's the angle Simon? Expiation of your clinical soul? Real down to earth spilling the guts by good old Nate. What's the use . . . the menu's served and I vomited twenty years ago.

DR SIMON SHORTER

Did you ever try to confront your mother about her behavior?

NATHAN PIERCE:

What . . . a nine year old tackling a thirty year old? <u>Not good odds</u> Bub . . . besides it wasn't like that.

DR SIMON SHORTER:

What do you mean?

NATHAN PIERCE:

I think mother in her own warped way used our time to feel comfort. Albeit at my expense but at that time knowing the 'old man' the way I did I wanted to make her feel important. It was only later on when I wanted to quit that . . . if you can understand what I'm saying.

DR SIMON SHORTER:

I only know that what you state makes sense for you Nathan. We
need to continue our talk next session.

NATHAN PIERCE:

Set match and whatever Si.

LIGHTS DIM — END OF SCENE ONE

ACT THREE SCENE TWO

(Dr Shorter is quietly reading a psychology text when the phone rings announcing his next patient Nathan Pierce. Dr Shorter responds with a smile and leaves his office returning with Nathan who is dressed in his 'magic cloak'. They sit opposite each other)

DR SIMON SHORTER:
How was your week Nathan?

NATHAN PIERCE:
Dynamically psycho or otherwise?

DR SIMON SHORTER:
Look Nathan the treatment process can be long and arduous. Improving self esteem learning to trust others' motives and beginning to feel secure is never a 45 degree learning curve. The trick is not to dwell on the troughs.

NATHAN PIERCE:
Validation . . . sense of worth . . . bolstering self esteem. I am what I am . . . you can lead me to water etcetera.

DR SIMON SHORTER:
What or whom . . . an important difference Nathan.

NATHAN PIERCE:
Mother seemed to think I was a 'what'.

DR SIMON SHORTER:

How so?

NATHAN PIERCE:

You once stated that mental health is concerned with quality of life. My behavior gave mother a quality of life to survive. Can you dig?

DR SIMON SHORTER:

You'll have to be more precise.

NATHAN PIERCE:

(takes off his 'magic cloak' drops it on the floor and begins to strip emulating an exotic dancer. When he gets down to his underwear he walks back to the chair opposite Dr Shorter sits down and pats his crotch)

Now do you catch my drift?

DR SIMON SHORTER:

Try and disclose your feelings Nathan.

NATHAN PIERCE:

I'm not able to . . . articulate the friggin drift . . . does that suffice?

DR SIMON SHORTER:

Your actions outside the office reflect what the problem is Nathan. Your method of coping with the memories of past abuse.

NATHAN PIERCE:

What . . . that I was complicit with mother's deviant behavior?

DR SIMON SHORTER:

Can you discuss your feelings Nathan?

NATHAN PIERCE:

What d'ya think? I feel crappy OK.

DR SIMON SHORTER:

Look . . . in a nutshell my job is converting this destructive . . . behavior to constructive . . . resolution . . . you know what I mean.

NATHAN PIERCE:

So I'm a greedy bastard . . . I take but I can't give . . .

(Nathan mimics Dr Shorter's accent)

'in a nutshell'.

DR SIMON SHORTER:

I'm simply saying that you have an opportunity to resolve the pain.

NATHAN PIERCE:

So what's the magical cure . . . reflecting on my problems over time? Is that going to do it?

DR SIMON SHORTER:

You've learned to take and not really give Nathan . . . at your expense.

III, ii, 198 | D.S. Hutcheon

NATHAN PIERCE:

Should I feel guilty?

DR SIMON SHORTER:

I think you've been punished enough Nathan. However lets talk about guilt. I believe the more guilt is understood the greater the chance of resolving emotional problems . . . how's that?

NATHAN PIERCE:

A consequence atoned by taking action.

DR SIMON SHORTER:

Yup but you chose the Planet Zachreb.

NATHAN PIERCE:

I have a lot of guilt about the past. I dramatize the present to avoid the pain is that what you're saying?

DR SIMON SHORTER:

I believe so.

NATHAN PIERCE:

Because I could have chosen not to.

DR SIMON SHORTER:

You were looking for empowerment.

NATHAN PIERCE:

I punished myself if society wasn't going to that was the driving force behind Zachreb . . . is that what you're saying?

DR SIMON SHORTER:

Nathan . . . the guilt you were feeling about the game you played with your mother impelled you to dramatize it to the outside world. To atone so to speak but look at the consequence.

NATHAN PIERCE:

OK my workmates think I'm a 'nutcase' so what.

DR SIMON SHORTER:

How do you feel towards your mother and father?

NATHAN PIERCE:

I love mother but hate her victimization.

DR SIMON SHORTER:

You mean your victimization.

NATHAN PIERCE:

She was victimized so I was victimized and that's why I'm here.

DR SIMON SHORTER:

The origin of your problem lies in your guilt Nathan.

NATHAN PIERCE:

Mother was made of polar opposites . . . superior vain prideful. Incomplete ugly inferior. She wanted a plaything to feel better and I was it.

DR SIMON SHORTER:

<u>You were seduced and eventually coerced Nathan.</u>

NATHAN PIERCE:

Remorse and gratitude makes Nate the dull boy . . . so I suppressed my feelings.

DR SIMON SHORTER:

Nathan you stopped running and designed the Planet Zachreb . . . that's how you attempted to cope.

NATHAN PIERCE:

What . . . I saw myself as bad and created an escape . . . <u>it's too pat Si.</u>

DR SIMON SHORTER:

Anyone who's been abused wants closure Nathan.

NATHAN PIERCE:

Why should I admit that I had a need?

DR SIMON SHORTER:

Because if you didn't the emptiness would have eaten you up. After Zachreb then what?

NATHAN PIERCE:

I'm having a dejas vu Si. When I tested you with the maps and calculations point counterpoint . . . remember? Well the past five minutes has reminded me why I'm here and you're there and I've got to go.

(Nathan stands up and shakes Dr Shorter's hand and begins to walk out the door)

DR SIMON SHORTER:

Nathan aren't you forgetting something?

(Dr Shorter points to the 'magic cloak' and Nathan's clothes strewn around the office. Nathan quickly collects his clothes and proceeds out the door calling as he leaves)

NATHAN PIERCE:

Save it 'till next time.

(a female scream is heard outside the closed door)

LIGHTS DIM — END OF SCENE TWO

ACT THREE SCENE THREE

(Dr Shorter is sitting in his chair reading a textbook when the phone rings announcing his next patient, Nathan Pierce. Dr Shorter drops down and completes five pushups stands slowly and leaves the office — returning with Nathan. Nathan walks to his 'magic cloak' hanging on a clotheshorse and places it carefully on the floor. He then drops down and lays on top of it facing Dr Shorter)

DR SIMON SHORTER:
Hi Nathan how was the past week?

NATHAN PIERCE:
Boring . . . monotonously boring and yours?

DR SIMON SHORTER:
A tad better I might say.

NATHAN PIERCE:
Treatment boundaries . . . are we proceeding appropriately Si?

DR SIMON SHORTER:
As I stated last session Nathan when we're abused we want closure and I think deep down . . . . a rationale for participating in the abuse.

NATHAN PIERCE:
That's easy Si it or I gratified a need an unresolved conflict . . . who knows I read that somewhere.

DR SIMON SHORTER:

I believe your mother found sexual relations with an adult over-whelming. you fulfilled an emotional need . . . her behavior towards you was not motivated by sexual desire.

NATHAN PIERCE:

What's being said here?

DR SIMON SHORTER:

Issues surrounding competency worth identity . . . a gross misuse of power. Nathan you were victimized.

NATHAN PIERCE:

<u>No kidding but so what</u> . . . where am I in all this crap?

DR SIMON SHORTER:

Nathan your mother functioned at an infantile level emotionally. She chose a child to fulfill her needs. This expectation tends to be reflected in members of an incestuous family. I believe your father encouraged your mother's behavior through non intervention. You carried this trauma for a long time . . . when the stress became too great you escaped to the Planet Zachreb. What d'ya think?

NATHAN PIERCE:

I think therefore I am Si . . . what d'ya want me to say?

DR SIMON SHORTER:

I think you have a lot of anger about what happened to you.

NATHAN PIERCE:

What are you saying?

DR SIMON SHORTER:

You need to feel valid inside.

NATHAN PIERCE:

You know Si these sessions tend to get tedious . . . <u>just about this</u> <u>time.</u>

DR SIMON SHORTER:

Look . . . I don't suggest this is easy stuff to disclose but my job is to confront your need to travel to Zachreb.

NATHAN PIERCE:

I read somewhere that a masochist is a depressive who still has hope.

DR SIMON SHORTER:

I think what we've discussed about your past gives us a clue. You felt connection when you were being victimized. This can produce an association between attachment and pain. When you were teased you learned that suffering was the price you had to pay in order to maintain a relationship with

(cut off abruptly)

NATHAN PIERCE:

<u>OK OK you know your stuff.</u>

DR SIMON SHORTER:

Your childhood needs further examination Nathan . . . let me go on.

NATHAN PIERCE:

(Nathan curls into a ball but nods his head to continue)

DR SIMON SHORTER:

Your childhood was filled with chronic loss . . . loss of self esteem loss of positive role models . . . loss of love. Your parents were often critical and made you feel guilty. You felt if you questioned the molestation it would be devastating for the family. I think you were there for your parents. In an odd way you felt a sense of loyalty . . . which has eaten you up. You were victimized . . . what legitimate choices did you have?

NATHAN PIERCE:

'Now I am grownup and literate and I sit in my chair as quietly as a fuse'.

DR SIMON SHORTER:

Poetry again . . . forget the 'smoke and mirrors' Nathan come out and lets dialogue.

NATHAN PIERCE:

(Nathan uncurls from the ball and lays on his back with his arms behind his head)

'And the jungles are flaming the underbrush is charged with soldiers the names on the difficult maps go up in smoke'.

DR SIMON SHORTER:

Margaret Atwood?

NATHAN PIERCE:

My rendition of Margaret Atwood . . . there's a difference Si.

DR SIMON SHORTER:

<u>Be real</u> Nathan . . . that's the difference I'm offering . . . <u>be real.</u>

NATHAN PIERCE:

The good Doctor implores the disturbed young man to <u>be real</u> . . . come out come out wherever you are . . . <u>fess up.</u>

DR SIMON SHORTER:

I think you're stuck in the misery loves company rhetoric. Nothing would make you feel better than if you could meet someone as miserable as you.

NATHAN PIERCE:

<u>Balls with a capital B.</u>

DR SIMON SHORTER:

When will you chose an end to the suffering?

NATHAN PIERCE:

Getting a touch worn out Si?

DR SIMON SHORTER:

Nathan I will not abandon you.

NATHAN PIERCE:

What would I have to do to be rejected Si?

DR SIMON SHORTER:

I'm not sure how to answer that question Nathan.

NATHAN PIERCE:

Come on Si you've parried my thrusts anticipated my thoughts and generally done a 'bang up' job. I'll ask you once again . . . what do I have to do to be rejected good Doctor?

DR SIMON SHORTER:

Spout some more poetry Nathan.

(Dr Shorter laughs)

NATHAN PIERCE:

(Nathan begins to laugh and then suddenly leaps to his feet and slides around the office using the 'magic cloak' as a skateboard stopping in front of Dr Shorter's diplomas hanging on the wall over his desk)

Si . . . have you ever compromised your professional ethics? You know . . . denigrated what you believed in?

DR SIMON SHORTER:

I've never betrayed my sense of what is ethical. Does that answer

(cut off abruptly)

NATHAN PIERCE:

But that's just it . . . you felt you had a sense of personal ethics to begin with.

DR SIMON SHORTER:

Your mother's behavior does not make you a bad person Nathan.

NATHAN PIERCE:

The old 'head heart' dilemma Si. Intellectually I know what you're saying. But in my heart I feel like a slut and when I travel to Zachreb I feel like a Prince . . . 'can you dig'?

DR SIMON SHORTER:

It's not an option the rest of society finds appropriate Nathan . . . that's why you're here.

NATHAN PIERCE:

Repeated research has stated that the emotional quality of the relationship between the client and the therapist is the highest correlated factor for success.

> *(Nathan falls into a 'push up' position on the floor and recites poetry at the extended 'up' position of each 'push up')*

'Now . . . I . . . am . . . grown up . . . and . . . literate . . . and . . I . . . sit . . . in . . . my . . . chair . . . as . . . a . . . fuse'

> *(upon finishing the poem in the 'up' position Nathan collapses to the floor breathing heavily)*

DR SIMON SHORTER:
More poetry Nathan I must be losing my touch.

NATHAN PIERCE:
I needed a 'quickie' before blasting to Zachreb Si.

DR SIMON SHORTER:
I wonder what Margaret Atwood

(cut off abruptly)

NATHAN PIERCE:
She would probably say that some people sexualize money some people flirt with power. I only know that if she was listening to my renditions of her poetry and liked what she heard I would invite her to Zachreb.

DR SIMON SHORTER:
Here we go again Nathan . . . can we return to the 'here and now'. Real world expectations and real world behavior and not to escape again.

NATHAN PIERCE:
I'm not sure yet Si . . . let's wait and see.

DR SIMON SHORTER:
Memories of childhood abuse traumatized you. You chose to escape to Zachreb where there are no expectations. Imposed rules and regulations do not exist in Zachreb. Is that real living Nathan?

NATHAN PIERCE:

No but it sure beats working nine to five Si.

DR SIMON SHORTER:

Look just how a person suffers reflects his personality. I believe you desired love and respect from your peers and although highly competent in your field got nothing

(cut off)

NATHAN PIERCE:

I feared authority figures and became super competent as a defense against criticism.

DR SIMON SHORTER:

It's much more than that Nathan . . . you carry baggage from your past which makes coping difficult.

NATHAN PIERCE:

Magical expectations Si . . . is that why I tend to 'con' people?

DR SIMON SHORTER:

More importantly you 'con' yourself into believing that fantasy life can replace <u>real living.</u> The 'give and take' of day to day living. Distancing yourself from responsibility . . . traveling to Zachreb. Is that using power in a responsible manner?

NATHAN PIERCE:

How do you see our progress Si?

(Nathan jumps up from the floor and begins to pace around the office. He stops in front of the wall of diplomas and begins to recite poetry)

'Now I am grown up and literate and I sit in my chair as quietly as a fuse'

DR SIMON SHORTER:
Ted Hughes again Nathan?

NATHAN PIERCE:
Not quite Si . . . Margaret Atwood.

DR SIMON SHORTER:
Nathan could we go back to the discussion at hand please?

NATHAN PIERCE:
What are the ingredients of choice and control Si?

DR SIMON SHORTER:
Nathan enough B.S did I once shun my professional responsibility when incest was disclosed? No . . . did I once misuse my power in the therapy sessions? No . . . did we challenge reliance on denial such as trips to Zachreb as a coping mechanism? Yes . . . did we attempt to improve communication patterns? Yes . . . did we demonstrate increased sensitivity to your emotional needs? Yes

(cut off abruptly)

NATHAN PIERCE:
(Nathan has not moved and is still looking at the diplomas on the wall)

Si could you have me committed?

DR SIMON SHORTER:

It would require two colleagues in Psychiatry to co-sign involuntary commitment papers, stating you are a danger to yourself, the community or other people. Why do you ask Nathan?

NATHAN PIERCE:

Would I survive in a Shrinkery'?

DR SIMON SHORTER:

I believe the residents in a Psychiatric facility would <u>fiercely challenge</u> your game Nathan.

NATHAN PIERCE:

I think I would like to end the session today Si.

(Nathan stands up abruptly and brushes off the 'magic cloak' before folding it over his left arm)

Do you mind if I bring someone next session?

DR SIMON SHORTER:

Let me think about it Nathan I'll let you know next week.

LIGHTS DIM — END OF SCENE THREE

ACT THREE SCENE FOUR

(Dr Shorter is reading a text when the phone rings informing him that the next patient has arrived - Nathan Pierce. Dr Shorter leans back and stretches then drops to the floor to complete five 'push-ups'. He then leaves his office and returns with Nathan who has brought his 'magic cloak' which hangs over one arm. He is also holding a large vinyl suit carrier in the other hand. Both men walk to their respective chairs and the session begins)

DR SIMON SHORTER:

Nathan how was your past week? I see you've brought something.

NATHAN PIERCE:

I have brought my cloak and a navy blue suit. What's it to yah?

DR SIMON SHORTER:

A navy blue suit?

NATHAN PIERCE:

Yes a navy blue suit.

DR SIMON SHORTER:

Nathan what gives?

NATHAN PIERCE:

Forgiveness is what gives and is a form of acceptance. But not all forms of acceptance constitute forgiveness. Enright et al I believe.

DR SIMON SHORTER:

No more 'tit for tat' please. I thought the revenge bit was over. Game Set . . . Match . . . Nathan?

NATHAN PIERCE:

As in I have wronged and wish to make amends Nate?

DR SIMON SHORTER:

But

(cut off abruptly)

NATHAN PIERCE:

But what provoked all this Nathan?

DR SIMON SHORTER:

You

(cut off)

NATHAN PIERCE:

You took the words right out of my mouth Si. Don't be so suspicious. You're conquering pathology . . . <u>you should be overjoyed.</u>

DR SIMON SHORTER:

Forgive my scepticism but I still remember the statement you made before leaving last time. Do you mind if I bring someone next session?

NATHAN PIERCE:

My my Si a touch of paranoia? I can recommend a good therapist if you want?

DR SIMON SHORTER:

(Dr Shorter laughs and then shakes his head)

May I look at the suit you brought Nathan?

NATHAN PIERCE:

All in due course Doctor . . . all in due course. One false move and I might relapse.

(Nathan laughs at his own joke)

DR SIMON SHORTER:

Nathan may I share something with you?

NATHAN PIERCE:

Why not . . . let it all hang out . . . go for it.

DR SIMON SHORTER:

Over time once the defences have diminished there is an increased tendency for the individual to express anger.

NATHAN PIERCE:

So what isn't that what you folks call catharsis? I mean isn't that what you want or in your rhetoric <u>desire</u> to happen?

DR SIMON SHORTER:

Often the person becomes more angry than before Nathan. I guess I'm wondering about that part of your personality.

NATHAN PIERCE:

I believe I have for all intents and purposes been a cracking good patient Si. I have attended these treatment sessions and played aggressive crappy games reflecting a microcosm of the rage I feel and I'm still coming to these friggin sessions Si. Is that what you want to hear?

DR SIMON SHORTER:

It's important to forgive Nathan. Acknowledge the anger and learn coping strategies which I can teach you.

NATHAN PIERCE:

I once read that shame is the sense of public scrutiny and subsequent embarrassment. Yes . . . teach me the friggin strategies if it makes you feel empowered Si.

DR SIMON SHORTER:

Look Nathan the shame becomes an added layer to the pain already experienced . . . coping with pain requires effective techniques

(cut off abruptly)

NATHAN PIERCE:

I have shame I am embarrassed and I want closure.

DR SIMON SHORTER:

I believe the time we've taken has been well spent don't you?

NATHAN PIERCE:

'Stumbling in the fever of a dream down towards the dark woods from the kindling tops' Ted Hughes you know.

DR SIMON SHORTER:

More games Nathan?

NATHAN PIERCE:

I think it's about time you see my suit.

DR SIMON SHORTER:

If it beats the poetry go for it.

NATHAN PIERCE:

My terms of reference Si?

DR SIMON SHORTER:

Your terms of reference Nathan.

NATHAN PIERCE:

(Nathan walks over to the chair where he left the 'magic cloak' and vinyl suit bag. He slowly puts on the 'magic cloak' and then proceeds to carry the vinyl suit bag over to the wall where Dr Shorter's credentials hang)

Si this is the beginning so listen carefully to my rules. I want you to describe the meaning of each diploma and professional membership on this friggin wall. With each definition Nate the crazy will take off one piece of clothing. <u>Only to my skivvies mind you</u> and then replace the old clothes with my nice new navy blue suit and matching dress shoes. Can you dig?

DR SIMON SHORTER:
Your terms of reference Nathan?

NATHAN PIERCE:
<u>My terms of reference Si.</u> Now lets begin . . . Bachelor of Arts Psychology.

DR SIMON SHORTER:
Entry level degree . . . four years duration . . . the precursor to graduate studies.

> *(Nathan takes off his 'magic cloak' theatrically and tosses it on the floor)*

NATHAN PIERCE:
Masters of Education . . . doesn't say in what.

DR SIMON SHORTER:
A graduate degree . . . in my case specializing in psychology. You can complete the degree with straight course work or by the thesis route. Your choice . . . but if you want to continue in graduate work the thesis route is recommended.

(Nathan takes off his shirt and throws back his shoulders making a muscle with both his arms raised. He tosses his shirt on top of the 'magic cloak')

NATHAN PIERCE:

Doctor of Education . . . doesn't say in what.

DR SIMON SHORTER:

The Ed.D . . . Doctor of Education . . . in my case specializing in Psychology. This degree is a practitioners doctorate as opposed to the Doctor of Philosophy which is a research degree. Your choice as to which stream you enter in grad school. The Doctor of philosophy is considered more prestigious.

(Nathan takes off his shoes and flings them dramatically over his shoulder)

NATHAN PIERCE:

Membership . . . British Psychological Society.

DR SIMON SHORTER:

Yes that one required a lot of application material to be reviewed completed and substantiated. You know the 'limeys'.

(Nathan kneels down and removes his socks and snaps them like a slingshot over to his shoes)

NATHAN PIERCE:

Membership . . . American Psychological Association.

DR SIMON SHORTER:

Yes that one I got after the British Membership. Amazing how quickly I gained American membership.

(Dr Shorter laughs Nathan looks perplexed)

Just kidding Nathan most practitioners join the APA. It was established in 1892 and will probably last another 100 years.

(Nathan takes off his pants twirls them around his head while doing a 'bump and grind' and throws them at Dr Shorter. Nathan begins to unzip the vinyl bag and takes out the navy suit which includes a pressed white shirt black socks and matching black shoes and tie)

NATHAN PIERCE:

Membership . . . Canadian Psychological Association.

DR SIMON SHORTER:

What can I say I was 'on a roll'. The CPA provides good discounts with Hertz and hey that's important eh.

(Nathan puts on the suit pants and spins in a circle on each foot with a giant smile on his face)

NATHAN PIERCE:

Membership National Council of Psychotherapists . . . Great Britain.

DR SIMON SHORTER:

Who knows I might emigrate someday. Nathan what can I say I like being qualified it makes me feel good.

(Nathan puts on the white shirt buttoning it up while humming a tune and swaying rhythmically)

NATHAN PIERCE:

Membership Canadian Evaluation Society.

DR SIMON SHORTER:

I like to evaluate . . . my training taught me the importance of worth statements.

(Nathan puts on both pairs of new socks still humming the same tune)

NATHAN PIERCE:

License to practice psychology.

DR SIMON SHORTER:

You require licensure to legally call yourself a psychologist which allows you to 'third party' bill using the registration number . . .see it on the side of the certificate Nathan.

(Nathan nods and proceeds to put on the tie knotting it by looking at the reflection in the glass frames of the diplomas)

NATHAN PIERCE:

Registration to practice as a Chartered Psychologist . . . The British Psychological Society.

DR SIMON SHORTER:

You guessed it again Nathan. I thought I'd try to get

(Dr Shorter affects a British accent)

qualified in the 'UK'.

(ends accent)

in case I emigrate someday.

NATHAN PIERCE:

Registration to practice psychology . . . Province of British Columbia.

(Nathan puts on the suit jacket spins around and begins to hum)

DR SIMON SHORTER:

What can I say . . . The Great White North . . . the land of hockey pucks igloos and the Royal Canadian Mounted Police.

(Nathan puts on the pair of black dress shoes and comes to military attention saluting Dr Shorter with a snappy wave of his hand)

NATHAN PIERCE:

Dr Shorter you are looking at the new improved Nathan Pierce. I look forward to our next meeting as today's 'song and dance' has taken a lot out of me.

(Nathan picks up his clothing including the 'magic cloak' and stuffs them in the empty vinyl suit bag. He salutes once again and disappears out the door remarking)

See yah next session Si get ready for a

(voice trails as a female scream is heard)

STAGE LIGHTS DIM — END OF SCENE FOUR

ACT THREE SCENE FIVE

(Dr Shorter is sitting at his desk when the phone rings announcing his next patient. He quickly 'drops down' and completes five 'push ups' in rapid succession and leaves the office. He returns with Nathan Pierce who is dressed in the dark blue suit. Nathan carries the 'magic cloak' over his arm and walks directly to the chair opposite Dr Shorter's desk chair. They both sit down in unison)

DR SIMON SHORTER:

Well Nathan I see you've arrived in the new suit that you tried on last session.

NATHAN PIERCE:

Sublimation Si sublimation.

DR SIMON SHORTER:

Sublimation?

NATHAN PIERCE:

Yes Simon sublimation . . . different

(enunciated for effect)

individuals have individual proclivities. Can you dig? I mean the suit that is.

DR SIMON SHORTER:

My understanding of sublimation refers to someone finding a useful even creative way of expressing problematic conflicts . . . what's yours?

NATHAN PIERCE:

Not this again . . . Jesus H. Christ Si and here I thought after last session <u>you</u> were getting the hang of me.

DR SIMON SHORTER:

How a person suffers reflects his or her personality Nathan. Oh yes . . . one more thing . . . a personality can be modified in treatment but not transformed. You can change the economics but not the dynamics . . . the old 'drive theory'.

NATHAN PIERCE:

<u>So friggin what Si . . . am I certifiable or what?</u> That's the 'bottom line' right? That's why the <u>big boys</u> at my company are paying you the <u>big bucks</u> right?

DR SIMON SHORTER:

Nathan clinical practitioners gain expertise by serving an extensive apprenticeship. Studying a variety of patients and

    (cut off)

NATHAN PIERCE:

What are you saying Si? Am I in that category you just mentioned? You know . . . a lab rat you can't train or in your lingo

    (sarcastic tone)

reinforce.

DR SIMON SHORTER:

We are talking free will Nathan. No one is forced to come to my sessions

(cut off)

NATHAN PIERCE:

I read somewhere that psychopathy and sadism are intertwined in the person's character with a touch of narcissism to boot. I have attended these friggin sessions to learn just enough . . . if you 'catch my drift' Si. The proverbial 'peaks and troughs' of mental illness . . . the 'ebb and flow' of manipulation

(Dr Shorter raises his hand abruptly)

DR SIMON SHORTER:

Clinical training attempts to cover the full spectrum of personality development. I only ask that you continue to attend the sessions.

NATHAN PIERCE:
(Nathan walks over to Dr Shorter's diplomas on the wall)

I see I missed one of your memberships last week Si. What in the hell is Orthopsychiatry?

DR SIMON SHORTER:

Orthopsychiatry refers to adjunct professionals . . . you know . . . psychologists, social workers, clinical counsellors that work in the field of psychiatry.

NATHAN PIERCE:
Do these orthopsychiatry folks consciously manipulate others as in Orthopsychiatric psychopathy? To quote your lingo.

DR SIMON SHORTER:
No but what's going on here is narcissistic twinning . . . cool it Nathan.

NATHAN PIERCE:
I read somewhere that malignant grandiosity causes a psychopath to sabotage therapy . . . is that right Si?

DR SIMON SHORTER:
Where do we go from here Nathan? You tell me . . . where do we go from here?

NATHAN PIERCE:
(Nathan takes out a pair of scissors from a coat pocket)

I think omnipotent control Si

(Nathan begins to cut up the suit jacket snipping quickly and efficiently as he talks)

omnipotent control

(cut off as Dr Shorter gets up quickly and begins to walk towards Nathan)

Back off Si.

(Nathan points the scissors menacingly at Dr Shorter who 'back-steps' to his chair and sits down calmly)

Do you find this perverse . . . I mean last week I had you convinced that the change of attire meant change . . . or in your words 'modification of personality' as in breakthrough or some such B.S Si. <u>Geez this is fun.</u>

(Nathan start to gouge and snip at the same time. The air is filled with material from the lacerated garment)

DR SIMON SHORTER:
I thought you were amenable to change Nathan . . . perhaps I was wrong?

NATHAN PIERCE:
I smell a rat Si . . . are you trying to 'limit set' good Doctor?

DR SIMON SHORTER:
I believe this relationship has gone its course Nathan.

NATHAN PIERCE:
I agree . . . I think the abuse has run its vexing course . . . if you 'catch my drift'.

DR SIMON SHORTER:
We've come 'full circle' Nathan. This behavior crosses boundaries of the real functioning world inhabited by real functioning people.

NATHAN PIERCE:
<u>Work shmerk Si. I mean who really gives a flying</u> . . . well you know the rest. We were never really that close Bub.

DR SIMON SHORTER:

Before you go Nathan may I request something?

NATHAN PIERCE:

What pray tell . . . <u>what?</u>

DR SIMON SHORTER:

The scissors Nathan . . . may I have them?

NATHAN PIERCE:

(Nathan responds in a childish voice)

I'm not sure Si let me think about it.

(laughs)

DR SIMON SHORTER:

Please Nathan . . . the scissors . . . that's all I ask.

(Dr Shorter puts hand out)

NATHAN PIERCE:

Well now if it isn't 'J.C coming off his cross'. <u>Si don't degrade yourself.</u>

(Nathan aggressively hands over the scissors. Dr Shorter places them in his bottom desk drawer and locks it without taking his eyes off of Nathan who stands nearby)

DR SIMON SHORTER:

I would like to end the session today Nathan.

NATHAN PIERCE:

I don't know about you but I'm feeling a little 'drafty' and that kind of vulnerability makes me feel like a 'scared bunny' Si. Honestly, between you me and . . . <u>I like omnipotence</u>

(starts to laugh)

like flying to the Planet Zachreb Si.

(Nathan falls to the floor and begins to hum for a few seconds and then suddenly jumps up and puts on the 'magic cloak')

Well I've got to go Si can we have one last

(emphasizes with facial contortions)

<u>termination</u> session. Isn't that what you call it Si . . . I mean you probably need a week to get over this one . . . <u>right quitter.</u>

DR SIMON SHORTER:

Yes Nathan one more session is probably a good idea. Let's call it a day and I'll see you same time next week.

(Nathan walks out of the office a female scream is heard. Dr Shorter draws a deep sigh leans over and shuts the door and sits down at his desk. He slowly picks up his phone and begins to dial pauses and begins to talk)

Alana . . . yes could you connect me with City Hospital's Forensic Assessment Unit . . . yes . . . I need to talk with Dr Johnson . . . yes that's right Alana . . . the In-Patient Unit.

STAGE LIGHTS DIM — END OF SCENE FIVE

ACT THREE SCENE SIX

(Dr Shorter is sitting at his desk when the phone rings announcing his next patient has arrived. Dr Shorter quickly drops down to the floor and completes five 'pushups' but at the last moment decides against it. He leaves his office for a moment and returns with Nathan Pierce dressed in a patched navy blue suit. The 'magic cloak' is hung over his left arm as he strides confidently to his favourite chair directly across from Dr Shorter's chair. Dr Shorter sits down slowly facing Nathan)

DR SIMON SHORTER:
How was your week Nathan?

NATHAN PIERCE:
Comprehensive Si comprehensive. It seems you called your colleagues at Forensic who took an active interest in my new suit. It's OK . . . strictly 'third raters' I fed them a line or several lines of . . . well . . . you get the idea.

DR SIMON SHORTER:
I'm sorry for the inconvenience I was concerned after our last meeting and thought a consult would

   (Dr Shorter loses concentration as Nathan stares intently at him)

NATHAN PIERCE:
Pray tell.

DR SIMON SHORTER:

Nathan let me digress for a moment.

NATHAN PIERCE:

Digress away Simon.

DR SIMON SHORTER:

Hans Kohut was a role model for me during my training days.

NATHAN PIERCE:

Yeh so d'ya wanna invite him over for a cocktail or something? Abstract and oblique statements have been my forte not yours Si. Please . . . fill in the blanks.

DR SIMON SHORTER:

Kohut based his theories on one major area of the psyche Nathan . . . narcissism.

NATHAN PIERCE:

I know I'm nuts right . . . so what?

DR SIMON SHORTER:

What I'm trying to say is that I truly believed I could help your situation with psychotherapy and I think I've errored or was too

(cut off abruptly)

NATHAN PIERCE:

I have a personality disorder Si don't feel bad.

DR SIMON SHORTER:

It's more than that Nathan. I have come to the conclusion that you might be better served in an in-patient

(cut off abruptly)

NATHAN PIERCE:

Meaning what?

DR SIMON SHORTER:

Meaning I want to talk to you about terminating our therapy sessions . . . for the time being.

NATHAN PIERCE:

Like friggin hell.

DR SIMON SHORTER:

Let me clarify

(cut off abruptly)

NATHAN PIERCE:

I've given up my freedom to let you challenge my . . . do you see the sacrifice GOOD DOCTOR.

DR SIMON SHORTER:

Nathan . . . I thought I could help . . . I believe you require hospitalization . . . for the time being.

NATHAN PIERCE:

(Nathan stands up abruptly startling Dr Shorter and begins to pace while talking)

You were a protective man . . . an influence in my life. Nate the snake versus the mongoose. Why quit now Si? The old man who feeds him seeds him . . . if you catch my drift good Doctor?

(Nathan begins to sing)

'Baby I need your loving. Baby I need your loving'

(stage whisper)

'Baby I need your loving'

(Nathan walks to the center of the stage and faces the audience)

DR SIMON SHORTER:

Nathan I'm not sure I can help you any longer

(Nathan smiles which turns to a scowl)

I wish to terminate our sessions . . . for the time being Nathan.

NATHAN PIERCE:

<u>For how long?</u>

(turns his head to the side away from Dr Shorter's view)

DR SIMON SHORTER:

I will have to assess how you do in hospital Nathan. That's all I can say at this point . . . that's all I can say at this point Nathan.

NATHAN PIERCE:

(Nathan turns his head to the audience lights become dim to near darkness)

I do not wish to end the sessions Si. NOT ON YOUR TERMS ANYWAY.

(Nathan wheels around 45 degrees his back to the audience and pulls a handgun from his jacket pocket)

You wanna know about pride . . . I'll teach you about pride Si.

(Dr Shorter slumps into his chair and does not move)

DR SIMON SHORTER:

You've got the gun Nathan.

NATHAN PIERCE:

(Nathan walks over to another chair and sits down dramatically about six feet from Dr Shorter)

We're going to play a game Si

(cut off)

DR SIMON SHORTER:

Nathan

(cut off)

NATHAN PIERCE:

Shut up and listen

(a long pause - Dr Shorter sits quietly)

I'm going to tell you something . . . you think I live an empty crap existence. That I depend on you the external . . . <u>expert </u>to help me by putting some phony friggin' mirror to my world. Well maybe you're right I needed a mirror. I'm going to play it back to you. But on my terms Si . . . my terms.

DR SIMON SHORTER:

I'm listening but please put the gun down Nathan.

NATHAN PIERCE:

(Nathan starts to spin the chamber of the revolver while he is talking)

<u>You want my terms</u> . . . 'I'm listening Nathan' . . . <u>you want my terms</u> . . . please put down the gun Nathan? O.K 'bigshot' <u>you got em.</u> You think you're so friggin smart . . . I will describe the game once Si. Just once and if you don't get it . . . Well let's hope you get it. As you see I brought a guest this evening . . . my .357 Colt Python to be exact with a four inch barrel to be more exact. I believe this weapon has 850 foot pounds energy at the muzzle Si. <u>Enough pop to frag somebody's ass </u>if you get what I mean. I can see you're aching to compete so here goes. I will recite a section of poetry and then spin the chamber there is one bullet in the gun . . . if you get it right I point the gun at <u>my head.</u> If you get it wrong I point the gun at <u>your head</u> . . . <u>got it?</u>

DR SIMON SHORTER:

(shaking)

Nathan

(cut off abruptly)

NATHAN PIERCE:

Got it?

DR SIMON SHORTER:

Got it.

NATHAN PIERCE:

WHAT I DIDN'T HEAR YOU SI.

DR SIMON SHORTER:

Got it.

NATHAN PIERCE:
(Nathan is very enthusiastic)

O.K here we go. 'Let there be light said God and there was light. Let there be blood says man and there's a sea' . . . Well?

DR SIMON SHORTER:

How long do I get Nathan?

NATHAN PIERCE:

Don't piss me off Si.

DR SIMON SHORTER:
(Dr Shorter is visibly shaken and begins to breathe in a slow and pronounced fashion)

It's one of the Romantic poets . . . lets see Shelley . . . yes Percy
Byshe Shelley . . . <u>Shelley.</u>

NATHAN PIERCE:

Wrong answer Si . . . SORRY.

> *(Nathan spins the chamber quickly while pointing the gun at Dr
> Shorter's head he pulls the trigger — Click — the gun does not
> discharge)*

I'm afraid the answer was Byron Si . . . <u>Lord Byron</u>

> *(Dr Shorter quivers in his chair and maintains the timed pro-
> nounced breathing)*

Aw . . . don't feel bad Si . . . here we go again where's your

> *(Nathan mimics Dr Shorter's accent)*

fightin' spirit amigo?

> *(Nathan spins the chamber of the gun while pointing the weapon at
> Dr Shorter's head begins to recite the next poem)*

'Beat beat drums blow bugles blow. Through the windows'

> *(Dr Shorter interrupts Nathan abruptly)*

DR SIMON SHORTER:

I already know the answer

> *(abruptly cut off)*

NATHAN PIERCE:

<u>Who the hell do you think you are it's my game Si.</u>

> *(Nathan aims the gun right into the face of Dr Shorter)*

DR SIMON SHORTER:

(Dr Shorter cringes and puts his head between his arms)

O.K O.K the answer is Walt Whitman . . . <u>Walt Whitman.</u>

NATHAN PIERCE:

Si . . . look I'm sorry . . . I didn't mean to . . . No that would be a 'ball faced' lie

(Nathan erupts into hysterical laughter)

<u>You guessed it.</u>

(Nathan quickly points the gun back to his own head and pulls the trigger - click — it does not discharge)

Look Si . . . we're even. Next poem . . . are you ready?

(no response from Dr Shorter)

ARE YOU READY?

DR SIMON SHORTER:

(Dr Shorter begins to sag in his chair. Nathan leans forward and aggressively pulls him up into an upright position at the same time pointing the gun against Dr Shorter's head)

Go ahead.

NATHAN PIERCE:

<u>Go ahead what Si? What kind of B.S is that?</u> . . . go ahead?

DR SIMON SHORTER:

<u>Do it . . . start the game.</u>

NATHAN PIERCE:

(Nathan shrugs)

If you insist.

(laughs)

Next poem . . . 'If I should die think only this of me that there's some corner of a foreign land

(cut off)

DR SIMON SHORTER:

I know the answer.

NATHAN PIERCE:

O.K big shot who? . . . WHO?

DR SIMON SHORTER:

Rupert Brooke . . . The soldier poet Rupert Brooke

(Dr Shorter's voice 'trails off' as he looks down)

NATHAN PIERCE:

(Nathan spins the chamber aggressively and aims the gun more meticulously at his own head and pulls the trigger - click there is no discharge)

Two to one for Si.

(Dr Shorter slumps in his chair and almost falls to the floor and once again is helped up by Nathan at the same time the gun is held against Dr Shorter's head)

DR SIMON SHORTER:

Nathan

    (cut off abruptly)

NATHAN PIERCE:

<u>Shut up.</u>

DR SIMON SHORTER:

Nathan . . . please . . . I just want to

    (pistol whipped across the face by Nathan)

NATHAN PIERCE:

SHUT UP SI. Next poem . . . IF YOU DON'T MIND. 'Jack fell as he'd have wished the mother said and folded up the letter that she'd read. The Colonel writes so nicely'. O.K 'big shot' who wrote it?

DR SIMON SHORTER:

Nathan

    (cut off)

NATHAN PIERCE:

WHO WROTE IT WHO WROTE IT WHO WROTE IT?

DR SIMON SHORTER:

(a long five second pause while Dr Shorter is deeply immersed in thought)

NATHAN PIERCE:

Zachreb to Si. . . . Times awastin.

DR SIMON SHORTER:

(Nathan moves the gun closer to Dr Shorter's head)

O.K O.K it's ah . . . it's ah . . .

(Nathan smiles and cocks the gun)

Yes by God it's William Butler Yates.

NATHAN PIERCE:

Wrong Si.

(Dr Shorter sinks in the chair and almost collapses to the floor utter-ing a loud groan. Nathan points the gun inches from Dr Shorter's head and pulls the trigger - click — there is no discharge)

Si . . . how 'bout Siegfried Sassoon

(Nathan begins to laugh hysterically)

It's two against two Si. Can you imagine a name like that? Siegfried Sassoon. Next batter up.

(Dr Shorter attempts to gather himself in the chair)

'The celluloid of a photograph holds them well six young men fa-miliar to their friends. Four decades that have faded and ochre-tinged'. O.K sport who wrote it?

DR SIMON SHORTER:

(Dr Shorter begins to do muscle relaxation exercises as his body tremor has become involuntary)

O.K give me time . . . O.K O.K . . . <u>O.K Nathan?</u>

NATHAN PIERCE:

O.K O.K but before you answer you need a 'pick me up' . . . You know.

DR SIMON SHORTER:

<u>A what?</u>

NATHAN PIERCE:

Don't play the wuss Si . . . you know . . . <u>a 'pick me up' pick me up'</u>
<u>pick me up'.</u>

DR SIMON SHORTER:

(pleading tone)

Nathan.

NATHAN PIERCE:

Si . . . see the 'magic cloak'

(Nathan laughs hysterically)

Put it on.

DR SIMON SHORTER:

What?

NATHAN PIERCE:

You heard me . . . <u>put it on.</u>

DR SIMON SHORTER:

(Dr Shorter leans over and picks up the cloak and rising slowly from his chair puts the cloak on)

Nathan

(cut off abruptly)

NATHAN PIERCE:

I wonder what the odds are now Si? I just can't imagine . . . Oh well . . . <u>What's the answer Si?</u>

DR SIMON SHORTER:

I believe the poet's name is . . . is ah . . .

NATHAN PIERCE:

(Nathan leans over and kisses Dr Shorter on the lips while simultaneously pointing the gun under Dr Shorter's throat)

Break the tie Si.

DR SIMON SHORTER:

Hughes . . . <u>Theodore Ted Hughes with an E.</u>

NATHAN PIERCE:

Excellent response Si.

(Nathan steps back and spins the chamber of the gun while placing the muzzle under his throat - click — there is no discharge)

What a rush Si . . . what a rush.

(Dr Shorter begins his muscle relaxation exercises — inhaling and exhaling while deep breathing through his nose)

Si Si Si

(Dr Shorter stops abruptly and sits upright in the chair as the theatre lights are dimmed)

Si the next poem . . . are you ready . . . that handy dandy cloak is your . . .

(Nathan begins to laugh hysterically)

sorry Si I couldn't resist . . . O.K for real . . . here we go.

(Nathan speaks in an affected dramatic manner)

'Each time I hit a key on my electric typewriter speaking of peaceful trees another village explodes'

(a pause for five seconds)

DR SIMON SHORTER:

Margaret Atwood . . . Margaret friggin Atwood Nathan . . . Now CAN WE FINISH THE GAME?

(the theatre lights are lowered to complete darkness)

NATHAN PIERCE:

(the noise of a spinning chamber is heard followed by a gun shot)

END OF PLAY - CURTAIN

THE THIRD AGENDA

CHARACTERS

Dr Walter Kemper - mid forties

Franz Hautman - mid twenties

Major Werner Ketterer - mid thirties

Erika - mid twenties (servant girl)

Dr Matthias Goring - mid sixties

First Gestapo Officer - mid twenties (Fredrick)

Second Gestapo Officer - late twenties (Rudy)

Third Gestapo Officer - late twenties

Julius Hattinberg - early twenties

Major Otto Dietrich - mid thirties

Speaker One - young man

Felix Lautner - mid twenties

Paster Kurt Brubaker - mid forties

3 — S.S Guards - mid twenties

3 - Gestapo Guards - late twenties

3 — film crew - young men

TIME: Spring — Fall 1936

PLACE: The Goring Institute in Berlin Germany. The Goring Institute is a Psychological Center serving both Inpatient and Outpatient

clientele. Dr Walter Kemper has been a practicing Psychologist for 20 years in Germany, the past three at the Goring Institute. He has been given a 'forced referral'. A political dissident, a young Nazi Officer who has until recently enjoyed a brilliant career in the Third Reich. Two weeks ago he struck a senior officer at a party and renounced Adolf Hitler. For this crime he has been declared 'unfit for duty' and referred for therapy against his will.

The stage lights are raised illuminating a small room with two chairs, a table, a couch and a window. There is a bookcase beside the door. Dr Walter Kemper is an informal man, 45 years of age, tall, slim and casually well dressed. He is unsure of Nazi Germany and the new German he is seeing in his practice these days. Franz Hautman is 24, disillusioned and at a 'crossroad' in his life.

ACT ONE SCENE ONE

WALTER KEMPER:

(a knock at the door)

Enter.

FRANZ HAUTMAN:

Herr Doctor my name is

(cut off)

WALTER KEMPER:

Yes come in Herr Hautman but let's drop the formalities. I'm Walter.

(Dr Kemper stands up and offers his hand)

FRANZ HAUTMAN:

I'm not sure what to say

(cut off)

WALTER KEMPER:

(Walter smiles and motions Franz to sit down)

Yes . . . you were sent here against your will to discuss your problems and you're nervous . . . would you like a coffee or tea perhaps?

FRANZ HAUTMAN:

Doctor I mean Walter . . . nothing.

(Franz looks down)

WALTER KEMPER:

(remains standing)

Franz if you don't mind I will indulge

(Walter pours a cup of coffee)

Please sit down . . . choose your comfort.

(Walter points to a chair and couch which produces a forced laugh from the younger man as he sits on the chair)

FRANZ HAUTMAN:

Thank you Walter I think I'll sit here.

(sits down and crosses his legs and stares intently at Walter)

WALTER KEMPER:

(Walter sits down on his regular chair by his desk and leans back)

Franz why don't you begin by telling me a bit about yourself . . . your background . . . family education and so forth.

FRANZ HAUTMAN:

(Franz smiles slightly)

I am from Leipzig originally born into an aristocratic family twenty four years ago. My father lost his inheritance at the gaming tables before the Great War. He was forced to marry mother . . . it was arranged her father was a very wealthy banker in Leipzig. A 'trade off' you might say . . . my father's title and its trappings for my mother's wealth . . . her dowry was in the millions you know.

WALTER KEMPER:

And that was pre inflation currency Franz.

FRANZ HAUTMAN:

(Franz laughs)

I'm glad one of us has a sense of humor Dr Kemper.

WALTER KEMPER:

I'm sorry . . . my feeble attempt at humor has often backfired . . . Please forgive me Franz and continue.

(motions with his hand to continue)

FRANZ HAUTMAN:

Thank you Herr Doctor let me see . . . the Fuhrer came to power three years ago . . . about six years ago I had finished Gymnasium with first class honors and was considering reading law at Stuttgaard. My father was taken ill and died within a week and mother was left alone. Her family had deserted her when she married my father a 'near do well'. Mother sent me abroad to England for a holiday at which time she gathered our resources.

WALTER KEMPER:

Gathered your resources?

FRANZ HAUTMAN:

She sold our estate near Leipzig and moved here to Berlin. She bought another home and I think became a lonely person. I on the other hand stayed a full six months in London enjoying myself seeing the sights. The British are entertaining their formality and protocol. I returned to Berlin and told mother I did not want a career in law. But rather I felt politics was the road I should follow. By now I was twenty years old and the world was ready to entertain my ambitions.

WALTER KEMPER:

Franz had you made many friends throughout your formative years while in Leipzig?

FRANZ HAUTMAN:

Yes a few school mates whom I still keep in contact. Why do you ask?

WALTER KEMPER:

Please continue.

(Walter motions again with the same hand movement as before)

FRANZ HAUTMAN:

Towards the end of 1930 I heard the Fuhrer speak a number of times and I believed his wisdom and became a disciple. I joined the army as an officer cadet and within two years received a commission. One year later Hitler came to power Hiddenberg died and we as junior officers made a fatal decision. I believe for survival as we knew this new force in Germany was too powerful to antagonize so we joined the National Socialist Party and pledged our allegiance to 'der fuhrer'.

WALTER KEMPER:

Like all of us you see him a great force uniting modern Germany

(cut off)

FRANZ HAUTMAN:

Then as now I was cowed by his brilliance and approval from the masses. Hadn't he labelled our greatest enemy 'the jew' and begun to purge our country of this . . . Yes I was mesmerized by this...

(sarcastic tone)

'great man' and declared allegiance to the death . . . My mother was horrified.

(Franz looks at the floor trembling)

WALTER KEMPER:

Franz what made you stay in the army?

FRANZ HAUTMAN:

I met a girl . . . a student at the University . . . someone I admired who understood my ambitions. Unfortunately it became a choice between two strong forces . . . love or loyalty to a cause. She made it obvious not so much in words but in actions that I must choose and I did. We separated and I became a Nazi. Hitler was my God whom I worshipped without shame.

WALTER KEMPER:

What became of the girl?

FRANZ HAUTMAN:

She was taken away to a camp for dissidents and taught to love Germany. I visited her once and begged her to give up her beliefs. She told me I was a fool and that Germany was no longer real. Seven months later she was transported east and I have not seen her since.

(Franz looks down and shrugs)

WALTER KEMPER:

Did your mother approve of her?

FRANZ HAUTMAN:

Mother was surprised and happy at my choice but said nothing to influence my decision.

WALTER KEMPER:

Proceed with your story you are a man of conviction.

FRANZ HAUTMAN:

Thank you Doctor I am the new Germany and will continue to love my country . . . whatever the cost. My story is just beginning . . . About eighteen months ago June 30th 1934 to be precise Hitler purged the S.A. Rohm was shot along with four hundred 'brownshirts' for treason. I had many friends who were killed and none were traitors to the Third Reich. It was at this time mother begged me to leave the army and continue my education. I was a 'bright light' she said too shrewd to be without a respectable career. This I might add was the only time my mother was forceful and opinionated. She loved me but very quietly and I admired that quality in her.

WALTER KEMPER:

You talk in the past tense Franz did your mother die?

FRANZ HAUTMAN:

I will tell you her fate in good time but first let me continue my story . . . Your colleague Dr Jung stated 'Hitler is the first man to tell every German what he has been thinking and feeling in his unconscious about German fate since the defeat in the Great War'. He also said 'Hitler's power is not political it's magic'. It was then I think . . . July 1934 that I made the decision to join the 'inner circle' . . . to follow 'der fuhrer' and learn the truth.

WALTER KEMPER:

How?

FRANZ HAUTMAN:

I met Dietrich the S.S Commander the man who arrested Rohm at Badwiessee. I knew Dietrich from friends of my father and through a mutual acquaintance was introduced to this 'cut throat'.

WALTER KEMPER:

What were your thoughts of Nazi Germany at this time Franz?

FRANZ HAUTMAN:

My thoughts were positive I was ambitious to be with the great minds who decided our fate. It was intoxicating . . . Dietrich's power played heavily on my mind. I used my title to gain Dietrich's favor and we reminisced about Leipzig and my father's estate. Dietrich had blond flaxen hair was arrogant and I pandered to his vanity. I was younger but smarter much smarter than he.

WALTER KEMPER:
Did Dietrich ask you to join the S.S?

FRANZ HAUTMAN:
No not then . . . he invited me to visit a brothel with him. His favourite 'Lebensbom' as he called it. You know 'stud farm' it was a glorious evening and from that day a friendship was formed. He thought as mentor . . . it was this weakness I exploited to win his favor and for a year I rose quickly in the Party.

WALTER KEMPER:
I did not hear of you in the media?

FRANZ HAUTMAN:
No I was behind the scenes promoting myself . . . getting known in the right circles. Playing the political game achieving my objectives. I joined the S.S in February 1935 working as Dietrich's first assistant. Before long I was privy to the party politics and deceit of the masses. It began to sicken me yet I stayed.

WALTER KEMPER:
How did you cope?

FRANZ HAUTMAN:
It was difficult I trusted no one in the Party. I met Himmler . . Dietrich's superior and impressed him . . . or so I thought. Dietrich's company began to bore me . . his obsession for power and obsequious nature around Himmler . . . once I saw him rape two 'serving girls' one after the other to prove his virility to Himmler. Himmler

laughed and toasted Dietrich's health. The girls were paid then led away . . . I never saw them again.

WALTER KEMPER:

I would like to ask you a few questions before we continue with your story Franz . . . may I?

FRANZ HAUTMAN:

Go ahead Doctor.

WALTER KEMPER:

What was your relationship with your father Franz?

FRANZ HAUTMAN:

He frightened me when I was young. As I got older I thought I respected him. He lived for today . . . on my mother's dowry. He didn't give a damn about other people's opinion of him. A sort of 'devil may care' fellow . . . you know the type.

WALTER KEMPER:

Did he demonstrate his affection towards your mother?

FRANZ HAUTMAN:

Yes once in awhile but nothing so obvious or frequent that would make you think he loved her deeply. I'm not sure whether he did or not?

WALTER KEMPER:

How did he discipline you?

FRANZ HAUTMAN:

He would scold me when I was young. When I was older he would threaten to withhold my allowance or banish me to my room.

WALTER KEMPER:

What did your mother say when he disciplined you?

FRANZ HAUTMAN:

My mother was fearful of my father's temper and would leave the room . . . he forbade her to become involved. Why do you ask Walter?

WALTER KEMPER:

Would you say your father was a proud German?

FRANZ HAUTMAN:

He was proud of being a German National but not proud of himself. No he did not like being a poor Baron nor did he like the 'dirt' fed to him by his in-laws.

WALTER KEMPER:

What did your mother do when he was demeaned?

FRANZ HAUTMAN:

Nothing . . . absolutely nothing. I think she quietly mocked the man and felt revenge when he endured these insults.

WALTER KEMPER:

How did this make you feel Franz? I mean over the years did the pattern change or worsen?

FRANZ HAUTMAN:

Father never forgave my mother but it didn't matter. She was too proud to let her feelings show . . . she accepted her life.

WALTER KEMPER:

But it must have effected you can you tell me how you dealt with your parent's problem?

FRANZ HAUTMAN:

Doctor I feel like a mouse caught in a trap and you're the hungry cat. I did not feel close to either parent and left the house when they argued. Yes I escaped . . . I did not become part of their struggle it was fruitless . . . <u>why must we go on?</u>

WALTER KEMPER:

Probably because a lot of your ambition and desire for power is a result of never feeling in control in your parent's household. Anyway enough 'cloak and dagger' interpretation . . . why don't we return to your fascinating story Franz?

FRANZ HAUTMAN:

Thank you Herr Doctor . . . I'm struggling where did we leave off? Oh yes . . . Dietrich and the S.S . . . I learned to hate the man and the S.S Director Himmler . . . . everyone involved in the S.S. By the autumn of 1935 last year to be precise I was looking for a way out . . . anything to escape the politics

(cut off)

WALTER KEMPER:

But you stated earlier you wished to be in the 'inner circle'. What did you imagine to find? Goldilocks?

(Walter laughs subtly at his own joke)

FRANZ HAUTMAN:

<u>You joke with my past Herr Doctor.</u> I am a man condemned as 'crazy' and you joke.

WALTER KEMPER:

Please forgive my indulgences Franz. I was only laughing at the irony.

FRANZ HAUTMAN:

May I begin again or should I leave?

WALTER KEMPER:

Please begin and I am sorry. Please . . . carry on.

FRANZ HAUTMAN:

About this time last year I believe it was October or so a memorandum came down from Himmler condemning all intellectual practice. Your very profession was denounced in the most vicious fashion. Himmler stated 'psychology is a trade union for pulling people's souls to pieces'. He attacked all forms of intellectualism and free speech . . . forgetting that many of his most brilliant officers had attended University. The S.S guards became even more fanatical in their attempts to find traitors within the ranks. I myself witnessed several beatings . . . men who were completely innocent of any crime dragged off and beaten. Dietrich was totally ruthless and it was then that I began to hate the Third Reich its philosophy . . . its corruption.

WALTER KEMPER:

Do you know what you say Herr Hautman? Do you see that picture on the wall.

(Walter motions to a picture of Adolf Hitler)

FRANZ HAUTMAN:

Yes yes call me a 'madman' and have me shot. I am not a traitor to Germany because I condemn the atrocities we are experiencing today in 1936. I have seen so much crime and feel sick. Hitler is a genius but must be stopped.

(Franz' voice lowers as he looks at the floor)

There . . . now you know.

WALTER KEMPER:

I know only that you are grieving many experiences and need to talk. Come lets have coffee . . . strudel.

(Walter leans over and pours two cups of black coffee and passes a cup to the young man)

FRANZ HAUTMAN:

(Franz drinks the coffee sparingly)

I must say this before we go on and to hell with the consequences. I joined an organization that is opposed to National Socialism. I made my decision a few months ago.

WALTER KEMPER:

<u>Franz . . . do you know what you say?</u> Your disclosure does not shock me but what prompted your change in attitude?

FRANZ HAUTMAN:

I think many things upset me the past six months. A failing belief in a tyrant leader . . . friends who became liars and enemies who wanted friendship. They are 'play actors' deceiving to achieve importance . . . something I also wanted but could not pay the price. I came home one evening to an empty house my mother was taken away earlier in the day and when I tried to find her they told me to wait until tomorrow. 'Please Herr Hautman your mother is fine we must ask but minor questions then she will be released'. I heard this for five days and then I received word she was dead. Forty seven years old and she died of heart failure. I did not see the body . . . I was shown a casket in the courtyard and told by the official that she died in her sleep. <u>I did not see her body. I believed the official and buried a casket.</u> These reasons became too important to forget or deny or manipulate in my mind. Four months ago I joined a group of people who felt as I felt <u>and I will die before I betray them.</u>

WALTER KEMPER:
(Walter leans forward and touches Franz' arm)

Franz your burden is Germany's burden.

FRANZ HAUTMAN:

(Franz stands up quickly and is composed)

Doctor what do you say? Do not play games with me . . . <u>what do you say?</u>

WALTER KEMPER:

I say only that I feel your anger. I know your sorrow you are not alone. I have witnessed many things as well. But most importantly I believe what you say and what you feel are real things happening in Germany today.

FRANZ HAUTMAN:

Doctor

(Walter raises his hand)

I mean Walter . . . you must hear everything from me because I am making a decision which I hope will effect the Third Reich.

WALTER KEMPER:

Please continue I am here to listen Franz.

FRANZ HAUTMAN:

Before I begin I must know something are you a National Socialist? You have a picture on the wall . . .

(Franz nods at the picture of Hitler)

that conveys a certain impression. Yet you speak or should I say indicate another impression. What I mean to say is . . . are you real and to be trusted or do you play a game?

WALTER KEMPER:

What difference does it make Franz. You are being followed by the Gestapo. Your credibility is lost in the Party and your referral to me is a last attempt to re-educate you. In their eyes you have no more 'rope'. You have nothing to lose Franz and everything to gain by being a

(Walter exaggerates with voice and body mannerism)

Good patient.

FRANZ HAUTMAN:

I understand only that you are a man who conveys two images and I need more time to trust.

WALTER KEMPER:

Take all the time you need . . . we are not racing for the cup in my hour Franz . . . my time is your opportunity.

FRANZ HAUTMAN:

Walter what is your background . . . may I be impertinent to ask such a question?

WALTER KEMPER:

I am Dr Walter Kemper . . . Doctor of Philosophy University of Vienna 1916. I am 45 years old single and love psychology. It is my passion. My dissertation was in Adlerian Psychology . . . I counsel people in distress and am good at my job. I visit a brothel like your Dietrich to 'clear my pipes' and enjoy American Jazz. I love my car a 1933 Stutz Bearcat . . . a present from an Aristocrat who was too possessive so I jilted her. I am a German who studied in Austria and lived with the Jews . . . gaining much knowledge from them. I returned to Germany before Hitler came to power. I . . . like you am attempting to formulate answers to this new regime. What else . . . I am a controversy in my field because I am opinionated . . . I demand truth and in the new Germany there is little truth to be found. There that is me and there are no hidden microphones . . . I know I checked this morning.

(Walter laughs at his joke)

FRANZ HAUTMAN:

Walter I will tell you something that may surprise you. I am half jew . . . My mother was jewish and no amount of money could save her from the Gestapo. I was christened a Catholic my father's religion and have those papers but I am half jewish which will haunt me to my death.

WALTER KEMPER:

Franz tell no one about this fact and no I'm not shocked. The Star of David was shining in your eyes all morning.

FRANZ HAUTMAN:

Walter I must take some time to think about today. I have told you so much it frightens me. Will you tell them there is progress with me?

WALTER KEMPER:

I will tell them nothing which will jeopardize my hour with you. That I promise . . . would you like more cake . . . coffee?

FRANZ HAUTMAN:

No thank you Walter I am afraid I must leave your company and return home. It is very lonely without mother . . . the servants are leaving one by one to seek other employment. I think they know to be seen with a dissident is fool hardy and I am not discrete in my opinions these days. So I must leave and return tomorrow with God's help.

(both men laugh)

WALTER KEMPER:

Franz please be careful and I will look forward to tomorrow's meeting.

(Walter shakes hands with Franz who leaves quickly shutting the door behind him)

STAGE LIGHTS DIM — END OF SCENE ONE

ACT ONE SCENE TWO

(The lights are raised — Dr Kemper and Franz Hautman are sitting opposite one another in Dr Kemper's office at the Goring Institute)

WALTER KEMPER:
Well Franz thank you for returning . . . before we start would you like some coffee . . . tea perhaps?

FRANZ HAUTMAN:
No thank you Herr Doctor.

WALTER KEMPER:
Franz are we back to formalities again?

FRANZ HAUTMAN:
I'm sorry.

WALTER KEMPER:
Please address me as Walter . . . Dr Kemper is too stuffy.

FRANZ HAUTMAN:
Walter I will try my best.

WALTER KEMPER:
O.K lets talk about you Franz Hautman. A bright spirited man who loves his country. May I come to the point . . . your behavior is not

crazy but in these times a discrete man is a wise man. The wisdom department does not appear to be your strong suit. The Gestapo see you as a traitor <u>preaching sedition.</u>

FRANZ HAUTMAN:
Doctor I mean Walter if this is so why do you take the time with me?

WALTER KEMPER:
Because I was ordered to treat you and I like a challenge and with you there is hope I think. I wish to talk about behavior . . . its cause its effect . . . consequential action you know psychology Franz . . . that is my strong suit. Maybe we can save you from yourself . . . you are impassioned and close to self destruction such emotionality in a totalitarian state is . . . not prudent.

FRANZ HAUTMAN:
I am me Walter as long as I breathe I will speak my mind <u>and the new Germany be damned.</u>

WALTER KEMPER:
Franz . . . could we talk about your association that came up in our last meeting?

FRANZ HAUTMAN:
That is my business Herr Doctor.

WALTER KEMPER:
Are you frightened I will betray you and betray the sanctity of my hour with you?

FRANZ HAUTMAN:

You speak of our meetings as something pure . . . we talk Walter that is all we do just

(cut off abruptly)

WALTER KEMPER:

I wish I could agree Franz but in one hour of talk you paint wonderful pictures about yourself. You reveal so much to me and that is why our time together is not just talk Franz.

FRANZ HAUTMAN:

Do you enjoy music Walter?

WALTER KEMPER:

Of course but not Wagner.

(Walter laughs)

FRANZ HAUTMAN:

Please tell me more about yourself Walter so our relationship has no secrets.

WALTER KEMPER:

This request is unusual . . . but the circumstances of your referral are unusual. I . . . like you feel impassioned but at my age recognize better when to show my 'trump card'. I learned to survive in the Great War . . . improvisation . . . one day each day . . . you bent your values to stay alive and buy time for one more day. Those who died could not adapt to the trenches . . . orders were obeyed to a point if you wanted to live. Strength became a 'game of wits' against yourself and your enemy. I took up chess after the war and the commonalities with war frightened me so I quit.

(Walter shrugs while Franz looks on intently)

FRANZ HAUTMAN:
You reveal much Walter . . . we are two men trying to survive.

WALTER KEMPER:
You are not doing as good a job Franz.

FRANZ HAUTMAN:
No but I have peace of mind and now no one frightens me.

WALTER KEMPER:
Franz your world in Germany is frightening and we are seeing a Country pretending to enjoy . . . pretending to care . . . pretending.

FRANZ HAUTMAN:
How do you know you are right Herr Doctor? Maybe both you and I are wrong about life in the Third Reich.

WALTER KEMPER:
Franz I have worked as a Psychologist many years. I too saw the rise of 'der fuhrer'. I have worked and observed and for three years survived as I did in the Great War. I hide my contempt . . . to survive. My path has become narrow . . . like trench fighting around the next bend could be certain death. So there is stalemate . . . strategy and much to ponder.

FRANZ HAUTMAN:

Walter join our group and fight with us . . . use this office as your weapon.

WALTER KEMPER:

I think not Franz I would not be a good partisan for I see no hope in futile action.

FRANZ HAUTMAN:

Herr Doctor . . . <u>the coward.</u>

WALTER KEMPER:

I won the Iron Cross First Class in the Great War . . . I see no hope in skirmishing for a death sentence.

FRANZ HAUTMAN:

Come once and meet my friends Walter you love Germany . . . please . . . come with me just once.

WALTER KEMPER:

I think not Franz.

FRANZ HAUTMAN:

These meetings I have with you what will be their meaning now that we understand each other?

WALTER KEMPER:

I think that is a question we cannot answer now. Let our meetings evolve over time and the Gestapo will be satisfied of a positive outcome. I think this route is the best.

FRANZ HAUTMAN:

Our group is not indecisive we are not comrades in name only. We plan to make a better Germany without 'der fuhrer'.

WALTER KEMPER:

You are perhaps eighteen or even eighty against eighty million. Eighty million German Nationals who revere 'der fuhrer'. Who see him as their savior. No Franz now there is no hope.

FRANZ HAUTMAN:

Are you going to sit in your office and see neurotics the rest of your life? This life I think is the more futile . . . you represent truth but turn your back on evil. This is hypocritical.

WALTER KEMPER:

No Franz I am a realist. Germany is not safe anymore. Like a tidal wave . . . do you build a dam against a tidal wave? No it will be crushed . . . you go instead to the higher ground to survive. Franz

(Walter leans forward and smiles)

my office is my 'high ground' my sanctuary does that make me a coward? Please understand it is how I endure.

FRANZ HAUTMAN:

So you will sit in your office your 'high ground' and do nothing . . . play the waiting game. <u>While we the common people drown like rats below. you are a coward.</u> While good Germans . . . yes German Jews are being brutalized everyday the 'good Doctor' hides in his sanctuary. <u>You make me sick with your pretence.</u>

WALTER KEMPER:

Young man I think this session is becoming

(cut off abruptly)

FRANZ HAUTMAN:

What Herr Doctor . . .

(feigned American Gangster accent)

'too hot to handle' When a man is in hospital a nurse will clean his wounds as well as his 'bed pan'. Maybe my comments upset the good Doctor and his sensibilities. I am true to Franz Hautman . . <u>you and your practice are a sham.</u>

WALTER KEMPER:

Franz . . . Germany is and always will be my first love.

FRANZ HAUTMAN:

Ah . . . so there is a conscience in Walter's brain after Patients have listened to Walter's logic and wooden heart. Herr Doctor you are human after all. Now I ask you to attend one meeting. If you love Germany you will fight for our cause. Walter this is your chance to fight . . . <u>come just once.</u>

WALTER KEMPER:

May I ask a question of you. What is the plan . . . the goal of this group?

FRANZ HAUTMAN:

We will rid Germany of this tyrant and establish a true democratic republic . . . without hatred . . . without corruption.

WALTER KEMPER:

Who is your leader? The masses need someone to follow.

FRANZ HAUTMAN:

I will not say now but come to our meeting and see for yourself.

WALTER KEMPER:

I will think about it Franz and now let us return to less emotional issues.

FRANZ HAUTMAN:

Walter as you said before it is my hour and to change the topic would betray the sanctity of our therapy . . .

(Franz presents a sardonic smile)

together.

WALTER KEMPER:

Franz your point has been made. I need time to think.

FRANZ HAUTMAN:

We need your talent Herr Doctor and you need peace Walter.

WALTER KEMPER:

(Walter stands and walks slowly around the room before looking out the window)

Franz when is the next meeting?

(Walter extends his hand to Franz and smiles warmly this action is reciprocated)

FRANZ HAUTMAN:

You will not be disappointed. I will tell you at our next appointment . . . our weekly sessions become good 'cover' . . . for both of us. Who would suspect the good Doctor Kemper of plotting against Hitler and who would suspect a traitor influencing the good Doctor.

WALTER KEMPER:

Franz I will trust no one in your group spies are everywhere.

FRANZ HAUTMAN:

Walter your identity is safe. Each 'cell' of our organization knows only its own members. If we are captured we cannot betray the total organization. We know only our 'cell' it is not perfect but for now it must do.

WALTER KEMPER:

I am not happy with this arrangement. But then I am not happy about a lot of things. In short these weekly meetings become instructional about the 'Cell's' activities am I correct?

FRANZ HAUTMAN:

Walter I am now under suspicion of treason and watched by the Gestapo. Let us be perfectly frank and clear about your role. I will be passing information to you through another man.

WALTER KEMPER:

'Mein Gott' I will be implicated before

(cut off abruptly)

FRANZ HAUTMAN:

Walter improvise. That's what you said must be done to survive. Aren't you the 'master psychologist'? You will be notified of further action in a few days. Right now the odds are on our side. I had to find a man I could trust . . . you are that man. Do not weaken. I must go now . . . lets set the next weekly appointment. If the Gestapo interrogates me I don't know how long I can survive they have ways of making anyone talk. Walter wisdom is your strength please remember your love for Germany.

WALTER KEMPER:

You speak with conviction . . . I will say goodbye and until next week good luck Franz.

(both men shake hands and Franz turns to leave)

FRANZ HAUTMAN:

Walter make our next appointment for next Wednesday . . .

(Franz gives Walter an intense glare)

exactly the same time. Please write my name in your daily calendar when I leave today . . . it could save your life in the future. Goodbye Walter and thank you.

(Franz leaves and shuts the door behind him. Walter returns to his desk sits down and opens up his large daily calendar — he turns the page forward and makes an entry after which he leans back and puts his arms behind his head)

STAGE LIGHTS DIM — END OF SCENE TWO

ACT ONE SCENE THREE

(The lights are raised Walter Kemper is sitting in his study at home. The time is 10:40 P.M he is about to retire for the evening. There is a knock at the door his servant enters the room with a message that a young Gestapo Officer is at the door and wishes to talk. Walter nods and the servant exits returning with a tall blond man of thirty — five. Walter stands extends his hand and offer the gentleman a chair the Officer accepts. Both men are seated opposite each other)

WALTER KEMPER:

Would you like a coffee . . . tea perhaps? Major . . .

(cut off)

MAJOR WERNER KETTERER:

Ketterer . . Major Werner Ketterer Doctor Kemper.

(Major Ketterer performs a quick officious bow with a nod of his head)

Regards are in order and thank you I would like a coffee please.

WALTER KEMPER:

(Walter rings a bell and the servant appears)

Erika could you prepare coffee we will be talking for awhile.

(Walter smiles and the servant girl exits stage left)

MAJOR WERNER KETTERER:

Kemper Ketterer Walter Werner a nice fit Doctor don't you think? I will come straight to the point. You have been treating a patient Hautman . . . an employee of the S.S who recently had a nervous breakdown. This young man has been under observation by the Gestapo for reasons I wish not to disclose at this time.

WALTER KEMPER:

I am treating this young man . . . yes . . . but he is an ex employee of the S.S. . . is that not so Major?

 (Major Ketterer nods as Walter continues)

I believe he was 'cashiered' from this elite group for controversial remarks about 'der fuhrer'.

MAJOR WERNER KETTERER:

Doctor . . . what is your diagnosis of Franz Hautman?

WALTER KEMPER:

I am not at liberty to disclose such information Major.

MAJOR WERNER KETTERER:

This is not your choice Doctor. Now <u>what is his diagnosis.</u>

WALTER KEMPER:

I am sorry.

 (Walter shrugs)

MAJOR WERNER KETTERER:

I could have you arrested for such insolence. The Third Reich is not your enemy . . . please

> *(interrupted by a knock at the door and the servant entering the room with a tray with two cups of coffee cream and sugar she places them on a table and leaves)*

Doctor . . . between you and I a person who defies our 'fuhrer' takes considerable risk in Germany these days. Your charitable act is a disloyalty and could result in severe consequences. A two year term in a re-indoctrination camp could be a brutal experience for a man of your social class and intellect Doctor. Some men have been released with disabilities . . . their mental faculties reduced if you know what I mean Doctor.

WALTER KEMPER:

Are you threatening me in my own house Major?

MAJOR WERNER KETTERER:

Doctor . . . what is this young man's affliction? Schizophrenia perhaps? acute depression? He was seeing a jewess you know . . . a student who tried to corrupt his mind. He is by all accounts a bright man and Herr Himmler speaks highly of him and then this 'breakdown' a short time ago

> *(Major Ketterer shrugs and shakes his head)*

hmm good coffee Doctor . . . may I have another?

WALTER KEMPER:

Major . . . I have observed the National Socialist Party rise from its humble beginnings. Hitler has been in power for three years and what do I see? A brilliant people rich in culture and heritage . . . influenced . . . persuaded . . . swayed . . . for what reason? I believe this progressive radicalization by Hitler's regime will have . . . or should I say has had a major . . . impact on our lives. Major I step off my 'soap box' and state categorically your business here has no meaning to me. Besides what is your concern with my therapy practice Franz Hautman is only one of twenty patients.

MAJOR WERNER KETTERER:

Doctor let us end the games. I need to know your diagnosis of young Hautman . . . what is your answer?

WALTER KEMPER:

Professional ethics mitigates against such disclosure Major.

MAJOR WERNER KETTERER:

I am sorry you are not willing to co-operate with the Third Reich Doctor. It was a referral from the government that sent this patient in the first place. Please

(Major Ketterer stands quickly and gives an abbreviated bow)

I will let myself out . . . we will be talking again soon Herr Doctor Kemper.

(Major Ketterer leaves the room exit stage left)

WALTER KEMPER:
(Walter leans over picks up a phone and begins to dial)

I would like to talk with Doctor Matthias Goring . . . yes . . . thank you. Doctor Goring . . . my esteemed colleague . . . yes yes . . . it is Doctor Kemper . . . yes . . . I need to meet with you immediately.

I am sorry for the hour of my call but I have received a disturbing visit from the Gestapo. Yes I could . . . yes

(Walter pauses hangs up the phone walks to the closet and puts on a top coat)

LIGHTS DIM — CHANGE OF SET

ACT I SCENE FOUR

(Lights are raised. Walter Kemper is sitting in a comfortable chair talking in earnest to the Director of the Goring Institute. Dr Matthias Goring is an elderly man in his late sixties also seated. He is related to Field Marshall Hermann Goring second in command of the Third Reich)

WALTER KEMPER:

Earlier this evening I was visited by Major Werner Ketterer of the Gestapo. It is my feeling that I am under investigation.

DOCTOR MATTHIAS GORING:

What makes you so sure Doctor Kemper?

WALTER KEMPER:

I received a visit from the Gestapo with no prior warning. I was then pressured to reveal the diagnosis of a patient I have been treating. I've only seen the young man twice in therapy.

DOCTOR MATTHIAS GORING:

What was his crime or may I state reason for referral Doctor Kemper?

WALTER KEMPER:

He insulted the Third Reich and was 'cashiered' from the S.S. They subsequently sent him to me as a condition of his release. He has powerful friends otherwise he would have been imprisoned. and now I am pressured to give the Gestapo a 'diagnosis'.

DOCTOR MATTHIAS GORING:

What is his name Doctor Kemper?

WALTER KEMPER:

Franz Hautman Doctor do you know of him?

DOCTOR MATTHIAS GORING:

(Doctor Goring leans forward intently)

Yes I must confess I do know a lot about him Doctor Kemper. A young man with a cause . . . he is disillusioned with the Third Reich.

WALTER KEMPER:

How do you know all this.

DOCTOR MATTHIAS GORING:

Doctor Kemper . . . Franz Hautman's family was German aristocracy. The father with no money but titled the mother a jewess from a rich powerful family . . . Leipzig I believe

(Walter nods)

yes I know the case Doctor Kemper. And now I must tell you something . . . it was I who the S.S called regarding Herr Hautman's erratic behavior it was I who the S.S called regarding Herr Hautman's erratic behavior several months ago. I told them to send him to you to seek help for his troubled mind.

WALTER KEMPER:

Doctor Goring he is a troubled man but not psychotic. He has a social conscience and could not stand the hypocrisy any longer. I have a duty to help him and not be harassed by the Gestapo Doctor Goring.

DOCTOR MATTHIAS GORING:

You have a duty to yourself first. Please use discretion with this case Herr Doctor. It appears our friends the Gestapo have quite an interest with our patient . . . and now you.

WALTER KEMPER:

(Walter is agitated and begins to raise his voice)

<u>Doctor do I stop treating this young man because of fear of reprisal from the Gestapo?</u> He has commited a crime against the State honoring his principles and was duly punished. Now he is being persecuted unjustly. <u>I will help him but to what end I don't know.</u>

DOCTOR MATTHIAS GORING:

Fine words Herr Doctor but come . . . listen to an old man. You have had a distinguished career you must not throw it away. Principles are fine and I commend you for showing such spirit but these times in Germany are not real. Everyday there is more injustice it will not stop with Herr Hautman being harassed by the Gestapo. The Third Reich is . . . extreme in its treatment of the Jew. The 'master race' concept is rubbish you and I know this but the masses follow like sheep.

WALTER KEMPER:

I can no longer live a lie Doctor. Pretend to be concerned pretend to be involved pretend to support the Aryan race ideology. Tonight you helped me make a decision. I was a coward and a fool for hiding behind my work . . . fear of reprisal has made us cowards good night Doctor Goring

(Walter stands abruptly)

DOCTOR MATTHIAS GORING:

Doctor please

(Doctor Goring motions Walter to sit down)

WALTER KEMPER:

(Walter sits down slowly)

Doctor Goring I have worked with this young man for only a short time but I believe . . . no let me rephrase my answer . . . I cannot nor will not state this man is unstable. I believe the Gestapo want me to declare him insane and use my testimony to further their cause. Their great cause . . . it sickens me and I feel I have no other . . .

(cut off)

DOCTOR MATTHIAS GORING:

Doctor Kemper if you follow your heart and support this man's cause you will be arrested and charged <u>with sedition.</u> You and he will perish and for what practical purpose . . . <u>principles?</u>

WALTER KEMPER:

(Walter jumps up from his chair and stands over Doctor Goring)

<u>To hell with practicalities I am sick of 'play acting'. The government manipulates everything we do</u> . . . they have access to our patients' files and we or more accurately <u>you</u>

(Walter points at Doctor Goring)

<u>do nothing.</u> Our patients believe in us and we are used as 'Judas Goats' to have them disclose their thoughts and beliefs which are used as indictments against them. <u>You talk of practicalities Doctor I talk of conscience.</u>

DOCTOR MATTHIAS GORING:

Doctor Kemper we live in difficult times as clinical specialists. The current regime has very strict rules of conduct for professionals. We are subject to the laws of the Third Reich and must obey or lose our jobs. These are difficult times please be prudent in all behavior. That is my statement to you this evening Doctor Kemper. I will try and forget your outburst and implore you to think of the consequences of your actions . . . these are not normal times. Goodnight Doctor Kemper . . . <u>Please.</u>

(Doctor Goring motions for the other to leave. Walter walks to the door briskly and leaves stage left. Doctor Goring picks up the phone and begins to dial)

STAGE LIGHTS DIM — END OF SCENE FOUR

ACT TWO SCENE ONE

(The interior of the Gestapo headquarters — Berlin. Walter Kemper is sitting on a hard backed chair in the middle of an interrogation room. There is soft light which inhibits the features of three Gestapo Officers seated behind a table in front of Walter. The table is long wide and presents a barrier dividing two points of view. Two armed guards stand beside Walter)

FIRST GESTAPO OFFICER:

Doctor Kemper my surname and rank are of no consequence . . . you may call me Fredrich. I will come straight to the point . . . we will ask a few questions of you and would appreciate your co-operation.

SECOND GESTAPO OFFICER:

Doctor Kemper . . . may we call you Walter?

WALTER KEMPER:

Go to hell. What have I done to be arrested and brought here against my will?

SECOND GESTAPO OFFICER:

Doctor Kemper I could break you like that . . .

(Second Gestapo Officer snaps his fingers loudly)

Let us not play games we know you have knowledge of a group of radicals opposed to the Third Reich. What are their names and you will be free to leave.

WALTER KEMPER:

I want my lawyer present.

SECOND GESTAPO OFFICER:

My my the good Doctor wants a lawyer present. Unfortunately we cannot oblige such a request from a political prisoner Doctor Kemper. Next you'll request democratic vote. Please . . . what are the names of these traitors.

WALTER KEMPER:

I do not know anything of these traitors you speak of. I have done nothing and serve my country to the best of my ability.

SECOND GESTAPO OFFICER:

Enough . . . come come Doctor let us respect each other's intellect. We are citizens loyal to the Third Reich. It has come to our attention you have knowledge of political activists who endanger our cause. We have our job of security as you have your job as therapist. Doctor Kemper one more time . . . please . . . tell us who are these traitors and you may leave with a clean conscience.

WALTER KEMPER:

Sir I am a practicing psychologist at the Goring Institute. I treat emotionally troubled people. I fought for Germany in the Great War . . . I am not a traitor to my country.

SECOND GESTAPO OFFICER:

Just so Doctor Kemper you would never consciously betray your Country. That is why we're here today. The Gestapo helps to cleanse the Third Reich of such impure contaminating thoughts. To protect all the Doctor Kempers from undesirable influences that see a person like you as a naïve vulnerable man. An intellect searching for a cause any cause his life is boring he has never married. No Doctor Kemper we are concerned for you and are interested in helping you correct an error by disclosing who these traitors are and helping us rid the Third Reich of such people. It would also help us assess you as a man who champions a cause. The masses need a hero who emulates Hitler . . . to give them the courage to make decisions that are correct. Are we understanding each other Doctor Kemper?

WALTER KEMPER:
I cannot tell you anything because I don't know anything.

SECOND GESTAPO OFFICER:
I had hoped it would not come to this Doctor Kemper. But you are a wilful man who needs further . . . efforts to see our point of view. Guard take our friend to the 'quiet room' and help him find his memory.

(both guards arm lock Walter and stand him up forcefully)

WALTER KEMPER:
YOU BASTARDS

(Walter's is punched violently in the stomach and sags to his knees)

SECOND GESTAPO OFFICER:
Walter . . . these men are brutal . . . they like to harm people and enjoy their work. I implore you to reconsider . . . these men will hurt you and very slowly. Time means nothing in these circumstances. They may have as much time as they need to make you talk and believe me you will talk. Everyone has a breaking point Walter. Tell

us what we want to know I can guarantee you will feel much better and one hour from now will have forgotten the whole affair.

(Walter lunges at the Second Gestapo Officer from across the table but is restrained by the Guards who punch him twice in stomach causing him to sag to his knees with his head lowered almost to the floor)

SECOND GESTAPO OFFICER:

My my Doctor Kemper such emotion from an intellectual. Under the circumstances I would show a little more restraint

(Second Gestapo Officer nods at the Guards and Walter is dragged away)

Doctor Kemper

(the Guards stop at the door)

we will be seeing you again when you are more willing to co-operate. I'm sorry we could not come to agreeable terms . . . Take him.

(Walter is removed from the room by the Guards the Second Gestapo Officer turns to his colleagues)

Gentlemen . . . this man has spirit . . . but is emotionally un-balanced. A weakened spirit easily 'brainwashed' with no sense of honor. Let the guards work on him . . . it is only a matter of time . . . he will break.

THIRD GESTAPO OFFICER:

You think the Guards will find out anything? Our source could have been mistaken it's not the first time an innocent . . .

(cut off abruptly)

FIRST GESTAPO OFFICER:

<u>Silence.</u> He is a proud man who will not give in easily. I believe he is guilty . . . gentlemen let us review the Hautman file.

(they open file folders on the desk in front of them)

I see his mother's family were Jews and had great wealth and his father was an Aristocrat.

SECOND GESTAPO OFFICER:

A strange case this Hautman situation. He is referred to the Goring Institute by Himmler's aide and Kemper is chosen to treat his affliction by the Director of the Institute . . . Matthias Goring who is first cousin to the Director of the Luftwaffe. Matthias Goring receives a call unsolicited by Doctor Kemper one night who is in a panic and begins to antagonize Doctor Goring with rhetoric opposing the Third Reich. The Director who is a patriot informs the Gestapo of his colleague's mental deterioration. It makes for a difficult decision gentlemen . . . if there is complicity between our friend Doctor Kemper and this Hautman who may be a member of a terrorist group and we intercede carelessly there could be complications . . . Goring has powerful friends.

FIRST GESTAPO OFFICER:

You muddy the issue there are no complications and we need Kemper. He will give us the answer and yes time is on our side.

SECOND GESTAPO OFFICER:

Can you be so sure Fredrick?

FIRST GESTAPO OFFICER:

The guards have a painful way of making causes anecdotes and principles appear futile. Kemper will lead us to the answer. We do this on our own initiative whether Hautman acts alone or with a group does it really matter? The facts remain clear that arresting insurrectionists who plot to overthrow a government is worth the risks involved. Gentlemen we know Kemper is hiding the truth we know his patient denounced the Third Reich and is half Jew. Let us seize the opportunity to further our careers are we agreed?

THIRD GESTAPO OFFICER:

Fredrick you are right I think we must let our good Doctor Kemper go back to his practice with our sincere apologies for today's misunderstanding. I see by his record in the Great War that he won the Iron Cross First Class. This man has honored the Fatherland but he is an intellectual whose mind is already corrupted by reading too much Freud . . . a jew you know. This young Hautman is trying to exploit Kemper's inherent character flaw . . . his elitism . . . he feels he is above the masses.

FIRST GESTAPO OFFICER:

Gentlemen then we are agreed. We will release Doctor Kemper and carefully observe his every move with the traitor Hautman. This is our recommendation and is an independent operation our superiors need not know . . . just yet.

THIRD GESTAPO OFFICER:

Fredrick when do we confide in our Superiors? When it is too late and Kemper has fled to Switzerland or Hautman to Brazil? I feel someone should know. Doctor Goring will also want an answer . . . what do we say?

FIRST GESTAPO OFFICER:

We say that we are still investigating all aspects of the case and will disclose nothing more at the present time. Gentlemen this is a golden opportunity a feather in our caps. Too much potential to be wasted.

(First Gestapo Officer picks up the telephone and orders the Guards to return Doctor Kemper to the room. A moment later Walter is led in to the room. His face is swollen his nose broken. The Guards push him to the chair in front of the table where sit the three Gestapo Officers)

WALTER KEMPER:

You swine you miserable

(cut off abruptly)

FIRST GESTAPO OFFICER:

Your insults do not help your cause and waste time Doctor Kemper. Now . . . who are Hautman's friends . . . their names Doctor . . . what do you say?

WALTER KEMPER:

I am aware my rights as a German National have been denied that I have been refused access to a lawyer. I will not rest until you pay for your CRIME. You are scum everyone

(Walter is quickly silenced by a Guard's blow to the head causing him to collapse to the floor)

FIRST GESTAPO OFFICER:

Revive him.

(water is thrown in Walter's face and he is sat forcibly on a small stool)

WALTER KEMPER:

What makes a man like you think he can play God? You

(Walter is slapped in the face by one of the Guards)

FIRST GESTAPO OFFICER:

Quite so Doctor Kemper my colleagues and I have reconsidered your situation and apologize for making such a regrettable error. You will be released immediately with a letter of apology. <u>Good day Doctor</u>

> *(the three Gestapo Officers stand in unison and give the Nazi salute shouting also in unison)*

<u>Heil Hitler.</u>

> *(Walter is dragged off by the Guards and led out of the room exit stage left)*

SECOND GESTAPO OFFICER:

And now it begins Fredrick. I hope you know what you're doing? The good Doctor will be more trouble than he's worth. It is too bad that intellectuals must contaminate their minds with absolutes. Their world expects a perfect Germany . . . everything in harmony like a symphony . . . too 'high minded' too corrupting of simple thoughts and simple obedience. Fredrick I know we are right to stop such corruption but where will it end?

FIRST GESTAPO OFFICER:

Simple thoughts allow drastic action in Germany these days. <u>We must be strong gentlemen.</u>

> *(the three Gestapo Officers salute shouting in unison <u>Heil Hitler</u> and subsequently file out of the officer exit stage left)*

STAGE LIGHTS DIM — END OF SCENE ONE

INTERMISSION

ACT TWO SCENE TWO

(Walter Kemper is sitting in a comfortable chair in his library at home. He is smoking his pipe and pondering his future in the Third Reich. His house keeper Erika appears at the doorway)

ERIKA:

Doctor Kemper a man is here to see you.

WALTER KEMPER:

Erika please tell him . . . <u>tell him I am busy and cannot be disturbed.</u>

ERIKA:

Doctor Kemper he came once before when you were not at home. He states it is imperative you see him tonight.

WALTER KEMPER:

Erika send him in but please stay nearby just outside the door. My visit with the Gestapo was enough excitement for 1936.

ERIKA:

Yes Doctor Kemper.

(Erika leaves the room and a young man in his early twenties enters the room and shuts the door)

JULIUS HATTINBERG:

Doctor Kemper my name is Julius Hattinberg thank you for seeing me. I will talk briefly as I know you are a busy man.

(Julius shakes Walter's hand warmly)

WALTER KEMPER:

My house keeper stated you were here before.

JULIUS HATTINBERG:

Yes Doctor I was here two days ago. Unfortunately you were not at home. Are you aware the Gestapo are watching your house?

WALTER KEMPER:

Herr Hattinberg or whatever your name . . . I will come straight to the point. I was arrested by the Gestapo two days ago and held incognito for six hours . . . as you can see

(Julius studies Walter's face and grimaces)

six hours is a long time to spend with the Gestapo. You think about freedom and your friends who are free and you wonder if you will ever return to your normal life again.

JULIUS HATTINBERG:

Doctor Kemper that is the very reason I came this evening alone. Our group is small but we are united in a common cause . . . to crush the National Socialist movement.

WALTER KEMPER:

(Walter begins to laugh which increases to guffaws)

Young man . . . in Germany today there are eighty million Nazi sympathizers. I will bet you could not find eight hundred German Nationals who would challenge the present regime. My error was treating a patient referred to me by the S.S. Logically this was followed with imprisonment and brutality by the Gestapo. What next . . . an eager young man shows up at my door sincerely interested in my devotion to a cause that is so stupid I wonder if my brain is damaged? Julius who ever you are . . . do you think I am so stupid to believe you? And considering the past week's events do you blame me?

JULIUS HATTINBERG:

Doctor Kemper I was an aspiring musician with the Berlin Philharmonic. I played the Oboe until the Gestapo pigs arrested my father and eldest brother and sent them to a re indoctrination camp. That was seven months ago and I have not seen them since. I was told they were placed there to be re indoctrinated in the Nazi code of conduct . . . whatever that means. Father was a Professor of Musicology at the University of Berlin. My brother a published poet. What risk to the Third Reich could they possibly be? For my own survival I quit the Philharmonic . . . my only contact with other Germans is with this group I've mentioned. Doctor . . . we think you are ready to join our cause Hautman speaks highly of you. Please re consider.

WALTER KEMPER:

(Walter laughs)

Thank you for thinking of me but I'm not interested in becoming a martyr. The Gestapo

(cut off abruptly)

JULIUS HATTINBERG:

Doctor Kemper do you agree with the government's policies? The encroachment of all values pertaining to personal freedom of German Jews for instance? Are you so blind to think things will improve in this crazy society?

WALTER KEMPER:

Germany is experiencing its lowest unemployment in

(cut off vociferously)

JULIUS HATTINBERG:

DON'T BE A FOOL.

(the door opens slightly but Walter 'waves off' the maid and the door is once again closed)

You were arrested and detained without 'just cause' because of your professional association <u>with an alleged mental defective.</u> A man sent to you by the S.S to be declared insane by the great Doctor <u>to eliminate any controversy about his condemnation of Hitler.</u> Hautman was esteemed by the S.S <u>by Himmler himself.</u> Do you think you are not under suspicion. <u>At this very moment your house is being watched.</u> Doctor Kemper whether you like it or not you are 'guilty by association'. Join us and contribute before it is too late for Germany. Doctor we need your knowledge.

WALTER KEMPER:

Julius I believe you think your cause is right and just but I must reiterate my position. Your cause is too late your number too small. How many of you are willing to die for this cause? Eventually you will be betrayed . . . I saw this in 1919 when the Bolsheviks tried to overthrow the Weimar Republic . . . they were hunted down like animals.

JULIUS HATTINBERG:

Doctor Kemper come to a meeting and judge for yourself. Our numbers are small but that does not mean we are weak. Come to our meeting I will be your contact. We need you Doctor . . . please come.

WALTER KEMPER:

Why are you so insistent I join? You and Hautman risk so much to recruit for this cause. To date I have not been disloyal to my principles or to the Third Reich but the past week's encounter with reality has been . . . illuminating . . . if only I could open my eyes.

(Walter smiles at his joke)

I am tired of pretending to agree with this regime . . . of being perceived as something I'm not.

JULIUS HATTINBERG:

Soon very soon I can give you further information in a week not before.

WALTER KEMPER:
(Walter walks to the window in deep thought and returns to his chair and smiles)

What is life without challenge Julius. When is your next meeting? I will probably regret my decision tomorrow.

JULIUS HATTINBERG:

I cannot elaborate on why we do what we do. Perhaps we can talk in the future when there is more time. Now I must go Doctor Kemper you will hear from me in one week. Please do not have a change of heart and remember the Gestapo watch your house and office day and night.

(Julius walks briskly to the door)

Doctor Kemper have a good evening I will let myself out.

WALTER KEMPER:

One last question before you go . . . what has become of Franz Hautman Julius? That you can tell me please.

JULIUS HATTINBERG:

You must wait to find out Doctor Kemper. Until our next meeting keep in good health and be alert. Good night Doctor.

(Julius leaves the room and Walter walks toward the window. Erika enters the room a short time later followed by a Gestapo Officer)

ERIKA:

Doctor Kemper this man is here to see you. I told him it was late and you were busy but he insists on meeting with you. Doctor he is with the Gestapo.

WALTER KEMPER:

Do I have a choice Erika please leave us.

(Erika nods and leaves the room shutting the door behind her)

MAJOR OTTO DIETRICH:

(Major Dietrich gives the Nazi salute and clicks his heels)

Heil Hitler Doctor Kemper. You have just met with a young man by the name of Julius Hattinberg . . what was the nature of your conversation?

WALTER KEMPER:

Major I am from the old Germany. That information is none of your business and if that is the reason for your visit let me escort you out of my house . . .

(Walter takes a step aggressively towards Major Dietrich)

physically.

MAJOR OTTO DIETRICH:

(Major Dietrich raises his voice)

Doctor Kemper I could have you arrested for making treasonable threats against a member of the Gestapo. . . That young man is under investigation by the Gestapo. Please let us talk like civilized human beings

(cut off abruptly)

WALTER KEMPER:

Who do you think you talk to . . . a child? You have insulted me with your stupid attempt at intimidation. I will state nothing.

(Walter pushes Major Dietrich towards the door violently and is subsequently whipped across the face with an Officer's baton that draws blood. This causes Walter to stop pushing both men stand facing each other glaring)

MAJOR OTTO DIETRICH:

Doctor Kemper I will leave but this is the last time I will come to you as a gentleman. You are treading very lightly . . . a charge of treason in the Third Reich is not a pleasant circumstance to find yourself. Even your reputation would not save you. But the hour is late and I must be going Doctor.

> *(Major Dietrich touches his cap and quickly leaves the room exit stage left)*

WALTER KEMPER:
> *(Walter paces back and forth for a moment and then calls Erika)*

<u>Erika please get my best Rhine Wine. I'm in a mood to celebrate.</u>

STAGE LIGHTS DIM - END OF SCENE TWO

ACT TWO SCENE THREE

(Walter Kemper is sitting in his office at the Goring Institute. It is late 11:00 P.M and Walter is tired but for some reason wishes to remain in his 'easy chair' smoke cigars and drink port. There is a low barely audible knock at the door. It has been one week since the visit from Major Dietrich)

WALTER KEMPER:
(slightly intoxicated)

Enter . . . ENTER.

JULIUS HATTINBERG:
Doctor may I come in?

WALTER KEMPER:
Hattinberg . . . Hattinberg . . . of course . . . my life is not worth an Aryan Deutchmark these days why not. Would you like some port? A brandy perhaps? A cigar? Please sit down.

JULIUS HATTINBERG:
(Julius is very nervous hands are trembling)

Doctor after meeting with you I was followed and subsequently detained by the Gestapo without legal representation for three days. They played a strange 'cat and mouse' game never allowing me to feel completely in control. Luckily my lawyer has connections and I was freed with token apologies. I have been hiding for the past week and can risk meeting with you at night only. Please get your coat . . .

(Julius jumps out of his chair and grabs Walter's coat from the coat rack)

we must leave immediately.

WALTER KEMPER:

Hattinberg . . . for a shrewd man you are not being wise nor prudent. Don't you remember I'm being watched day and night. I expect the Gestapo to come crashing through the door at any moment.

JULIUS HATTINBERG:

Doctor you must come with me now at once.

(Julius attempts unsuccessfully to put Walter's arms into his over-coat while Walter is still at his desk providing mock resistance in his drunken state)

The meeting will begin in less than one hour and you must be present.

WALTER KEMPER:

I'm not sure

(cut off abruptly)

JULIUS HATTINBERG:

Doctor there is no time. Please come.

(Julius grasps Walter under his armpits and pulls him up to a standing position and this time succeeds in getting Walter's arms into the overcoat)

WALTER KEMPER:
(Walter begins to stagger in his drunken state and requires constant support from Julius)

Why not my life has been so boring the past month. Why not add to the tedium. Should I bring my Luger? Perhaps my Sabre from Ypres? Better still my invisible cloak to disappear from the Gestapo.

JULIUS HATTINBERG:
Come Doctor follow me and have trust I take you to a better Germany.

ACT TWO SCENE FOUR

(Both men leave Walter's office as the Stage Lights dim. When the lights are raised Walter Kemper is sitting on a crate in a dimly lit cellar. There is one candle burning in the center of the room. A small band of individuals sit in a semi circle around the candle. A well dressed man sits in front of the group. He is identified as Speaker One of the First Cell. Julius Hattinberg stands by Walter Kemper)

SPEAKER ONE:

Let us begin the meeting . . . I wish to thank you all for coming and the risks and danger in order to attend these meetings. For new members you are designated by number. I'm sure the need to shield our respective identities is obvious . . . thank you once again for attending.

WALTER KEMPER:

Thank you for 'shielding' my identity but I am still not sure why I have been chosen to attend? Surely there must be other individuals who are willing and even adamant to challenge the Third Reich.

SPEAKER ONE:

Speaker eight as you will be known. You were chosen because we trust you. You made a comment several years ago I believe in 1928 . . . that to join the National Socialist Party 'flatters the lowest instincts of the mass' which several 'brown shirts' took exception to after the interview. However . . . that is another time and this is another place. You may call me Speaker One . . . please . . . we must begin our agenda. First on our list is armaments. Number seven do you have the information we requested?

SPEAKER SEVEN:
(Julius Hattinberg begins to speak)

Yes Speaker One there are several factories on the outskirts of Berlin manufacturing heavy industrial materials for war. In addition the Institute for Consumption Research in Nuremberg has just delivered a major shipment of dye. Last month a large shipment of ball bearings arrived from Leipzig. To date forty two shipments of major industrial materials have arrived from other cities in Germany. Initially Nazi propaganda stated our military support and alliance with the Spanish Nationalists would account for such increases. But even this cannot be the reason for so much war material coming to Berlin.

SPEAKER ONE:
Thank you for the information Speaker Seven you may sit down. Keep surveillance on the factories then shifts hours of work number of people employed . . . any 'turn over' in staff . . . do you understand Speaker Seven?

SPEAKER SEVEN:
I will Speaker One.

(Speaker Seven bows his head curtly and remains sitting)

SPEAKER ONE:
To our new member . . . you are the second of three agenda tonight. Please feel free to talk . . . we are interested in your opinion . . . by all means speak freely amongst friends.

SPEAKER EIGHT:
(Walter stands slowly slightly intoxicated in speech)

I am . . . Number . . . I mean Speaker . . . whatever. I am employed in the City of Berlin and believe our political system is shaken. We are living in a psychotic state and there is no hope no cure for this current regime. Maybe that is why I am here. Although I am cynical of . . . making a difference we are too few and Hitler too powerful.

(Walter sits down abruptly but continues to speak a murmur begins to be heard from amongst the other members)

Maybe I am here because I seek justice and attending this meeting makes me feel less ashamed of what I have become

(cut off vociferously)

SPEAKER ONE:

Speaker Eight you are here because Hitler insults your sense of dignity and to survive we compromise compromise and compromise until nothing remains of our dignity and shame takes over. Hitler hates minorities . . . he 'scapegoats' Jews and will provoke war with Europe . . . trust the facts this will happen. In 1933 there were 500,000 German Jews who controlled the country's finances. In 1936 it is illegal for a Jew to be a German citizen. Did you know that ten German Jews have won the Nobel Prize for Science since its inception over thirty years ago? In 1929 the per capita income of Jews in Berlin was twice that of other residents in our city. So what . . . maybe they worked harder. Enough . . . my point is simply stated . . . the plight of a civilized and scholarly race is at stake. I am not Jewish but have watched their demise for the past three years with fear and amazement why nothing is done. There is no social conscience in the Third Reich. The life blood of a society is its empathy and fairness to all classes of people . . . all races of people. Today's Germany is anaemic . . . dying under this mad regime. We need you Speaker Eight and look forward to your comments.

(Speaker One abruptly sits down)

SPEAKER EIGHT:

(Walter stands slowly)

Speaker One for the past three years I too have been aware that opposition to this racial persecution has been non existent. I know I was one of the cowards who did not want to be involved. Your speech just now was articulate and enlightening . . . but again I state . . . <u>what can we do?</u> What will our lives purchase? We are fighting a machine . . . a sick bureaucratic machine that has contaminated the thinking network of Germany. It is 1936 and we live in a totalitarian state where there is total suppression of the Arts . . . the Press . . . Freedom of Speech. I am risking everything to be here. What is your strategy how will you fight I must know this before I commit.

SPEAKER ONE:

You have nothing to fear from the First Cell Speaker Eight. But before you make a decision please wait a few moments. Our leader has not arrived . . . he is our third agenda item.

STAGE LIGHTS DIM

ACT TWO SCENE FIVE

(The lights are raised and a new arrival is sitting amongst the group. It is Franz Hautman and begins to speak in a slow articulate manner)

FRANZ HAUTMAN (LEADER OF THE FIRST CELL) :

Thank you all for attending the meeting. My friends I'm sorry I was late but I thought I was being followed and decided to take an extra Street car connection and 'double back' on foot to be safe. Thank you for coming to the First Cell as always I am proud to be a member. I wish to outline a plan I devised in theory and require its critique and refinement by the Cell. As you may have guessed most of us are intellectuals who detest the Third Reich. The Nazi propaganda is clever and has manipulated the populace with three themes heard 'ad nauseum' since the twenties. The first describes the Jews being the major recipients of the Capitalist exploitation of the German people. The second is the Jew's alliance with the Marxists of Russia and the third and most deadly in my opinion is the Jews conspiring against the 'aryan' interests in Germany. I propose we use Hitler's philosophy against Hitler.

(the group begins to agitate and compliments are heard)

My friends let me continue . . . Hitler stated in Mein Kampf 'whoever wants to live must therefore fight and whoever does not wish to do battle in the world does not deserve life'. He believes a Nation must earn its right to live. I believe we must fight a war of truth against the lies of Nazi propaganda. To do this we begin to print our own philosophy of truth <u>and let the populace know there is an option.</u>

SPEAKER EIGHT:

(Walter stands abruptly)

May I make a small statement before I leave. Your plan is heroic in a Country whose treatment of minority groups is a disgrace. The effort you propose is undoubtedly the last peaceful option. However I believe it is too late to change Germany . . . the course is set. Your attempt to expose the Third Reich and offer a just society is not realistic.

(the members agitate Walter raises his voice)

<u>Our Nation believes its leader's charisma</u>

(agitation diminishes and Walter lowers his voice)

and his promises of a thousand year Reich in a perfect Aryan Nation.

(Walter turns to Franz Hautman)

<u>You will not be heard.</u>

(Franz vehemently shakes his head causing the group to begin to agitate amidst cries of 'traitor')

Yes . . . disbelieve and fight for your cause but not with me as your comrade. I am tired of fighting battles that are lost before they begin. <u>Now I wish to return home.</u>

(Walter sits down abruptly crossing his arms amidst cries of 'traitor' and 'coward')

SPEAKER ONE:

Be quiet . . . <u>be quiet</u>

(the group settles down)

Not so fast Speaker Eight. The German Socialists have an acquired habit of waiting for things to happen rather than acting to make them come about. I believe there is a 'window of opportunity'. Let's discuss options further . . . please wait and continue to discuss options Speaker Eight.

SPEAKER EIGHT:
(Walter does not stand but continues to sit while he speaks)

Speaker One anti-Semitic prejudice is throughout all facets of the German nation. The anti semites have succeeded again and again during the past ten years in placing the 'Jewish Question' in all facets of politics within our Country. Anti semitic thinking is beyond the fringe . . . it is 'main stream' number one 'a subversive race' according to the National Socialists. <u>Joseph Goebbels has made sure of that.</u>

SPEAKER ONE:
Look there are some rivals to the National Socialists even as we talk. Paramilitaries . . . communists and others . . . they are not organized but could be influenced to become so with the right media campaign against the current regime.

SPEAKER EIGHT:
<u>Are you insane.</u> In 1932 nearly 10,000 'brown shirts' were wounded in street battles. After 1933 the vengeance against their enemies was perpetrated <u>with impunity.</u>

SPEAKER ONE:
I believe the middle class will become disillusioned with the current regime. They need an impetus to move . . . to take action Speaker Eight.

SPEAKER EIGHT:
I have witnessed brutal violence . . . a disgrace to our Fatherland many times over since Hitler took power three years ago. The marches . . . the street violence . . . for respectable 'middle class' this seems incidental and not a threat. They do not see the disaster looming and you think propaganda against the current regime will stir anti government sentiments. The communists 'Red Flag' has been banned . . . copies of this book confiscated . . . more than 1000 arrests during the past year.

SPEAKER ONE:

I believe the 'middle class' will become disillusioned with the current regime. They need an impetus to move . . . to take action Speaker Eight.

SPEAKER EIGHT:

Hitler has treated the communists as criminals who plan illegal acts and will pay the consequences. Concentration camps have opened for political dissidents . . . all over the Country the communist . . . jew . . . gypsy . . . homosexual have been labelled 'enemies of the state'. What are we to do? <u>Sit and do nothing Speaker One.</u> I look to history for our answer . . . and why

> *(states with sarcastic tone)*

'propaganda' will fail and fail and fail. Hitler stated two years ago to his 'brown shirts' never let yourselves be distracted for one second from our 'watch word' the destruction of the marxists'. They have been defeated and imprisoned . . . along with the new 'scapegoat' the Jew. No Speaker One we are too few . . . <u>and your approach is futile.</u> A mass exodus of Intellectuals from the Universities and State funded clinics has been ongoing for three years. The degree of Nazi brutality and cowardice will become many times more powerful. We as a 'Nation of Free Thinkers' . . . a cultured people proud of our heritage are lost.

> *(a collection of <u>boo's</u> and <u>traitor</u> can be heard amongst the group)*

<u>I must go now.</u>

> *(Walter stands up quickly and walks out of the cellar amidst a chorus of boo's and hisses — exit stage left)*

STAGE LIGHTS DIM - END OF SCENE FIVE

ACT TWO SCENE SIX

(Two weeks have passed since Walter Kemper met with the First Cell. He is sitting at his desk in his Office at the Goring Institute. It is early evening — a knock is heard at his door Walter calls out 'enter'. Major Otto Dietrich of the Gestapo enters the room)

WALTER KEMPER:

What a delightful surprise Major . . . please . . . take a seat.

   (sarcastic tone)

Would you like some port? A cigar perhaps?

MAJOR OTTO DIETRICH:

Your flippant manner will someday cost you dearly Herr Doctor Kemper. Yes . . . a drink would be nice.

   (Major Dietrich carefully chooses a chair opposite Walter removes
   his hat and slowly sits down)

I would like to talk to you this evening Dr Kemper.

WALTER KEMPER:

Your wish is my command Major. Please . . . if you don't mind I will also have a drink to celebrate this occasion. Are we battling wits or 'locking horns' this evening. You have me at a disadvantage Major.

MAJOR OTTO DIETRICH:

Dr Kemper would you tell me your whereabouts on September 14th of this year?

WALTER KEMPER:

Let me check my day book. Yes here it is . . . I am sorry to disappoint you but I have an alibi Major. I had a full schedule of patients that day.

MAJOR OTTO DIETRICH:
(removes a small book from the breast pocket of his uniform)

Dr Kemper . . . you were seen leaving the Institute at 19:35 hours with a young man who has been identified as Julius Hattinberg. This man has been linked to a small group of insurrectionists disloyal to 'der fuhrer'. Doctor by association alone with this criminal of the Third Reich you could be arrested for treason.

WALTER KEMPER:

Major this man came to me seeking help in my professional capacity as a therapist. What must I do? Run a police check on every new face that seeks help from me?

MAJOR OTTO DIETRICH:
(Major Dietrich turns several pages of his note book and begins to talk)

Our agents followed you for two hours and then lost sight.

WALTER KEMPER:

Ah yes it was a foggy night.

MAJOR OTTO DIETRICH:
(continues to read his notes as he talks)

Doctor . . . you returned home at 23:19 hours that same evening . . . alone. Where did you go for what . . . almost four hours?

WALTER KEMPER:

We walked for over three hours talking philosophy culture the newest cars built by the Third Reich. You know . . . a 'free association' of thoughts. An intellectual diatribe between two men pondering life. This is rare in Berlin these days Major.

MAJOR OTTO DIETRICH:

(Major Dietrich frowns and then puts his notebook back into his breast pocket)

I find that hard to believe Doctor. Our glorious city is ruled by the 'middle class' who think in terms that are . . . too pedestrian for a man of your intellect I think. But enough debate . . . let me put you at ease and talk in terms that are comfortable for both of us. I myself chose to join the Nazi Party in 1930 as it promised to rid our society of Bolshevism. I witnessed the atrocities of the Bolsheviks in our Country in 1919. I am a committed German who loves his country. I came here tonight to gauge your loyalties to the Party. Are you a member Doctor Kemper?

WALTER KEMPER:

Major before I discuss my Party loyalties let me have another drink to stimulate my collective conscience. I mean conscious thought.

(Walter pours another large glass of port from the decanter and drinks half of it at once before settling back in his seat across from Major Dietrich)

I am not a member Major . . . although it is my impression that Hitler rose to power to unite a weakened dispirited Germany. In three years he has accomplished what no man expected of him. Almost 100% employment and zero inflation. I know you agree with these startling facts Major. As you would undoubtedly confront me with illuminating insight if you knew I was wrong.

(Walter's is showing signs of intoxication)

MAJOR OTTO DIETRICH:
Please continue Herr Doctor this is fascinating.

WALTER KEMPER:
Your glass is empty Major . . . you have me at a disadvantage already. Your brain is clear and mine is . . . clouded. However . . .

(Walter stands quickly losing his balance and nearly falling over Major Dietrich who braces himself. Walter regains his balance and begins to pace in his office while talking)

it is my opinion that Hitler rose to power because the 'middle class' German had few alternatives. Hitler's radical ideology prompted by the economic depression in the 'twenties' made his platform of truths and promises all the more convincing. There were many pressing economic and political problems he blamed for Germany's plight. His convincing oratory with an audience of civil servants . . . teachers and yes Psychologists seduced us all. Made us believe his evangelism. I myself listened to his speeches and believed his vision for a new Germany. He promised to eliminate Capitalism Socialism International Extremism and the Depression. He was Major . . . a God to worship larger than life . . . a sun to be orbited by a Nation of followers. So be it your initial question . . .

(Walter almost loses balance as he takes another large gulp of port and continues to pace while he talks)

was . . . 'Why have I remained a mere citizen of Berlin'? Instead of a Nazi Party member? Major our heritage . . . our culture is steeped in 'demi gods' . . . Beethoven Einstein Freud Handel Bach Wagner . . . the list goes on and on . . . and on. And now we have a man who is a total God. A God for all times for which we orbit. At this point I draw a parallel Major. The sun is a magnificent Planet from which we draw light . . . and our lives. We mere mortals are totally dependent on this 'ball of fire'. The earth's orbit is fixed at a distance where it receives the sun's light and continues to orbit. But what happens if our . . . alignment becomes too close with this sun . . .

(Walter sways around his chair nearly falling over Major Dietrich before falling into his chair)

Major . . . I am apolitical. Please

(Walter motions with his port glass hand to the decanter)

have another drink you must be bored with this discussion.

MAJOR OTTO DIETRICH:

Quite the contrary Doctor Kemper. You have intrigued me . . . you made several references to Jews in your analysis of . . . 'demi gods'.

WALTER KEMPER:

(Walter takes another large gulp of port)

Please Major let me remind you of a fact you will be familiar with I'm sure. The Jew living in Germany before the Third Reich advanced both legally and illegally in a manner that few races could match. There are many Jews who attained the highest rank in Professions the Sciences Commerce and Political life . . . yet they represented less than one percent of our population. Appearing more visible Major . . . luminescent you might say

(Walter is cut off abruptly)

MAJOR OTTO DIETRICH:

Doctor when are you joining the Nazi Party? I must have your answer before I leave. I will strike a proposal with you. Your membership for a drink Doctor how is that?

WALTER KEMPER:

(Walter begins to giggle which accelerates to an extended laugh and then to a guffaw which slowly declines as Major Dietrich abruptly stands and places his cap on his head)

You strike a difficult bargain . . . let me ponder your proposition Major

(Walter begins to laugh again and mimics Major Dietrich)

'ponder your proposition'. Flippancy is not my 'long suit' but sometimes I wear it when the party is tedious.

(Walter closes his eyes and begins to sway trying to maintain balance. He places his hands over his cheeks in mock concentration)

Hmm . . . my answer is (stage voice) <u>No Major</u>.

MAJOR OTTO DIETRICH:

(Major Dietrich pulls a whistle from his tunic jacket and blows three shrill times. Within seconds two large S.S Guards enter the room with their guns drawn)

Doctor I'm placing you under arrest with charges of seditious contempt for the Third Reich and intellectual debauchery. You are a dangerous man Herr Doctor. <u>Take him away.</u>

(Both Guards clasp Walter firmly under his armpits and half drag half march the drunken man whose struggles are in vain — exit stage left)

STAGE LIGHTS DIM - END OF SCENE SIX

ACT THREE SCENE ONE

(The lights are raised. Walter Kemper is sitting on a bed in a prison cell he shares with two other men. He is in the basement of the Gestapo Headquarters in Berlin. The date is November 21, 1936)

WALTER KEMPER:
Gentlemen my name is Doctor Walter Kemper. I am here as a political prisoner. I preached sedition against the Third Reich and have exhibited intellectual debauchery and my head hurts from too much port. What is your crime against humanity?

FELIX LAUTNER:
Doctor your courage of conviction is contagious. How do you know one or all of us are not Gestapo agents? Anyway I know you by reputation and will follow your lead willingly. My name is Felix Lautner I am a Civil Servant in the city of Breslau and my crime? I had 'relations' with my second cousin who is quarter Jew.

(both men laugh)

WALTER KEMPER:
That is a lot of math to follow and a crime with a friendly weapon Herr Lautner. I would have thought your decision to copulate with a quarter Jewess was prudent . . . she was probably in love with you . . . is this a correct assumption?

FELIX LAUTNER:
Yes we were in love Doctor. Not just 'lovers' certainly not in this regime. What about our neighbor here. What is your crime against humanity Sir?

PASTOR KURT BRUBAKER:

My name is Kurt Brubaker. I am a Protestant Pastor with a congregation in a village outside of Berlin. I have been arrested for negotiating the freedom of Jews from this oppressive regime. Doctor I have heard of you as well. By reputation you are a good and fine man.

WALTER KEMPER:

Pastor Brubaker . . . may I call you Kurt?

(Pastor Brubaker nods and smiles)

I guess I should have said more prayers when I was growing up. God only knows it might have helped.

(three men laugh which turn to nervous gaffaws)

I too have heard of you by reputation. It is an honor to be imprisoned with a hero and hopefully not a martyr Pastor.

PASTOR KURT BRUBAKER:

You Felix and I have been fated together. Felix for his carnal relations with a Jewess. Yourself

(Pastor Brubaker nods at Walter)

a man of distinction who is a traitor to this mad regime and I a lowly Village Pastor who betrayed the laws of Germany by helping some intellectual zealots defect . . . who happened to be Jewish.

(three men laugh)

WALTER KEMPER:

Felix what are your views of the Nazi regime? Obviously you share their love of Jews.

(three men laugh)

FELIX LAUTNER:

As a Civil Servant I am supposed to be apolitical. However intellectually my views are this. To Hitler Jews are an ethnic race alien to the German people. He encourages a brutal solution to the German Jew after manufacturing the concept of 'Jewish World Conspiracy'. For instance since 1933 racially prejudiced laws incarceration deportation and I think in the future annihilation of this race. It sickens me as a German . . . Doctor do I pass my thesis?

WALTER KEMPER:

At times I can be stupid Felix.

(Walter offers his hand which is accepted by Felix)

FELIX LAUTNER:

No problem Walter. I simply answered your question.

PASTOR KURT BRUBAKER:

Gentlemen we are united in our politics. But what is our fate as Germans? Hitler views politics as war. He crushes any free thinking. Germany does not care anymore and Hitler uses the Jew as his 'scapegoat' to meet his needs for power. Where is the world while this is happening? What do the English think? I hear they view Hitler as a great man who turned the tide of depression.

(Pastor Brubaker shakes his head as the sound of the Guards are heard opening the cell door)

S.S GUARD:

(cell door is opened quickly and the S.S Guard steps into the room)

<u>Stand to attention you men.</u> Be alert you are to meet the committee to decide your fate. Keep your wits about you Jew lovers.

(Guard laughs and signals the men to march out of the cell which they do in single file — exit stage left)

STAGE LIGHTS DIM – SET CHANGE. WHEN LIGHTS ARE RAISED THE THREE CELL MATES ARE SITTING IN FRONT OF A LARGE TABLE BEHIND WHICH SIT THE THREE GESTAPO OFFICERS SEEN EARLIER. MAJOR OTTO DIETRICH PRECIDES AND IS SITTING IN THE MIDDLE OF THE TABLE BETWEEN THE GESTAPO OFFICERS.

ACT THREE SCENE TWO

MAJOR OTTO DIETRICH:

Gentlemen . . . welcome . . . I hope you have enjoyed getting acquainted . . . how is the cuisine? We try to do our best . . . under the circumstances.

(Major Dietrich and the Gestapo Officers laugh)

WALTER KEMPER:

Your best is a compliment to Nazi efficiency Major. Caging Jew lovers together . . . exemplary thinking . . . it reduces the confusion.

MAJOR OTTO DIETRICH:

(stands suddenly startling his colleagues and the three prisoners)

SHUT UP CLEVER MAN

(the Gestapo Officers tug at his uniform and motion him to sit down which he does slowly while glaring at the prisoners)

WALTER KEMPER:

Major Major you surprise me with this outburst and I thought you were a man of cold calculating logic. It only goes to show . . .even I make mistakes.

(Walter is slapped in the back by the Guard's rifle butt and he winces nearly falling to his knees but manages to maintain his upright posture)

MAJOR OTTO DIETRICH:

That Doctor Kemper is a painful solution to your insolence. Anymore comments please . . . feel free

> *(Walter spits at Major Dietrich and is clubbed with a rifle butt and falls forward unconscious to the floor)*

Revive him.

> *(the same Guard leaves the room returning with a bucket of water which he throws on Walter's face and upper torso. The other prisoners attempt to come to Walter's aid and are motioned to stand at attention by the second Guard. Walter begins to groan and slowly moves his head)*

Doctor Kemper as I stated in your office I admire your courage and your spirit but not your politics. We are the Aryan race . . . you had an opportunity to join the Party and chose not. You cannot win.

WALTER KEMPER:

> *(Walter is groggy but able to speak with volume while laying on the floor)*

You fool.

> *(Guard raises rifle butt and is motioned to stop by Major Dietrich)*

MAJOR OTTO DIETRICH:

Stop. Let the prisoner speak.

WALTER KEMPER:

The German people gave up their democratic rights to live in a police state. Three years ago Hitler came to power . . . they lost their virtue . . . we must organize to be a free Nation again.

(Walter passes out)

MAJOR OTTO DIETRICH:

Intellectual 'claptrap' . . . for a bright man he is a stupid idealist. Now gentlemen . . . listen to reason . . . Doctor Kemper thought he could impress the Gestapo with his stupid attempt at heroics. The fool. I personally hate violence but will use it to defend the honor of our Nation. NOW TELL ME THE NAMES OF YOUR ACCOM-PLICES . . . and you are free to go. A bargain . . . I will let you think about it for one minute. Guards . . . revive the good Doctor.

> *(once again the Guard leaves the room to fill the bucket with water returning quickly and pouring its contents over Walter's face and upper torso. He begins to groan and move slowly and is immediately pulled to his feet and made to stand at attention at which point he slowly looks around in a concussed stated)*

MAJOR OTTO DIETRICH:

Who are your friends in the 'First Cell' Doctor Kemper? This group is known to the Gestapo. Please no more games.

WALTER KEMPER:

> *(stage whisper)*

Go to hell.

> *(Guard lifts his rifle butt and is waved off by Major Dietrich)*

MAJOR OTTO DIETRICH:

Walter . . . listen to reason . . . God knows you have courage. But to continue this struggle.

> *(Major Dietrich clicks his tongue and shakes his head)*

We have ways of making you talk . . . <u>have no doubt that you will talk Walter.</u>

(Major Dietrich stands up and walks around the table and kneels down to within a few inches of Walter's face)

Please reconsider Walter . . . no one will be the wiser.

WALTER KEMPER:

(Walter looking up at Major Dietrich swallows a number of times before responding)

I am a slow learner Major . . . <u>Go to hell.</u>

(Major Dietrich leaps up and kicks Walter in the stomach. After a short period Walter opens his eyes and responds in a stage whisper)

That is my answer Major.

(Guard raises his rifle butt but is motioned to stop by Major Dietrich)

MAJOR OTTO DIETRICH:

(Major Dietrich looks at Walter and motions the Guards to pick him up which they do and motions the prisoners to support him while standing between them. Major Dietrich marches around the desk takes off his cap and sits down quickly)

PASTOR KURT BRUBAKER:

(Pastor Brubaker strains under the 'dead weight' of holding onto Walter who is nearly unconscious)

Major . . . Doctor Kemper is a man of conviction even if his principles betray the Third Reich. <u>Please this once show mercy.</u> Let him go . . . he knows nothing. If you must punish . . . deport him Major.

Deport him. He was a hero in the Great War he does not deserve this. Not

(cut off abruptly)

MAJOR OTTO DIETRICH:
Pastor unfortunately I cannot 'turn cheek'. It has gone too far. This man has spit on the Third Reich . . . insults are not taken lightly these days.

FELIX LAUTNER:
Major

(cut off)

MAJOR OTTO DIETRICH:
Ah the Civil Servant mouse can speak. The traitor who sleeps with a Jewess . . . how was she mouse? Eager? Passionate? Did she climax?

FELIX LAUTNER:
Major you can 'bait' me and it wasn't like you said. Now if I may speak?

MAJOR OTTO DIETRICH:
Of course mouse speak as much as you like.

FELIX LAUTNER:
I too had an opportunity to remain loyal to the Nazi Party but failed when I remained loyal to a friend . . . who happened to be a Jew.

MAJOR OTTO DIETRICH:
I agree mouse . . . you failed to control your Freudian libido with a Jewess.

FELIX LAUTNER:

I'm afraid to disappoint you Major but my friendship with Miss Lowengard was a beautiful experience. A cherished memory. I kept my morality and sense of ethics when I began to realize the delusions Hitler stood for. His hatred of the Jewish race is inhuman Major. You are a pawn

(cut off vociferously)

MAJOR OTTO DIETRICH:

I WANT HIM SHOT. TAKE HIM AWAY

(the guards club Felix who falls unconscious to the floor. He is dragged from the room by the legs while the two other prisoners are held at gunpoint by Major Dietrich)

PASTOR KURT BRUBAKER:

(Pastor Brubaker falls under the weight of holding up Walter alone. Both men end up laying in a heap on the floor in front of the table)

Please don't kill this young man Major. Hitler views himself as a savior to the German people . . . in his eyes another Christ. Unfortunately he distinguishes the German Jew from the German people. We are all Aryans in the eyes of God . . . please don't kill this young man.

MAJOR OTTO DIETRICH:

SHUT UP JEW LOVER.

(Pastor Brubaker shrinks back in response to the volume and Major Dietrich takes a few seconds to compose himself)

Hitler does not error. Hitler has brought Germany out of its poverty. He is a great leader. So what if a few miserable Jews are deported.

I would not go back to the old ways. Hitler offers us freedom from the 'jewish conspiracy'.

PASTOR KURT BRUBAKER:

(sits up and moves to a kneeling position holding Walter's head who has lapsed into unconsciousness)

Major there were 500,000 Jews living in Germany in 1930. Their rights have been systematically removed . . . they number 200,000 in 1936.

(gunshots are heard — Pastor Brubaker surrounds his head with both his arms and begins to weep loudly)

MAJOR OTTO DIETRICH:

Say a prayer for the mouse Pastor. He was good at speeches. Gentlemen we will continue this discussion tomorrow.

(the guards return and march to stand behind both fallen prisoners)

Guards take them away.

(Major Dietrich stands to attention with the Gestapo Officers. They give a Nazi salute and shout in unison)

Heil Hitler.

(each guard drags a prisoner by the collar to the door and exits stage left dragging the prisoner through and out the door)

STAGE LIGHTS DIM - END OF SCENE TWO

ACT THREE SCENE THREE

(Walter Kemper and Pastor Kurt Brubaker are sitting on their respective beds inside of the Prison cell in the basement of the Gestapo Headquarters)

WALTER KEMPER:
(Walter slowly swings his legs off the bed and stands)

I tried to remain apolitical from the time this regime came to power . . . but I could not forget the old Germany.

PASTOR KURT BRUBAKER:
(Pastor Brubaker sits then lies on the bed)

Racial persecution of the Jews 'turned my stomach'. Anyone seen talking to a Jew was suspected of sympathizing with them. How absurd . . . to defy this stupid rule I purposely met with Rabi Goldstein on Saturday evenings at his Synagogue to play tarot.

WALTER KEMPER:
Excellent Kurt and what became of Rabbi Goldstein?

PASTOR KURT BRUBAKER:
He was found hanged in his apartment four days ago. Some say 'foul play' . . . I don't know . . . I think he just gave up. Maybe the tarot games were too much.

(both men laugh)

WALTER KEMPER:

Last year a young female lawyer in Dusseldorf was arrested by the Gestapo for managing the legal affairs of emigrating Jews. I am told she was marched off to a Concentration camp for political reeducation. Along the way they beat and raped her.

PASTOR KURT BRUBAKER:

Walter what will you do if they spare your life? You must have connections throughout Europe you could start your practice outside of Germany . . . Britain perhaps?

WALTER KEMPER:

Kurt I would stay in Berlin . . . I would stay and fight as long as I could breathe.

PASTOR KURT BRUBAKER:

Doctor Kemper I should point out that open condemnation of the Nazi regime could place you at considerable risk.

(both men laugh)

WALTER KEMPER:

If I am to die today is as good as tomorrow. Enough is enough. I had to have a student radical shame me to react to this horror <u>Mein Gott</u>.

PASTOR KURT BRUBAKER:

When Hitler came to power he did so by legal pretence. I did not perceive he would alter and then undermine the entire German government. The public expected Hitler's regime to maintain law and order as they did in the riots last year. I have been disgusted by the apathy Germans have shown towards the treatment of the Jew. As a theologue and a man I cannot abide by any of this. Denial of their property and culture . . .

(Pastor Brubaker is interrupted as two Guards enter the cell with a beaten bloody man. They dump him in the center of the cell on the floor and leave slamming the cell door. Both Walter and Pastor Brubaker attend to the man)

WALTER KEMPER:

Franz Hautman.

(Walter and Pastor Brubaker help Franz to his feet and then help him onto one of cell cots where he supports himself by leaning against the wall and letting his legs dangle over the edge of the cot)

FRANZ HAUTMAN:

(slow deliberate voice)

The Gestapo raided our meeting. Several First Cell members tried to escape but I fear were captured and faired no better than I . We were betrayed . . . by whom I don't know.

WALTER KEMPER:

(screaming is heard in the background the men look at each other)

There is your answer Franz. It really doesn't matter.

FRANZ HAUTMAN:

(Franz tries to suppress crying while speaking)

The Gestapo are good at their job and damn slow about it.

(the screaming reaches a crescendo and then abates quickly)

WALTER KEMPER:

Franz do you have any broken bones?

FRANZ HAUTMAN:

I don't think so Walter. I am just tired and in pain. They know their work Walter. I believe the Americans call it 'softening up'.

WALTER KEMPER:

Franz did you give them any information?

FRANZ HAUTMAN:

<u>I am not a traitor.</u>

(Franz begins to cough spits blood)

WALTER KEMPER:

Franz this is Pastor Kurt Brubaker. Maybe you've heard of him? He has risked his life many times for the Jews and hates the Nazi.

FRANZ HAUTMAN:

Walter I don't know this man like I know you. I prefer to mistrust the unknown.

(Franz begins to cough and puts his arm over his mouth)

WALTER KEMPER:

As you wish Franz.

(screaming is heard again and then subsides to moans)

FRANZ HAUTMAN:

Like our companion next door we wait for the end. Unless you have a 'magic cloak' Doctor?

(the three men laugh)

PASTOR KURT BRUBAKER:

Someone once stated 'illness is a disgrace to be managed by health control'. The Nazi have taken this statement one step further to mean 'misery can only be removed by exterminating the miserable' I read that somewhere.

(Walter and Pastor Brubaker laugh)

WALTER KEMPER:

Well stated . . . destroying the Jews and political dissidents is a purification of the old Germany and we produced Goethe Beethoven Thomas Mann.

FRANZ HAUTMAN:

Doctor Kemper . . . I mean Walter. You once discussed your life in the trenches during the Great War. I remember you said compromise kept you alive in the trenches. That death and fear tested your courage but compromise kept you alive.

WALTER KEMPER:

Yes I said those things.

FRANZ HAUTMAN:

Civil liberties don't creep into our lives and if you believe in what is right you make a personal decision to fight. What is pathetic are your friends neighbors colleagues who have no purpose. They just agree and agree and agree.

(Franz begins to sob and is consoled by both men)

WALTER KEMPER:

Franz sometimes we lose our will to fight when we grow old. I'm glad we met.

(Walter strokes Franz shoulder and looks at Pastor Brubaker)

PASTOR KURT BRUBAKER:

Someone said it is the fight for the principle that is the important part of life. Not whether you win or lose. I hope we win. I find criminal life a little unnerving.

(the three men laugh heartily)

Young man what did you study in University?

FRANZ HAUTMAN:

It doesn't matter now. Can you believe I was in the S.S twelve months ago. Walter remembers our first meeting.

WALTER KEMPER:

Yes Franz as I recall it was a 'forced referral' by the S.S. Your former employees felt you had gone mad condemning the Third Reich and they referred you to be formally declared insane for such views. But alas . . . the good Doctor Kemper did not discover such a malady.

(guards are heard marching down the corridor and stop in front of the cell door)

GUARD:
<u>You in there stand to attention. The tribunal has reconvened.</u>

(The three men stand up and are let out of the cell in single file by the guards)

STAGE LIGHTS DIM - END OF SCENE THREE

ACT THREE SCENE FOUR

(The lights are raised. The three men are sitting in front of a court tribunal chaired by Major Otto Dietrich. The men sit on three chairs in the middle of the room facing three Gestapo Officers sitting behind a large table flanking Major Dietrich)

MAJOR OTTO DIETRICH:

We meet again gentlemen. But what have we here another traitor to the Third Reich? Franz Hautman the Jew lover . . . welcome.

FRANZ HAUTMAN:

Well Well the demented Otto Dietrich.

> (knocked to the floor by a Guard)

MAJOR OTTO DIETRICH:

Revive him . . . can you believe he was once a colleague of mine. But now I must say I question my own sanity associating with this traitor.

> (Major Dietrich shakes his head and looks at his colleagues)

WALTER KEMPER:

I provide Mental Status Examinations Major.

> (Walter is knocked to the floor by a Guard)

MAJOR OTTO DIETRICH:

Silence . . . revive him.

PASTOR KURT BRUBAKER:
Major end this game. Pass sentence and let us die like men.

MAJOR OTTO DIETRICH:
Shut up.

(guard knocks Pastor Brubaker to the floor)

Guard get our good Doctor Kemper to his feet.

(Walter lying on the floor barely conscious is roughly picked up under the armpits by both Guards who stand him to attention)

That leaves you again Doctor Kemper . . . should we pick up from yesterday? Your courage was impressive . . . but a stupid waste of time.

WALTER KEMPER:
(Walter's speech is slurred and he begins to lose balance as the Guards hoist him up into an upright 'attention' position)

Hitler's Germany demands blind obedience . . . an agreement with racial superiority. Major . . . do you see the men in front of you agreeing with this madness?

MAJOR OTTO DIETRICH:
Doctor I once wrote a text for 'der fuhrer'. A speech at Heidelberg two years ago. In this text I quoted a great German philosopher whose name I've forgotten . . . 'only that which is fruitful is true'. In Germany today we must be industrious to survive and if we are to survive we must kill those enemies of the State deemed impure. Do you see this point Doctor?

III, iv, 344 | D.S. Hutcheon

WALTER KEMPER:

My eyes are a little misty Major. The platitudes rained on my friends and I

(Walter begins to lose consciousness and sags. The Guards hoist him into an upright 'attention' position)

forgot . . . give me some time to remember.

(Walter faints and is revived — a Guard takes the water jug on the table and throws it into Walter's face which revives him. The Guards hoist him back into an upright 'attention' position)

MAJOR OTTO DIETRICH:

Guards the Doctor is clever . . . Walter I admire your spirit but there is no way out of this dilemma. One more thing . . . we will be filming our interrogation this afternoon . . . for posterity you understand.

(a Guard leaves the room and returns with a large film camera)

Guards take these Jew lovers away.

(Major Dietrich points to Pastor Brubaker and Franz Hautman)

They make their peace with God.

(Pastor Brubaker and then Franz Hautman are separately dragged out of the room as the Guard with the cameral films the proceedings)

Doctor Kemper . . . Walter . . . can you hear me?

(Walter is held up by the remaining Guard)

How long have you practiced at the Goring Institute Walter?

WALTER KEMPER:

A number of

(Walter sags and is hoisted up by the Guard)

years Major. Is this 'sham' really necessary?

(The Guard raises his hand to slap Walter and is stopped by the Major raising his hand in protest)

You plan to kill us eventually . . . why the games? Is your ego that deficient?

MAJOR OTTO DIETRICH:

Your training and experience has allowed you to understand the human psyche and how it functions under stress Doctor.

WALTER KEMPER:

Apparently so . . . these past two days convince me your statement is correct and also provides empirical evidence

(cut off abruptly)

MAJOR OTTO DIETRICH:

Shut your mouth. Enough 'pap' Doctor. What would you say if I stated Hitler's concept of Germany can be described in three words . . . power will and surprise?

WALTER KEMPER:

I would only be surprised at any concept Hitler claims as his own Major.

MAJOR OTTO DIETRICH:

One last time Doctor. Are you or have you ever been a member of an 'underground' terrorist group called the 'First Cell'?

WALTER KEMPER:
Your question begs impertinence Major 'No I haven't'.

MAJOR OTTO DIETRICH:
Doctor would you describe to the Tribunal your relationship with the former S.S Officer Franz Hautman.

WALTER KEMPER:
Franz Hautman was referred to me for treatment by the S.S approximately three months ago.

MAJOR OTTO DIETRICH:
Would you describe to the Tribunal the nature and course of events that transpired in your treatment sessions with young Hautman.

WALTER KEMPER:
That is confidential information Major. However I will say he enjoyed my strudel but the coffee I'm not so sure.

MAJOR OTTO DIETRICH:
DO YOU DARE TO INSULT THIS COURT.

(Major Dietrich takes his Luger from its holster and lays it on the table in front of him)

WALTER KEMPER:
Major the excitement of the past few days. The camera you know. I lost control.

(Guard raises his hand to strike but is motioned to stop by Major Dietrich)

MAJOR OTTO DIETRICH:

Doctor are you aware that Franz Hautman is a Jew?

WALTER KEMPER:

If I did it did not matter in the slightest. Therapy does not discriminate by racial attributes Major.

MAJOR OTTO DIETRICH:

Doctor 'der fuhrer' does not agree with such statements and his word is law in Germany. Hitler views the Jewish spirit as evil and its embodiment manifests itself in all forms of conduct against the Third Reich.

WALTER KEMPER:

Memorized clichés Major. Do you have one original

(cut off vociferously)

MAJOR OTTO DIETRICH:

MY PATIENCE RUNS SHORT DOCTOR . . . <u>Listen for once to a practical statement.</u> You intellects 'muddy the waters' of all logic. You are the reason Germany fell into disgrace after the Great War. Hitler is a genius that will save Germany from further dishonor. <u>Can you see the logic why he demands change Doctor.</u>

WALTER KEMPER:

Major as I have no alternative but to listen please continue. But talk slowly so I may comprehend this philosophy of change.

MAJOR OTTO DIETRICH:

(Major Dietrich stands up abruptly and begins to pace behind the table keeping his Luger on the table)

Our politics in Germany thanks to this great man are about struggle. A struggle for excellence . . . a quality of living space which will allow our Nation to be biologically and spiritually pure. Racial purity and controlling the numbers of racially impure . . . non Aryans is our first priority in the new Germany. Domestic policy has become the attainment of this goal. The Jew must be eradicated in all forms. Racially of course . . . spiritually and practically including all their bourgeois inventions of democracy socialism and communism. Did you know that Karl Marx was a Jew Walter?

WALTER KEMPER:

I was aware of this fact Major.

(Walter stares at the luger on the table while Major Dietrich continues to pace)

MAJOR OTTO DIETRICH:

In short politics becomes an engine for war Doctor. Our living space when purified of the spiritual Jew will be invaded by other European countries desiring to live in perfection. Of course the logical extension of this obvious conclusion is what Doctor?

WALTER KEMPER:

In the living room or the bathroom Major? There is a distinction I'm told.

MAJOR OTTO DIETRICH:

Doctor.

> *(Major Dietrich stops pacing behind the table directly in front of the luger picks it up and then replaces it on the table in the same spot. He then looks directly at Walter)*

Walter . . . I'm losing patience. Please consider your options carefully.

WALTER KEMPER:

I believe Pastor Brubaker made a statement earlier today . . . he wanted to die like a man. I share his sentiments Major. I'm also tired so let's finish this before your rhetoric bores me to death.

MAJOR OTTO DIETRICH:

You will have your wish Doctor. Guard bring in the Jew lovers I want them hooked first.

> *(one of the Gestapo Officers stands up abruptly and leaves the Interrogation Room returning with a large wagon-like contraption. It has a seven foot wooden wall with three equally spaced 'meat hooks' fastened at the top of wooden wall)*

Doctor . . . have you ever watched a man die slowly and in great pain? It is not a pleasant experience believe me. They scream . . . they beg and cry for mercy and then they die. It takes a long long time. NOW ONE LAST TIME WHO REPRESENT THE FIRST CELL? GIVE ME THE NAMES.

WALTER KEMPER:
(stands upright and shakes his head)

MAJOR OTTO DIETRICH:
Doctor in front of you is an instrument of torture. We use it on enemies of the State and today it will be used to silence your traitorous friends. I am tired of your insolence. Maybe witnessing this spectacle will loosen your tongue.

WALTER KEMPER:
Please Major let them die with honor.

MAJOR OTTO DIETRICH:
Doctor my colleagues have chided me in the past for showing mercy with traitors. Your comrades are being revived as we talk and will be here shortly. In the meantime collect your thoughts. I'm sure you will think of something brilliant to say.

WALTER KEMPER:
Yes I have something to say Major. I wish to make a full confession. you have won this battle . . . I require some writing paper if you don't mind.

MAJOR OTTO DIETRICH:
(Major Dietrich is visibly shocked)

Walter . . . Guards stand easy.

(Major Dietrich takes out his notebook from his tunic breast pocket. While his attention is preoccupied Walter rushes forward and grabs the Luger off the table. He is shot at point blank range by one of the

Guards and falls onto the table. Major Dietrich pushes the body off the table with his foot. Walter's body lands on the floor with a thud he is obviously dead)

That was a good way to die Walter . . . <u>Guards</u> . . . place Doctor Kemper's body on the center hook.

(stage lights begin to dim as Walter's body is dragged by the legs to the base of the wooden contraption and both guards begin to lift the body from under the armpits onto the center hook)

END OF PLAY

I AM MYSELF ALONE

The Play is three acts and entails events leading to the Lincoln assassination in 1865 by John Wilkes Booth. The major characters speak with a distinct Southern Maryland accent. The wardrobe, manner and extended latency of response, reflect the courteous formality adopted in America during this period of history.

CHARACTERS

John Wiles Booth - mid twenties, dark features with moustache, medium height, slim build, very handsome. Has a tendency to be theatrical in temperament and copy the inflection, grammar and vocabulary of his companions.

Mary Mitchell - early twenties, red hair, attractive

Edwin "Ned" Booth - late twenties, elder brother of John Wilkes Booth

Annie Graham - mid twenties, blond hair

Emma Starr - early thirties, Madame of Washington's largest brothel

Mary Sarratt - early forties, dark hair, medium height, attractive woman

Bessie Hale - early twenties, very pretty, slim, as tall as John Wilkes Booth

Clement Clay - early fifties, heavy Alabama accent, bearded, politician, stately in appearance

George Sanders - late fifties, politician, bearded, portly body

Jacob Thompson - early forties acts much older, clean shaven southern politician, handsome dark features

John Garrett - (voice off stage)

ACT ONE SCENE ONE

JOHN WILKES BOOTH

My name is John Wilkes Booth, Wilkes as called by my family and friends. Talent I possess but have been called a 'handsome young man', 'a rascalian' living off my family's reputation. In this regard great minds are closely aligned, as people pursued my father, so I am pursued. As people adored my father's spirit so mine is apotheosized. As father's acting talents were loved so mine have inspired affection. But the fact remains that our family's creative powers though talented has been fatal. It killed my father before his time, which leads me to a humorous statement of fact. At father's funeral, laid out in his coffin, people thought he appeared alive and called the doctor to pronounce him dead, which of course he was. That being said the Booth acting legacy has endured public fascination for thirty years. I have to date received many compliments which could be misconstrued, but which I accept at face value, to quote 'splendid athletic beauty', 'irresistible to women', 'a leader amongst men' 'courteous, kind and forthright'

(pause)

but you be the judge.

(lights dim, set change to a dingy dressing room circa 1858 in Richmond, Virginia)

ACT ONE SCENE TWO

EDWIN BOOTH

Wilkes you're mother's darling, the stage you play is the world you see. Men and women performing in a make-believe construed world. And you ask yourself can acting be a fulfilling career? Can it replace the routine mediocrity of real living? Boredom was never your strong suit brother, you yearn for excitement, always have, always will.

JOHN WILKES BOOTH
(stripped to the waist, well defined physique)

Theatre in the round Ned, my future is theatre in the round, such is life for this young

(interrupted)

EDWIN BOOTH

Balderdash Wilkes, you speak as a visionary but play act a charlatan. With hard work you could become the best actor of the family, with hard work mind you.

JOHN WILKES BOOTH

I'll make my way on my own accord brother, mark my words. In the meantime whom I consort with along the way remains my business

(Booth puts on a shirt, waistcoat, cravat and velvet dinner jacket)

and now I must pay a visit.

EDWIN BOOTH

An audition I presume?

JOHN WILKES BOOTH

Boudoir politics brother, it takes its toil.

(strides past his brother and turns as he reaches the door)

Mary Mitchell is her name and she's been cast as my Juliet. I'm going to be a fine leading man someday. I've toiled for three long years as a stock actor learning my craft, in more ways than one.

(Ned laughs)

I want success Ned, I have the intensity and desire to succeed and the critics will not be fooled. But now I must be going.

(Booth opens the door abruptly, turns and bows courteously, leaves closing the door quickly)

EDWIN BOOTH

(Monologue - facing the audience)

My brother is a man of many gifts, as for the so called 'rivalry' between us, there's none from my point of view. Wilkes is a far better actor than I and will someday rival our father's talent, let that be said. Our profession and name is our passport to all endeavors, which makes us accessible to diversion and intrigue. That aside Wilkes will become a great actor rest assured through hard work, devotion and talent. He is an optimist at heart, a man possessed with a passion to prove his worth. I, or more accurately we as a family never encouraged Wilkes to act. It's a sordid business but we're connected by father's legacy to perform and perform we must. Like his father before him Wilkes wants to lift the acting craft to its greatest heights in America. Like his father before him Wilkes totally immerses himself in the character he portrays, which can lead to a troubling dilemma,

(pauses)

over identifying with the falsity of theatre life, juxtaposed with real world consequences off stage. To speak in plain English one achieves perfection in performances or at least near perfection by saddling the courage to enter into the abyss of your personality and soul. This feat was a total damnation for my father and might be as well for young Wilkes. Careful mentorship is required as Wilkes is destined for glory but at what cost I wonder.

(stage lights dim, set change to semi darkness, a hotel room in which a man and woman lie naked in bed)

ACT ONE SCENE THREE

JOHN WILKES BOOTH

I must declare your passion and loveliness overwhelms me Mary, I am spent. Give me time though and I'll arise for the occasion.

(both laugh)

MARY MITCHELL
(red hair, youthful appearance, age 22)

Wilkes, take your time and pleasure will follow in carnal affairs. Don't worry your manhood will take up the cause

(pauses)

for the glory of the South.

(both laugh)

JOHN WILKES BOOTH

Mary you're play acting my temperament. I'm a driven, passionate man but can also love with a tender manner. AND YOU are a tom-cat of desire Annie, ready and willing as always.

(both laugh)

MARY MITCHELL

Our preamble to ecstasy was delicious Wilkes, matching your fight in Richard the Third. I'm sure we've never been equalled in bed or on the stage.

(both laugh)

JOHN WILKES BOOTH

I don't know about that Mary, my father was a confirmed womanizer. A genius in life both on and off the stage. My brother Ned is first rate but without guts and I can be genteel in my ways when it suits me. What else, ah yes, my father told me not to be an actor, but if I did, not to be a failure disgracing the family name, am I succeeding?

(both laugh)

MARY MITCHELL

Wilkes you'll be outstanding in your profession. Your winning ways and demon temper are irresistible to the public.

JOHN WILKES BOOTH

Yes Mary I guess they are. I've chosen this profession and live life as a melodrama, through thick and thin. Both its strengths and vices have touched my character deeply.

MARY MITCHELL

Wilkes you're creative, your wilful emotions and talent with its Caliban ways. I on the other hand have no desire to be great. To be loved yes, but to be great is too much a burden.

JOHN WILKES BOOTH

Mary there's always a lull before the storm. When I was young mother instructed me about piety, truth and honesty. I felt somehow disqualified to meet these criteria and regretfully her hopes were dashed when I pursued a career on stage. Deep down I knew I wanted adventure, reckless adventure, which limited my life as a puritan.

(Mary laughs)

MARY MITCHELL

Wilkes I'm a country without boundaries waiting to be conquered and part of your charm, nay your talent, lies in deflowering damsels who invite the chase. I know because I was one of them and I've watched you and your game is skilful.

(Mary makes a circle with both hands and then makes an aggressive motion forward with her right hand fingers extended. Booth laughs with gusto)

The preamble is always the same, Southern manners and politics. John Brown aside it's a polite diversion from the task at hand - namely conquering the wench.

(both laugh)

With respect to your dear mother's training, you're a Caliban Wilkes, both on and off the stage and well earned. I do not lie and you know it.

JOHN WILKES BOOTH

Mary it's a well known fact that I've a passion for the fairer sex, storming the Bastille when the wind blows and the sails billow

(pauses)

if you catch my drift?

(both laugh)

That being said my devotion to mother has no bounds. I'll love her 'till my dying breath, on the other hand acting is a vice of which I'm addicted. The accolades and hero's welcome are adorned with camp followers in every town, but what of it.

(Booth shrugs and Mary laughs)

MARY MITCHELL
(sits up suddenly baring her naked torso)

Wilkes, enough, enough, enough. Please, continue your journey through my continent, stopping wherever, doing whatever, you know the drill so well.

(Booth pulls Annie down beside him)

JOHN WILKES BOOTH
I'm most often aroused and easily conquered by femme fatales Mary

(rolls on top of Mary who squeals in mock terror)

you know that

(Booth begins to kiss Mary as he talks)

please view this afternoon's performance as a harbinger of future excursions into your

(pauses)

country.

(both laugh)

(END OF SCENE, LIGHTS DIM, CHANGE OF SET)

ACT ONE SCENE FOUR

(Chicago 1862, backstage in a dingy dressing room after a performance)

EDWIN BOOTH

Wilkes you were brilliant as Richard the Third. Father would be proud and mother, I can't imagine what she'd say. Well done younger brother, WELL DONE.

JOHN WILKES BOOTH

Ned, how do you go on. Remember I've toiled on the stage for five long years. The public appreciates my talent, the critics, yes the critics, now there's the rub, with their uppity words and whimsicality. In their eyes I shine like a mirror, so don't be surprised by the outcome. Over time I've built my reputation on their confidence with my performances being real, truly real as in true living Ned. The audience jells when I perform, like a mink glove sliding 'cross your body, the critics can feel the momentum Ned, that's all.

EDWIN BOOTH

Whatever the cause Wilkes, tonight you WERE Richard the Third. A great performance worthy of acclaim by all who take notice.

JOHN WILKES BOOTH

Ned it's an affair of honor. I love my craft and have spent long hours perfecting my skills. Simply put I need the stage more than it needs me.

EDWIN BOOTH

Wilkes your performance was pristine. The audience loved every nuance of the character you portrayed. You reached the pinnacle tonight brother, what's next on your agenda?

JOHN WILKES BOOTH

The Corsican brothers, Julius Caesar, the Western sisters, Helen and Lucille.

(laughs with a devious smile)

Rebellious to the end dear brother.

EDWIN BOOTH

Wilkes please.

JOHN WILKES BOOTH

(climbs on a chair and begins a monologue with much gesturing)

What's the world coming to? Am I equal to the appointed task one asks? The South, the glorious South where art thou? A wicked purulent gob has lifted your skirts for all to see. His cunning ways and means have prepared this wench for debauchery. In his mind cruelty and injustice have become more right than wrong.

(Ned has a startled expression)

Those of us with honor will defend this damsel in distress. Even play actors can serve notice to a bully Ned.

(Wilkes pirouettes on the chair and jumps to the floor in one movement)

EDWIN BOOTH
Then it's true Wilkes, MY GOD IT'S TRUE

(pauses)

Please dear brother say it isn't so.

JOHN WILKES BOOTH
(laughs with gusto)

If the Yankees conquer the South I'll die a thousand deaths, let that be stated in no uncertain terms.

(smiles broadly at his brother)

EDWIN BOOTH
Mother would sour like curdled milk if she heard you speak so. Give it up Wilkes, give it up before it tears you down.

JOHN WILKES BOOTH
(laughs)

Ned I'm having you on, who plays the fool now dear brother?

(Ned roars with laughter and hugs his brother stepping back grinning broadly)

EDWIN BOOTH
Wilkes, Wilkes you ARE a consummate actor, father would be so proud.

JOHN WILKES BOOTH
(shrugs and then smiles)

Next week I travel home to Baltimore. I'm looking forward to my engagement as Richard the Third. Annie will be my co-star, I'm very fond of her company, last time she stated my performance worthy of

(pauses briefly)

nay, commanded admiration, which one you ask?

(Ned laughs, lights dim, end of scene, change of setting to a hotel room in 1862. Wilkes and a young woman with blond hair are naked in bed)

ACT ONE SCENE FIVE

ANNIE GRAHAM
Wilkes you're an outstanding athlete, both on and off the stage, but you know that.

JOHN WILKES BOOTH
Annie, dear sweet Annie how long it's been, a year, eighteen months? You're too kind, but I can also be delicate and oblique

> *(pauses)*

if you catch my drift.

> *(Annie laughs)*

ANNIE GRAHAM
You keep me in suspense Wilkes, last time it was delicious soixante-neuf. But other times you over-play your part and leave me

> *(pauses)*

well you know

> *(pauses)*

serving your purpose. And yet other times the liaison is exacting and carefully rehearsed, which conquers my soul, leaving my body quivering like a leaf.

> *(Wilkes laughs)*

JOHN WILKES BOOTH

Annie you're a touch poetic and I thank you as a man performing his duty as a man.

ANNIE GRAHAM

Another notch Wilkes? Please stop, you speak enough.

(Annie sits up suddenly, her naked torso is visible to the audience. She leans over and puts on a robe while still in bed. She climbs out of bed and walks around the room while talking, eventually standing in front of the bed listening to Wilkes)

Are you staying in the South Wilkes? I hear your performances in Chicago and New York were superb.

JOHN WILKES BOOTH

Yes on both 'counts and according to the critics I was better than passable, but you know the critics. I miss the South Annie, working in the North impersonates real living. For example, a few months ago a man came to my mother's house lookin' for Dr. Booth. I thought instantly he must be thinkin' of my brother Joseph who was a medical student in Philadelphia awhile back. Alright I said and asked if he needed quinine for he looked like a wounded soldier on leave. He nodded and I laughed which made him laugh and I eventually told him the truth. This story only goes to show that war impersonates theatre Annie and I can't help but improvise real life experiences when given the opportunity. This war after one year of fightin' has not touched, nor even caressed the undergarments of the North, not yet anyway. But I digress please forgive me

(pauses)

how've you been this past eighteen months?

ANNIE GRAHAM

Missing you, missing your advances, missing our liaisons.

JOHN WILKES BOOTH

(laughs with gusto)

I've returned to fulfill your every wish, need and whatever Annie

(pauses)

both on and off the stage.

(both laugh)

ANNIE GRAHAM

(regains composure)

Wilkes stop it, your pleasure can be my pain and you know it, casting a spell on every wench to whom you make advances.

JOHN WILKES BOOTH

(mimics Annie)

'Wilkes please stop it'.

(pauses)

Annie I'm a virile young man with unnatural desires, lusting and conquering every which way. Using both types of intimacy to better the wenches. Is that what you want me to say? That whomever strikes my fancy becomes a challenge to be conquered is that it?

(pause)

Please Annie remember this always

(pause)

Your presence dignifies my soul

(slight pause)

but for now I must go and rehearse.

(Wilkes emerges from bed naked with his back to the audience and quickly puts on his long underwear. Annie walks to the side of the bed, takes off her robe and enters the bed sliding under the sheets. Wilkes continues to talk as he dresses)

The parts I play are tragedies Annie. You and I aren't tragic, but that being said what lies in my future is a path for freedom. A path built on dignity and respect, for as we speak the South is being sullied. Its character and noble spirit dragged through the mud and I'll not stand by like a cowardly . . .

(pauses to regain composure)

I must go now dear sweet Annie, please keep cozy and the bed warm, I'll see you soon.

(Wilkes fully dressed strides to the door, turns suddenly facing the audience and bows quickly to Annie. Annie in return blows him a kiss. Wilkes opens the door and leaves abruptly)

(LIGHTS DIM, END OF SCENE, CHANGE OF SET TO A MAJOR STATE ROOM OF THE ST. LAW-RENCE HOTEL, MONTREAL QUEBEC 1864)

ACT TWO SCENE ONE

(Clement Clay is present in the room)

JOHN WILKES BOOTH

I've recruited allies for the cause Mr Clay, willing to abduct this tyrant Lincoln without bloodshed. It can be done in a fortnight, what say you?

CLEMENT CLAY

Election is two months away and security tight, is such a plot feasible Mr Booth?

JOHN WILKES BOOTH

It can be done if we make haste Mr Clay. I've the right contacts but need to speak with Marshall Kane before we proceed. If not he then maybe Jacob Thompson your associate up here. Lincoln's blockade of the Southern ports means direct travel back home is dubious at best and I don't fancy spending exorbitant rates, travelling to and from Canada by way of Bermuda Mr Clay.

CLEMENT CLAY

Kane's not in Montreal and can't be reached and Jacob Thompson represents the State Department not the War Department Mr Booth. However to placate your mood may I state emphatically that compatriots will be targeting Union officials in the North. I can put you in touch Mr Booth.

JOHN WILKES BOOTH

Who are they pray tell?

CLEMENT CLAY

Simply put

 (pauses)

at this time in the city of Montreal they're plans to invade the North. The war does not bode well for the South. A more clandestine approach is required to achieve victory. Canada is a neutral country, an obvious place of refuge and you Mr Booth are a famous thespian. We can use your obvious talents to help liberate the South. What say you?

JOHN WILKES BOOTH

My life's a drama Mr Clay and that rubber neck, gander goose has to be stopped. Money, fame and influence will allow me to achieve something remarkable. I know this to be a fact Sir.

 (pauses)

In my youth a fortune teller told me I'd die young which I believe to be true. It's been a fast and furious life thus far Mr Clay, filled to the brim at every turn, filled to the brim.

 (pauses)

I humbly accept your request and will be your servant. In any event there must be an end to coasting, milksop politics.

 (pauses)

There's a saying in my neck of the woods Mr Clay. Poor white trash inheriting gold get greedy and end up poor white trash. This ape, baboon has overstepped and will be stomped down, mark my words.

CLEMENT CLAY

Can you at least state your plan in a general sense mind you. My associates and I

(interrupted)

JOHN WILKES BOOTH

As yet my plans are not finalized Mr Clay. Let me return to Washington, with your leave

(pauses)

we'll keep in touch.

CLEMENT CLAY

Yankees view our cause as treasonable, see us as marginalists, posing a threat to their political agenda Mr Booth and their ideas about the South. It's as simple as that. From now on it'll be very dangerous for you, take care in these desperate times

(pauses)

and trust no one.

JOHN WILKES BOOTH

I'm a play actor performing a role Mr Clay and for those big city, impudent Yankees who challenge me off stage

(steps forward dramatically with both hands holding his jacket lapels and begins to recite in a theatrical manner)

'I've toiled long hard years to be a success in the largest cities of the North and won your praise and recognition. Please, let's be brothers in these, foul and turbulent times'. AND THEY BUY IT HOOK LINE AND WHATEVER.

(slaps his knee and pauses turning his head slowly to look directly at Clement Clay)

Mr Clay I've no fear of anything and will be conquered by no one.

CLEMENT CLAY

Lincoln is a slippery, vain rascal from a ten cent State, who must be taken down Mr Booth. He's undermined the liberties of the South by challenging the '57 Dred Scott law. Negro's ain't citizens so how can you fight for them. It don't make sense, but that being said I fear he's swayed the Yankee vote and will win the election this November.

(sits down on a chair and looks towards the audience)

JOHN WILKES BOOTH

Lincoln's conspiring against the South, its ways of life and grandeur. His ways will be placed in check, I give you my word on that Sir. But right now my colleagues await my return, that's all I can say. Please excuse my leave but there's work to be done. It's a difficult journey home and I must be off.

(Wilkes bows deeply and walks quickly to the door, he leaves shutting the door quietly behind him)

(LIGHTS FADE, END OF SCENE, SET CHANGE TO A HOTEL ROOM IN WASHINGTON, DC - FALL 1864)

ACT TWO SCENE TWO

JOHN WILKES BOOTH
(two distinguished gentlemen are standing in a hotel room with Booth)

Gentlemen as you know the Confederate Congress recently approved five million dollars for a political mission to Canada. Largely comprised of 'copperhead' extremists to quote the Yankee papers.

(pauses holding a brandy snifter takes a quick drink)

I've hatched an easy plan to abduct this rogue giraffe and sue for peace.

(other men laugh)

GEORGE SANDERS
Sir, we admire your pluck

(his companion nods)

but I believe the Yankee President is too closely guarded as election draws near. It's less than a month away, what's the hope for success as time runs down?

JACOB THOMPSON
(heavy Southern accent)

Mr Lincoln despairs of the November election against McLellan. His guard's down, but that's only my opinion gentlemen. Voters will be deciding on a new constitution which outlaws slavery. Why just last month I was at a slave auction in Mississippi, where only five dollars, five dollars mind you, could purchase a negro regardless of age or physical health.

(pauses)

We're at war mind you.

(pauses)

I am and always will be a loyal Southerner, but I fear my democratic friends in the North have lost their fighting spirit.

(pauses and clasps his hands together)

Mr Booth I'm ancient as well as being old before my time, please tell us your plan, the time is late and the evening runs short.

JOHN WILKES BOOTH
(walks around the room drinking from the brandy snifter, as he talks he punctuates his remarks with sudden movements)

Mr Lincoln is known to ride unescorted mind you to 'Soldiers Home' a few miles north of Washington. An easy mark for a group of men to overtake his carriage and transport his hide to the Virginia backcountry. Gentlemen it can be done, IT CAN BE DONE. We could then sue for peace, prisoner exchange, you name it.

(Booth spins in a tight circle and slaps his thigh, takes a large drink from the brandy snifter and refills it from a brandy bottle located on a nearby table)

The life of the Confederacy could be saved gentlemen. I have a contact you may know by name of Conrad.

(other men nod)

I've been able to convince him of secrecy, but don't ask me how

(other men laugh)

and at the same time got the approval of the Confederate War Department to go through with an abduction of

(pauses and takes a quick drink)

this bumptious fanatic.

JACOB THOMPSON

He's got something George, if Lincoln is abducted he could be used as a 'bargaining chip' to have Confederate prisoners released from Camp Douglas way up Chicago way. We could organize a rebellion in that region which would further divide the Union.

GEORGE SANDERS

Spoken like a true 'Copperhead' Thompson, but we think ahead of our plan. Is it reasonable to assume we can trust Mr Conrad? Will he follow through if the chips are down? These are treacherous times gentlemen, treacherous times.

JOHN WILKES BOOTH
(frowns and is agitated)

I believe in Conrad's spunk Mr Sanders and in my heart and soul have faith the plan will succeed with Conrad at the helm, yes indeed. I meet with him later this week and will

(mimics Sanders accent)

'gauge his pluck'. But over everything else his strength of will and commitment to a just cause will pull him through gentlemen.

(pauses and takes a big drink from the snifter)

His royal highness of the stump, the demigod giraffe was never more than a sectional candidate anyway. Trumped up to win the election of sixty after he so called beat Douglas in the '58 debates. During this war El Diablo's administration has been a reign of terror led by an imbecile deluding himself, a King Tut so to speak.

(Booth takes a big drink from the brandy snifter before continuing and begins pace up and down the room as he talks, punctuating the air with hand gestures to make his point)

Your passivity smells to high heavens Sanders.

(Sanders steps back suddenly but is motioned to be calm by Jacob Thompson)

It speaks of concession, compromise and 'boot lickin'.

(Booth turns to glare at Sanders who stands motionless and glares back at Booth)

His royal highness the ignominious gob will insist on a Confederate surrender, mark my words. Nothing less than capitulation will be his demand. This is not an option for any true Southerner NO SIR.

(Booth is now inches from Sander's face before spinning away to pace up and down the floor)

This tyrant baboon wants the end of slavery and certain rights maintained by Southern aristocracy FOR OVER ONE HUNDRED AND FIFTY YEARS MIND YOU

(pauses and takes a big swig from the brandy snifter)

will be nullified just like that.

(snaps his fingers)

Why even Thom Jefferson had a parcel of slaves up there in New York, THOM JEFFERSON MIND YOU

(pauses and takes another swig from the brandy snifter)

Gentlemen I've spoken at length and let my guard down so be it, I am what I am.

(takes a final swig to empty the contents of the brandy snifter)

It's time I departed but will stay in touch, be rest assured our cause shall not be vanquished

(Booth tosses the empty brandy snifter onto a chair and walks to the closet. He takes out his coat and cape and puts them on dramatically. He strides to the hotel door, turns and makes a full length theatrical bow, the cape flowing behind him. He opens the door quickly and walks out closing the door behind him)

(LIGHTS DIM, END OF SCENE, CHANGE OF SET TO A BEDROOM IN A WASHINGTON DC BROTHEL)

ACT TWO SCENE THREE

(Wilkes is naked in bed with prostitute Ella Starr, Madame of the largest brothel in Washington DC - 1865)

JOHN WILKES BOOTH
(Booth stares at the ceiling while Ella Starr kisses his face and neck)

Miss Starr I'm spent.

ELLA STARR
Ella, please Wilkes just Ella.

JOHN WILKES BOOTH
Ella then

> *(pauses)*

thus far my career has been successful, certain perks have fallen my way and I've developed, if I may say boldly, a steady fascination for the fairer sex. I find them robustly different in temperament which is appealin'

> *(pauses)*

from a distance mind ya and their bodies are warm too.

> *(Ella laughs)*

ELLA STARR

Wilkes what inhabits your mind? You've easy acquaintance with women of all classes, why then fornicate with a trollop these past three years?

JOHN WILKES BOOTH

Frankly and with deference to your mindful psychology, the male species is weak in matters of the flesh and one other thing

(pauses while choosing his words)

I've been pampered

(pauses)

pampered by my sisters and a mother whom I adore.

(pauses as he clasps his hands behind his neck and stretches his shoulders)

I've come to expect this adoration and use charm to conquer all queen bees who feel a need to drop anchor at my doorstep. This I say in confidence Ella, as I pay for your time and pleasure I must insist on your discretion.

ELLA STARR

You ask the discretion of a fallen woman Wilkes, I am impressed.

JOHN WILKES BOOTH

As I'm my mother's love, you've become the receptacle of all my fears. Is that so complex Ella? How're you different y'ask? My answer is simple and straight forward, but first a preamble. My fans have ripped my clothin' in a frenzy believin' the character I portray on stage is ME FOR GOD'S SAKE. I get a hundred love letters 'aweek statin' eternal love and devotion smittin' with my

(accentuates a nasal affectation)

'greek god looks' WHAT POPPYCOCK. The world is upside down this past four years and I've no one to talk to, share my fears, support me when I'm down trodden. These are calloused times with martial law imposed, precludin' sharp words and dialogue that are needed I might add. But you Ella, you're my standard bearer. I enjoy your company, velvet wit, mind and body aligned like gold.

(pauses)

Can you understand the meanderins' of an artist dear Ella?

ELLA STARR
Let's get back to business Wilkes. Your manhood has never been challenged in my lodgins', the time is late.

(Booth laughs)

JOHN WILKES BOOTH
Why Miss Starr you're my coach and conductor and what have we here?

(both look down at Booth's midsection)

Exquisite logic Miss Starr.

(both laugh, turn to embrace and kiss when Booth suddenly sits up)

ELLA SWEET GOD IN HEAVEN

(pauses)

I've a pressin' engagement that can't wait. Please forgive my hasty retreat but I'm off like a scalded cat.

(Booth leaps naked from bed and runs to the closet putting on his clothes quickly. All the while Ella laughs hysterically. Booth fully clothed, preens in front of the mirror, adjusts his hair and moustache. He bows courteously to Ella and places several bank notes on a dresser by the door. Prior to leaving the room he blows Ella a kiss which she returns. Booth leaves closing the door behind him)

(LIGHTS DIM, SET CHANGE , AS LIGHTS ARE RAISED THE SET IS THE INTERIOR OF A LIVING ROOM OF A MODEST WASHINGTON HOME)

ACT TWO SCENE FOUR

JOHN WILKES BOOTH

(a middle aged woman, early forties stands in front of Booth)

Mrs Sarratt I'm charmed as always, thank you for seein' me at such short notice.

(bends over and kisses Mrs Sarratt's hand while she curtsy's in return)

I'm here to offer my sincerest apologies for the other evenin' and to doubly apologize for the fear my friends and I caused yah. Our undignified, revoltin' behavior, actin' like common vulgarians, I was out of my mind to threaten you harm and the oath takin', be damned Lucifer I was out of my mind, it's as simple as that.

(pauses and stares intensely at Mrs Sarratt)

Please, I ask most humbly that you remain with our cause dear woman. As you can see my temper is never mediocre and I feel ashamed of creatin' great fear and trepidation in any woman's heart, 'specially yours.

(stands close to Mrs Sarratt and grasping her right hand with both his hands kisses her hand and begins to sob)

MARY SARRATT

(comforting tone and gentle manner)

My dear young man, yes your behavior was the devil at work, my very soul was in peril. But forgiveness is in my heart as these are harrowin' times and our love for the South must transcend differences. Have these words passed your test of faith Mr Booth?

JOHN WILKES BOOTH
(continues to clasp Mrs Sarratt's hands and stands face to face look-ing intently into her eyes)

Mrs Sarratt your mistrust at this time is indeed warranted. But must I alone be solely to blame for this misdeed? I think not for we live in perilous times and the stress of war can bring out a purulent evil which hides inside as never before.

(pauses)

Be as it may I would consider it an honor if you'd allow me to call you Mary.

MARY SURRATT
(visibly startled, steps back but regains composure)

Sir there's almost twenty years difference in age.

(pauses and then steps closer to Booth)

But yes, you may call me by my Christian name. You showed pluck and determination callin' here today, after the other evenin's goin's on

(pauses)

and I like Southern men who show character and grit

(pauses)

'specially Southern Maryland dandies in sheep's clothin'.

(Booth laughs and bows dramatically)

JOHN WILKES BOOTH

Mary, as you stated so adroitly, I've character but with accursed flaws. I'm reckless and secretive, for these days no one can be too careful, yet I feel

(pauses)

nay I know I've got the brains of twenty men, a photographic memory for detail and love the company of fine southern women such as yourself. In all my life I've not met such a handsome, refined woman as you. Please accept my sincere apology for the other evenin's digression. I will be a true friend you wait and see.

(Booth smiles and steps back to admire Mary)

Mary I'm excitable and cantankerous and want my way in all things, it was a mistake, just a mistake amongst friends.

MARY SARRATT

Mr Booth your friends drew guns and demanded my oath of secrecy in a plot to kidnap the President of the Yankee States. I've been and will continue to be complicit with these nefarious plans. That counts for somethin' AND YOU KNOW IT.

(pauses)

Threats aside, these men were raw, crude-oil raw, without Southern charm and gentility. Why d ya' 'sociate with inferiors who behave like riff-raff. Usin' words like jezebel and harlot in a woman's presence, why I blushed like a rose.

(pauses)

NO SIR I'LL NOT TOLERATE SUCH BLASPHEMY

(pauses)

in my house or anywhere else NO SIR.

JOHN WILKES BOOTH

Mary the deeds of mankind should be swept clean when vengeance is held sacred. That night reckless actions came from the devil's own mouth.

(Booth pauses, speaks in a seductive manner)

Please Mary

(pauses)

be my friend.

(Booth begins to weep then regains composure)

Forgive me when I say I'm deeply embarrassed and sorry. If you were to cast me aside I would not blame you now, or ever more.

MARY SARRATT
(embraces Booth who faces the audience and smiles)

You're forgivin' Wilkes, please stay with me awhile and recite some poetry.

(pauses)

You've been painted by some as a free thinker, by others a Methodist and still others a Catholic and a Jew, but in my home you're just plain Wilkes, my dandy, my sweet Southern dandy.

JOHN WILKES BOOTH
(Booth lowers himself slowly to bended knee and looks up at Mrs Sarratt)

You're a true angel and a dear woman and should know that I live in the presence of others, not with them. I'm a stage actor blamed for living life through art.

(Booth stands up slowly maintaining eye contact with Mary Sarratt)

But now I've been stoked by war ravaged against the South. A frustration so great is deep within me, it feels no limits. Carryin' the burden causes me to act on dreams and fantasies to improve my beleaguered existence. There is evil drivin' our Nation, our glorious South has been violated like a precious child slapped down for no reason.

(pauses)

Our path is just, our case for freedom is now and forever. God the almighty surely loves a child who'll stand up and fight for a belief, no matter what the consequences bear.

MARY SARRATT

Wilkes I believe in our cause, in my heart I'm with ya, you know that

(Booth nods)

but fear invades my spirit, that's all I can say. I need a young man's strength.

(pauses and looks at Booth for several seconds)

Come Wilkes stand by the hearth and recite some poetry.

(Booth nods and strides to the hearth as Mary Sarratt looks on)

(LIGHTS DIM, END OF SCENE, SET CHANGE TO A HOTEL ROOM IN WASHINGTON DC - 1865)

INTERMISSION

ACT TWO SCENE FIVE

JOHN WILKES BOOTH

(alone in a hotel room drinking from a brandy snifter pacing the floor)

Food, manpower, rifles, supplies they're slim to none. Lee's army is stagnant at Petersburg, envoys suein' for peace have been declined, irregular warfare, Beall's hangin' this past February, where's it all end? I'm surrounded by a crew a' cutthroats, down to low life, greasy malcontents without an inklin' between their ears, Atzerodt isn't the only culprit. I'll nullify those witnesses who profess bravery 'round the dinner table, but talk a blue streak when caught. Clarke, Weichman, Mudd, Herold, Arnold, O'Laughlin, I must ensure complicity to preserve their silence. If our plot is ruined they'll meet the same fate as I.

(takes a large swig from a brandy snifter and slaps his knee before twirling on the spot)

I'll take McCulloch to Crystal Springs and scout the area. The stable boy will see us together, know our names and testify to the fact. I must leave dear Bessie Hale 'outta this. In all my life she's the only woman to rival mother's love and sincerity. When she leaves for Spain I'll abduct the hairy panderer, whose nothin' but a trumped up Yankee mouthpiece anyway. Surratt, Arnold, Herald, Azerodt use the same Livery stable as me and my trusted, one eyed mare.

(pauses and takes a swig from the brandy snifter)

I must lie and lie and lie for the glory of the South. must not be vanquished

(pauses)

and for my friends, witnesses and cut throat crew,

(pauses)

the end justifies the mean. Trusted friendships are truly depleted, that's for sure, lest my plans make me dizzy with anticipation, I'm ready and my brain tells me the time is right.

(pauses and takes a large swig from the brandy snifter)

The Yankee Solomon will be sittin' in the box at Ford's and can be abducted, then taken from Washington, how you ask?

(completes a full bow with arms extended while holding the brandy snifter aloft)

Arnold on my cue can seize the bandicoot ape and one of the other's can get 'em backstage and outta the buildin' under escort. As usual steppin' out for a quick one is his bodyguard, an idiot minion too concerned for drink to be cogitatin' 'bout foul play. This makes the plan easy, a quick carriage ride due south and from there we ransom his hide for prisoner exchange. Tonight I give my last theatre engagement, from this day on I rebuke play actin' as a farce of life and in these hard times I AM MYSELF ALONE.

(howls and takes a swig from the brandy snifter)

After visitin' Ned these past months the contrast in Yankee style and grace sickens my stomach to knots. The war and its sacrilege have made me an outcast. Why only the other day my opinion was challenged

(takes a big swig from the brandy snifter)

HOW DARE YOU SIR.

(pauses while collecting his thoughts)

But in short time I will astonish the world, mark my words. Ned and his Yankee ways, he gloats over their victories and thinks me a fool for not

(mimics Ned's voice)

'readin the writin' on the wall dear brother'. My lovin' mother prays for my health and my broken heart despairs 'bout what I'm goin' to do?

(takes another swig from the brandy snifter until it's empty. Booth sits down slowly onto the floor cradling the empty snifter, rolling it from one hand to the other)

The fall of Richmond, the army in full retreat, no food, no rifles, no supplies. A Confederate surrender imminent but the glory of the South vindicated. How say you Sir?

(pauses)

YES SIR VINDICATED.

(takes a look inside the empty brandy snifter lifts it up and attempts to drink, shakes his head and slowly stands up nearly falling as he struggles to his feet. Booth then refills the snifter from a bottle on a nearby table)

King Solomon Mr high and mighty has the audacity to mention in a speech that Thom Jefferson and John Adams died on the fourth of July, the anniversary of our great nation and then with the same breath gave votin' rights to the negro, can you believe it? After one hundred and fifty years includin' Gettysburg and Vicksburg

(pauses)

CITIZENS OF THE UNITED STATES?

(pauses, swaying in the air almost losing balance)

I'LL RUN THE VILLAIN THROUGH BY GOD.

(pauses, takes a large swig and puts the brandy snifter carefully on the floor caressing the glass before sitting down, examining the snifter as he talks)

Just four short years ago abolitionists were condemned for causin' war and now they're loved and venerated

(pauses and suddenly throws his arms in the air, brandy spills from the snifter covering the floor around Booth)

SIC SEMPER TYRANNIS.

(begins to pace)

Runnin' backstage I'll escape by horseback and ride like the devil. Panic, fear and confusion will be my passage to safety by God.

(facing the audience stands erect and begins to speak in a flat, methodical manner)

I'm handsome, well bred and articulate, a Southern gentleman and not a common ruffian. I can easily pass the sentries guardin' the bridge out of Washington. They'll not yet be warned of the scoundrel's demise and I'll pass curfew as a genteel young man out for a ride, as the moon is bright and the evenin' fresh. This'll not be out of the ordinary by any means or stretch of the imagination

(pauses and smirks)

besides the war is over.

(pauses)

I'm an actor first and foremost, my charm will breach any conflict of thought, like it has with maidens on the couch. Which reminds me, during frequent forays into Southern cities of charm and gentility, I learned to make friends easily, many of whom were of the fairer sex. Although my leisure activities included horseback ridin', billiards and sword fightin' women found their position moved higher on my list of priorities after a few

(pauses)

frivolities, that was for damned sure. My perfectionism in the female situation was never so adroit than when playin' parlor games, where my ability to comprehend, embellish and use my actin' talents conquered the evenin' and sometimes the damsel. How so you wonder, with a quick verse sung to the high heavens says I. A renderin' of 'Bonnie Blue Flag' which was forbidden to be sung as declared by the Yankee authorities. Of course this placed me in the highest regard by those damsels present who often said 'Wilkes stop that you overstep your boundaries'. But in my way of thinkin' their meaning was 'Wilkes go 'way closer I'm hungry for your attention' which I was.

(Booth smiles and turns slowly, he walks to the door opens it slowly and exits, end of scene)

(CHANGE OF SET TO THE PARLOR OF THE HOME OF MISS LUCY "BESSIE" HALE, DAUGHTER OF SENATOR JOHN HALE - LATE SPRING 1865)

ACT THREE SCENE ONE

(a pretty young woman in her early twenties enters the Parlor unannounced and stands quietly beside Booth - she looks at him intently)

JOHN WILKES BOOTH

Bessie my love.

BESSIE HALE

(steps back)

Wilkes you smell of drink and look the worst for wear. What's the problem dear love?

JOHN WILKES BOOTH

Bessie one look from you can slay a dragon, or a platoon of naval marines. Yes, I'm distressed and in need of support may I speak frankly?

BESSIE HALE

Please my love speak openly and from your heart, you're safe here, I'm all ears.

JOHN WILKES BOOTH

Calamity has befallen the South.

BESSIE HALE

(pauses and shrugs before speaking)

Wilkes, old news is dead news as the saying goes. But I'm being flip, please forgive me. There's something different in your voice and I think what's made Wilkes so fearful? Our love is a treasure never stolen, I'm here to help you over any hurtle. When you come to me drunk and fearful this is territory unmapped. We're trading hats my love, in the past you were my shield, my

(interrupted)

JOHN WILKES BOOTH
I'm not sure now.

BESSIE HALE
(smiles and looks lovingly at Wilkes)

Wilkes build a bridge with your words and articulate your thoughts. You're never at a loss.

JOHN WILKES BOOTH
I'm engaged on a mission to end tyranny I work to end tyranny.

BESSIE HALE
(startled puts her hands in front of her face and then looks down letting her hands fall to her side)

Wilkes, dear Wilkes, what's come over you, the drink's addled your brain, you know I'll be at your side always, through thick and thin, pray speak openly.

JOHN WILKES BOOTH

In the past I had definite ideas on what I held sacred, we've argued about your views on abolition, but other virtues you possess commanded my love and high regard. You know that Bessie, I'm being sincere. As an actor I was often brilliant according to critics like Winter who stated I was a great talent and would one day attain a high position

(pauses)

but for my tendency to be excitable and eccentric offstage. Bessie don't for a second mistake those theatrical gimmicks for what I've always felt about the South and its dilemma. Richmond has fallen, Mobile and Montgomery the last vestiges of Southern aristocracy will soon follow suit, we are lost, mark my words, we are lost.

BESSIE HALE
(implores Wilkes to continue)

Wilkes.

JOHN WILKES BOOTH
(pauses)

I'm on a mission to correct certain wrongs made by this Yankee state. Mark my words Bessie Hale, these wrongs shall be vindicated, mark my words.

BESSIE HALE
(begins to cry, places her hands over her face after awhile she regains composure)

Wilkes please stop, you babble on with talk of vengeance. THE WAR IS OVER. We're free to start our lives again, we can be together for all times. Please Wilkes I know the armistice has made you rage within, but wait and see how our great Nation will heal the wounds between North and South. Things will work out for the better, just wait and see.

JOHN WILKES BOOTH
(embraces Bessie and begins to stroke her hair)

I feel alone in this most devilish world, my heart is truly broken, the war was a tragedy devised by the Yankees, a house built by straw

(pauses)

to live and die alone, without you by my side is too much to bear. Bessie you'll soon travel to Spain with your father

(looks at Bessie intensely)

and I'll be left behind alone, with my heart and soul forgotten, what will become of us?

BESSIE HALE
(pulls Booth close to her and looks at his face)

Don't speak of terrible crimes and deplorable endings for we'll never end and don't admonish me for leaving. I must be chaperoned as virtue dictates, but will return to be with you always.

JOHN WILKES BOOTH
(flippant, infantile tone)

I wish the best for both of us then. Let's part knowing our love will continue whatever happens.

BESSIE HALE

Wilkes please stop.

JOHN WILKES BOOTH

Yankee agents of the government infest Washington, they plan my demise as we speak.

BESSIE HALE

(distressed voice)

Wilkes you must challenge fact from fiction, get a grip my love, get a grip.

JOHN WILKES BOOTH

What I know for damned sure is my code of honor to the South. That platitudes of lies spoken by villains in power insult our dignity and that injustice must be rectified.

BESSIE HALE

Don't talk with such malice Wilkes, it hurts me so to see you like this.

JOHN WILKES BOOTH

Bessie the rights of each State of our Union I truly respect and support with vigor. The South cultivated a life that was deemed no longer viable and will be a forgotten memory in future times. People's lives have been changed forever and who's to blame? Not the South mind you, it was killed off bit by bit, she fought on to the end but was conquered. There was passion in her struggle, a brave courageous spirit like a never ending parade but her wish to breathe clean and maintain glory was defeated, her head severed at the neck.

(Booth begins to cry and attempts to regain composure while speaking)

Bessie I seek vengeance as any man with a passion for a cause and I'll always love you, our times together, your laugh, your dignity as a woman refined. But I must go now and journey home, please let me look at you one last time so my spirit is made stronger knowing you love me so.

(Booth quickly embraces Bessie kissing her deeply. He then pushes past her to exit the Parlor, turning quickly to give a large theatrical bow. She curtsy's in return and then covers her face)

(LIGHTS DIM, END OF SCENE, SET CHANGE, THE PARLOR OF MARY SARRATT'S HOME IN WASHINGTON DC)

ACT THREE SCENE TWO

JOHN WILKES BOOTH

(paces the floor)

Surrender of Lee and his whole army. Grant's terms accepted

(tempo increased, repeats the phrase)

Surrender of Lee and his whole army. Grant's terms accepted.

(Mary Sarratt enters the Parlor and stands in front of Booth)

Mary, the papers the past few weeks, all they speak of is uncondi-tional surrender by Lee. I can't believe the madness, total capitula-tion, why Mosby and his boys are still fightin' in the hills north of Washington.

(Mary Sarratt shakes her head and turns to leave)

No Mary wait, I was at that scoundrel Lincoln's speech the other day, close enough to hit him with a rock. Now listen to the poppy-cock he told the audience standin' up there in the balcony so high an' mighty. I will recite from memory, please, I beg your indulgence

(Mary turns back to face Booth as he begins his recitation Booth mimics Lincoln's high pitched voice)

'We meet this evenin' not in sorrow but in gladness of heart. The evacuation of Petersburg and Richmond and the principal insurgent army, give hope of a righteous and speedy peace whose joyous ex-pression cannot be restrained'.

(looks directly at Mary)

Then can you believe the charlatan imposter gave votin' rights to the negro. VOTIN' RIGHTS MIND YOU. They'll be citizens of the world next, wait 'n see.

MARY SARRATT

Wilkes I told you awhile back that the Yankees would prevail. Why just the other day they arrested Gus Howell on spyin' charges. I'm goin' on his behalf to talk with General Augers and if that don't work to Judge Turner to secure his release.

(pauses)

Now listen close, after talkin' with our friends I was able to locate and secure guns, brand new saddle carbines like you told me to get. They're hidden in the back of that Tavern outside of town we talked about.

(Booth begins to pace)

JOHN WILKES BOOTH
(talks while pacing punctuating the air with both broad and refined gestures reflecting the emotional interpretation of each word)

Mary, Lincoln's abduction is becomin' more ensnarled with too many cooks and not enough chefs if you catch my drift. As a result things are happenin' every which way. More darin' is required for the plan to work. He's a hero to the Yankees, a goddamn hero but with a fatal weakness, he enjoys his outins' and that's the way we get to 'em.

(pauses)

I've arranged to meet with our friends at a tavern soon enough to change the plans made a fortnight ago.

MARY SARRATT

Which tavern Wilkes?

JOHN WILKES BOOTH

The Metropolitan downtown, but before then I need to talk with Atzerodt and another at Herndon House

(pauses to look at Mary and then walks towards her)

Mary

(Booth embraces Mary and looks fondly at her while facing the audience)

If anythin' goes wrong and you're implicated your life will be in danger. Your bravery and dedication to the cause are beacons for us all. Have you made plans after it's over?

MARY SARRATT

That's of no consequence now

(pauses)

I wish to say somethin' Wilkes, may I speak frankly from my heart?

(Booth nods)

In the past your energy ignited people like a tempest in a teapot, you were by reputation a philanderin' cad like most young dandy's and I was wary of your masculine ways. But with time, for me any-ways, you were the great inspiration of all our efforts. I loved your spirit of attack, no quarter asked nor given. The 'cut and thrust' of life lived too quickly on the edge.

(pauses)

That bein' said I'm obliged and beholdin' and will always stand behind you. I accept the consequences of my actions, anythin' awaitin' is in God's hands now, I'm prepared.

(Wilkes begins to weep then regains composure)

JOHN WILKES BOOTH

Rehearsals for 'Our American Cousin' have ended, accordin' to the papers the gala performance will be attended by Lincoln and his entourage good friday the fourteenth. Those watchin' the Play will see the end of tyranny and the honor of the South vindicated, I give you my word on that kind lady.

MARY SARRATT

I'll take a carriage this evenin' from Howard's Livery Stable and drive to the Tavern outside of town. I'll get those 'shootin irons' ready, if you need 'em they'll be waitin'.

(pauses)

Wilkes after it's over ride like there's no tomorrow.

JOHN WILKES BOOTH
(kisses Mary's hand and bows quickly

Mary I go now to attend to things most urgent. Be aware that no Yankee vigilantes will take Booth alive.

MARY SARRATT

Good luck young man and may the South arise when we're gone.

(Booth bows deeply and turns to leave, prior to reaching the Parlor entrance he turns to look one last time at Mary before leaving)

(END OF SCENE, LIGHTS DIM, SET CHANGE TO A WASHINGTON HOTEL ROOM, THE AFTERNOON OF APRIL 14, 1865 - CLEMENT CLAY IS PRESENT)

ACT THREE SCENE THREE

JOHN WILKES BOOTH

Mr Clay I've just left a lady friend with more passion for the South that I can shake a stick at. If we had fifty thousand like her during the war the South would've prevailed, mark my words. Her manner and grit were most inspiring.

CLEMENT CLAY

I come to you

(long pause before shaking his head)

I thought a compromised peace could regain the White House, I was dead wrong Mr Booth and the devil will steal my soul, can you forgive me?

JOHN WILKES BOOTH

Mr Clay both our efforts failed. In '61 Southerners thought a return to the Union would restore their way of life. Sanders thought that too and was wrong, dead wrong. No one ever thought with such political savvy, but he was wrong.

(pauses and begins to pace up and down the room)

No sir, we can still correct this calamity and transform the South to its former greatness, you wait and see. WE PAY HOMAGE TO NO ONE. If frontier justice is the last resort so be it.

(slaps his knee and turns to stand directly in front of Clay)

What say you?

CLEMENT CLAY

Conservatives wanted Lincoln defeated last November, he was not. Three years ago our government wanted the war stopped at any cost, it was not. Treasonable action was taken to achieve unconditional peace it failed and the war waged on and on and on.

(pauses)

In the end no one will judge poorly your honor to defend the South Mr Booth.

(Booth bows)

It will take whatever it takes to build back its glory. Stanton the reprobate has tried to strike terror in our hearts and he's failed at every juncture. We're now more than ever stronger in determination to regain our glory. I accept the fact and responsibility that during the past four years our government has bent rules, rules of conventional warfare that will appear beyond defense by the Yankee government. And we will no doubt be prosecuted for our actions, that's for sure. Our cabinet on many occasions discussed burnin' cities, incitin' riots and deprivin' Yankee prisoners without the decencies provided soldiers of war. For these actions I condemn our government and its Cabinet which felt justified in this way of thinkin'. But on the other side of the coin, Sherman can and will go to hell for eternity for what he's done to our beloved South. No plan of action suggested by any Cabinet member ever equaled, or came close to his flagrancies to the South and its good people NO SIR. What say you Mr Booth?

JOHN WILKES BOOTH

In a few hours time the fatal blow will be dealt Mr Clay and may God have mercy on our souls.

CLEMENT CLAY

Before we depart let me read if you will an article by Townsend to lift your spirits and courageous heart for tonight's deed.

(Booth is startled then bemused as Clement Clay puts on his reading glasses)

I quote "vital beauty the thoughtfully stern sweep of two direct dark eyes, meanin' to women a snare, and to men a search warrant. He seemed thoughtful of introspections, ambitious self-examinins, eye studies into the future, as if it witheld him to somethin' to which he had a right".

JOHN WILKES BOOTH

(laughs and strikes a theatrical pose before shaking Clement Clay's hand)

My days on the stage are long gone Mr Clay, that critic sang my praises in happier times. After tonight I envision a better tomorrow for I've purchased time from the devil to commit this deed, that's all I can say

(pauses)

but now it's time to bid farewell.

(Booth wearing a cape over his jacket makes a theatrical bow bending at his waist. The cape flows around and behind him, Booth exits stage left)

(END OF SCENE, LIGHTS DIM, SET CHANGE, BOOTH IS SITTING AT A DESK IN A WASHINGTON HOTEL ROOM, ALONE WITH HIS THOUGHTS. HE TURNS TO THE AUDIENCE AND BEGINS A SOLILOQUY)

ACT THREE SCENE FOUR

(Booth mimics a black southern accent while sitting alone)

'Ned did ya hear what that 'ol scoundrel did last month? He travelled down to Jeff Davis' house in Richmond, leaned his legs over a chair and squirted tobacca' juice all 'ova da' flo. Somebody 'outta kill 'em daid'.

(cheering is heard in the background Booth turns his head in acknowledgement before speaking with his own southern Maryland accent)

The revelry and candles outside

(pauses)

the South has been vanquished, flung to the ground and trampled underfoot led by a sorcerer baboon. I feel like carryin' a rebel flag up and down the street on the fastest horse in the South yellin' DEATH TO TYRANNY.

(pauses and begins to sob then regains his composure)

Autocracy must end now, self servin' decision makin', the higher law concept of right and wrong. It all smacks of powers beyond the normal acceptance, a devil's brew that will stop tonight. As with Lincoln goes Seward, an extremist who must be retired, a man with a deaf ear to the people of the South. A man called Secretary of the State, SECRETARY OF THE STATE MIND YOU, whose very doctrine has made him a target of the people, the Courts and his Congress. His ambitions multiplied by his brains and vanity bought him a seat in Valhalla

(pauses)

beside that long eared, trumped up, bearded ape, mark my words.

(pauses)

Mother, dear sweet mother whom I adore. For some reason I've been chosen for a more noble cause than play actin' and will give my life for this cause tonight. My benefactor and lady friend says her rosary while prayin' for my intentions, for this I must prevail. Last month while watchin' McCullock sleep I wept like a baby, he was so peaceful in his dreams, for this I must prevail. Princes and Princesses 'round the world will know my name shortly and will gaze more closely at their Kingdoms after tonight's deed. If nothin' else 'an eye for an eye' will appease our shame, for this I must prevail. The negro may take cause to look closely at change for it will be a long, bloody and unforgivin' challenge MARK MY WORDS, for this I must prevail.

(slowly and deliberately Booth stands and faces the audience, he walks to the center of the stage)

I go now and face destiny, I'll take a life and my chances for heaven or hell be damned. What awaits me is only peace of mind through courage of action, thus always to tyrants SIC SEMPER TYRANNIS.

(LIGHTS DIM, CHANGE OF SET TO AN INTERIOR OF A BARN - PORT ROYAL, VIRGINIA, APRIL 26, 1865)

ACT THREE SCENE FIVE

JOHN GARRETT

(Voice outside of barn, actor not seen by audience)

Mr Booth we have arrested and placed under guard your accomplice Mr Herold. I am John Garrett son of the owner of this farm. I have been deputized by Lieutenant Conger of the 16th New York Cavalry to negotiate a surrender. What say you sir?

JOHN WILKES BOOTH

(aside to the audience, kneeling behind hay bales stage left, reduced lighting)

I am alone, they have taken Herold who surrendered thinkin' he's safe. Horse feathers, he will be hung, jerkin' on the rope spittin' blood like a rabid dog. I will choose my fate more carefully. I did my duty freein' the South from Yankee oppression. I will go down a fightin' man, mark my words.

(responds to John Garrett in a lilting Irish accent)

Who are you again, are you sure you've got the right man? I'm an infantry soldier, I fought with the New York 'Fightin' Irish', you know, the 69th. I'm down here lookin' for work, after all the war has been over almost a month.

JOHN GARRETT

Give it up Mr Booth, we are fully aware of your true identity. Surrender your arms and come out. We have surrounded the barn, you can't escape by any means. Give it up sir, GIVE IT UP.

JOHN WILKES BOOTH
(aside to the audience)

This simpleton stooge knows not who he trifles with and his Yankee troops are green includin' the officer leadin', otherwise they would've rushed me by now. I'll play for time, my brain works like a hummin' bird in times like this. I can talk a blue streak and get out of any predicament, you watch.

(pauses)

How's that for negotiatin' a peaceful resolve?

JOHN GARRETT

I've been instructed that in five minutes we torch the barn Mr Booth. Hand out your arms first or we will shoot you dead. Please give it up Mr Booth, we want no bloodshed.

JOHN WILKES BOOTH
(switches to his own Southern Maryland accent)

Mr Garrett I have to remind yah of three important details you're missin'. I'm here and you're there and I ain't comin' out. My eyes and body know the inside of this barn and you fellas don't and lastly, and for your sake probably the most important, it's gunna be light in the next few hours and I can see your uniforms real fine, if yah catch my drift?

JOHN GARRETT

Mr Booth your time is almost up and we've laid kindlin' of pine needles and twigs 'round the barn, please give it up for God's sake.

JOHN WILKES BOOTH
(aside to the audience)

I'm not dyin' like a petty tramp caught stealin' apples from an orchard. Would you give it up? I told Herold not to say anythin' 'bout my shootin' irons, my best friends right now are my two Colts and a Spencer carbine. They'll do ma' talkin' when the time comes, wait and see.

(responds to Garrett)

Young man I'd advise you, for your own good not to come here again.

(pauses and calls out)

Anyone listenin' out there who is truly a man ... I'm a cripple but will meet in mortal combat with a chosen man from your brave unit. If this is acceptable please have the courtesy to move the remainin' force back, let's say a hundred yards to give both sides a fair to middlin' fightin' chance. Now there's a bargain, what say you?

(aside to the audience)

As you see there is no answer as they're being coaxed to contemplate my request. Once again I've won the game of wits. I had a dozen times the chance to shoot the leader but held off. Then they sent that farm boy they recruited as a peace maker, I can't believe it. For some reason my decision has charmed their sentiment and weakened their strategy.

(responds to soldiers)

Look here, make it fifty yards, still close enough to feel confident of capturin' me if I win the contest. This is a bargain not a fool's errand, consider seriously my offer gentlemen.

(aside to the audience)

Their lack of spirit and witless passivity is beyond reason.

JOHN GARRETT

Time is up Mr Booth, the barn has been set afire.

JOHN WILKES BOOTH

(aside to the audience)

I would've done the same

(pauses)

but a long way's back in time. They're fools if they think I'll surrender.

(responds to Garrett)

WELL BOYS PREPARE A STRETCHER I AIN'T COMIN' OUT

(a gunshot is heard, lights fade slowly to darkness)

END OF PLAY

CPSIA information can be obtained at www.ICGtesting.com
Printed in the USA
LVOW10s1156021016

506983LV00001B/4/P